Logistics

The strategic issues

Edited by
Martin Christopher
Professor of Marketing and Logistics
Cranfield School of Management

CHAPMAN & HALL

London · New York · Tokyo · Melbourne · Madras

Published by Chapman & Hall, 2–6 Boundary Row, London SE1 8HN

Chapman & Hall, 2–6 Boundary Row, London SE1 8HN, UK

Chapman & Hall, 29 West 35th Street, New York NY10001, USA

Chapman & Hall Japan, Thomson Publishing Japan, Hirakawacho Nemoto Building, 7F, 1-7-11 Hirakawa-cho, Chiyoda-ku, Tokyo 102, Japan

Chapman & Hall Australia, Thomas Nelson Australia, 102 Dodds Street, South Melbourne, Victoria 3205, Australia

Chapman & Hall India, R. Seshadri, 32 Second Main Road, CIT East, Madras 600 035, India

First edition 1992

© 1992   Chapman & Hall

Typeset in 10/12pt Palatino by Graphicraft Typesetters Ltd, Hong Kong
Printed in Great Britain by Hartnolls Ltd, Bodmin, Cornwall

ISBN 0 412 41550 X

A catalogue record for this book is available from the British Library

Library of Congress Cataloging-in-Publication data

Logistics: the strategic issues / edited by Martin Christopher. –
   1st ed.
      p.   cm.
   Includes bibliographical references and index.
   ISBN 0–412–41550–X
   1. Business logistics.   2. Strategic management.   I. Christopher, Martin.
HD38.5.L65   1992
658.5–dc20   91–41056
                                                                    CIP

Contents

Contents

Contributors

– **Warren Blanding**
  Chief Operating Executive
  Marketing Publications, Inc.
  Silver Spring, MD, USA

– **Dennis E. Blumenfeld**
  Operating Systems Research Development
  General Motors Research Laboratories, Michigan
  USA

– **Joseph L. Bower**
  Donald Kirk David Professor of Business Administration and
  Senior Associate Dean for External Relations
  Harvard Business School
  Boston, MA, USA

– **Donald J. Bowersox**
  John H. McConnell University Professor of Business
  Administration
  Michigan State University, East Lansing, Michigan, USA

– **Alan Braithwaite**
  Managing Partner
  Logistics Consulting Partners, Colchester
  Essex, UK

– **Lawrence D. Burns**
  Operating Systems Research Development
  General Motors Research Laboratories, Michigan
  USA

– **Phillip L. Carter**
  Professor of Operations Management
  Michigan State University
  East Lansing, MI, USA

– **Martin Christopher**
  Professor of Marketing and Logistics
  Cranfield School of Management
  Bedford, UK

- **William Copacino**
  Arthur Andersen & Co.,
  Boston, MA, USA

- **John I. Coppett**
  Professor of Marketing
  Houston University
  Texas, USA

- **Carlos F. Daganzo**
  Department of Civil Engineering
  University of California
  Berkeley, California, USA

- **Michael C. Frick**
  Operating Systems Research Development
  General Motors Research Laboratories, Michigan
  USA

- **Christopher Gopal**
  Manager, Manufacturing and Cost Management Group
  Price Waterhouse, Los Angeles
  California, USA

- **Randolph W. Hall**
  Department of Industrial Engineering and Operations Research
  University of California
  Berkeley, California, USA

- **J.H. Van der Hoop**
  Logistics International
  'S Gravenwetering 50
  Rotterdam, Netherlands

- **John B. Houlihan**
  Vice-President
  Booz, Allen & Hamilton
  London, UK

- **Thomas M. Hout**
  Vice-President
  Boston Consulting Group
  Boston, MA, USA

- **George A. Isaac   III**
  Partner
  Touche Ross & Co.'s Management Consulting Division, Chicago
  IL, USA

– **Thomas C. Jones**
   Booz, Allen & Hamilton
   Cleveland,
   Ohio, USA

– **C. John Langley Jr**
   Professor of Marketing and Logistics
   University of Tennessee
   Knoxville, TN, USA

– **D. Little**
   Dept. of Industrial Studies
   University of Liverpool
   Liverpool, UK

– **Robert M. Monczka**
   Professor of Materials Management
   Michigan State University
   East Lansing, MI, USA

– **J. Mosquera**
   Dept. of Industrial Studies
   University of Liverpool
   Liverpool, UK

– **R. Keith Oliver**
   Vice-President
   Operations Management Services in Europe
   Booz, Allen & Hamilton
   Cleveland, Ohio, USA

– **Hans-Ulrich Pretzsch**
   Director
   BMW, Germany
   München, Germany

– **Daniel W. Riley**
   Vice-President
   Booz, Allen & Hamilton

– **John H. Roberts**
   PA Consulting Group
   Manchester, UK

– **Donald B. Rosenfield**
   Arthur D. Little
   Acorn Park
   Cambridge, MA, USA

– **Roy D. Shapiro**
  Associate Professor in Production and Operations Management
    Harvard Business School
    Boston, MA, USA

– **Graham Sharman**
    Director
    McKinsey & Company, Amsterdam
    Netherlands

– **Roy Dale Voorhees**
    Professor of Logistics
    Iowa State University
    Iowa, USA

– **Michael D. Webber**
    Vice-President
    Operations Management Services in US Eastern region
    Booz, Allen & Hamilton
    London, UK

– **A.M.A. Wild**
    Midas Consultants
    London, UK

– **Richard Yallop**
    Managing Director
    Customer Service International Limited, Norwich
    UK

Preface

In selecting the twenty articles for this book I became even more aware of how fast-changing the logistics scene has been these last two decades. New concepts and techniques have emerged at a rapid rate and the acceptance of these ideas – at least by the leading edge companies – has been most impressive.

Almost thirty years have elapsed since Peter Drucker wrote his pioneering article on distribution entitled: 'The economy's dark continent'. The implication of the title and the thrust of his argument was that management knew and understood little of the opportunities that existed for profit leverage through logistics. What he said was:

> Physical distribution is today's frontier in business. It is the one area where managerial results of great magnitude can be achieved. And it is still largely unexplored territory.

For many companies this, unfortunately, still holds true. For many more, however, the adoption of the concept of integrated distribution and subsequently of logistics management has brought with it many rewards.

Along with this growth of interest in logistics has come an enlarged definition of its scope. The reach of logistics extends from managing supplier relations through to the management of final demand via intermediaries on to the final customer. Today's logistics manager will most likely adopt a definition of logistics along these lines:

> Logistics is the process of strategically managing the acquisition, movement and storage of materials, parts and finished inventory from suppliers through the organization and its marketing channels, in such a way that current and future profitability is maximized through the cost-effective fulfilment of orders.

At the same time the organization has also had to adapt to new and challenging competitive pressure. In many markets significant inroads have been created by companies – often from overseas – that have recognized the importance of providing customer satisfaction through quality in its widest sense. Thus 'conformance to requirements' from product characteristics through to delivery performance has become the battle-cry of the late twentieth century.

The response of organizations to the challenges posed by these new competitive pressures has been varied. However, one emerging trend is apparent, and that is the growing emphasis that is being placed upon logistics management as a means of achieving a closer integration between the market place and the firm.

The mission of logistics management is to plan and co-ordinate all those activities necessary to achieve desired levels of delivered service and quality. Logistics is therefore the link between the market place and the operating activities of the business. The scope of logistics spans the organization, from the management of raw materials through to the delivery of the final product. However, in addition to the operational aspects of logistics there is a strategic dimension which is of even greater importance to the achievement of competitive advantage.

It is this strategic dimension of logistics that provides the focal point for the book and I have sought to select articles and papers that reflect the key strategic issues where logistics has a role to play.

I have selected just five issues which I believe are increasingly going to occupy the thoughts of senior executives in the 1990s:

(1) The customer service explosion
(2) Strategic lead-time management
(3) Organizational integration
(4) Throughput management
(5) Globalization

Not all of the twenty papers that I have included in this book fit neatly into one of the five areas above, but between them they throw a clear light on Drucker's so-called 'dark continent' and provide practical guidelines for managerial action.

THE CUSTOMER SERVICE EXPLOSION

So much has been written and talked about service, quality and excellence that there is a danger that these vital issues will become clichés. However, there is no escaping the fact that the customer in today's market place is more demanding, not just of product quality, but also of service.

As more and more markets become in effect 'commodity' markets, where the customer perceives little technical difference between competing offers, the need is for the creation of differential advantage through added value. Increasingly, a prime source of this added value is through customer service.

Reflecting this crucial contribution that service can make to competitive advantage, four of the contributions in the book make this their major theme:

(1) Get leverage from logistics
    R. Shapiro
(2) Customer service logistics
    W. Blanding
(3) Audit your customer service quality
    M. Christopher and R. Yallop
(4) Logistics for service support in the computer industry
    D. Little, J. Mosquera and A.M.A. Wild

Customer service may be defined as the consistent provision of time and place utility. In other words products don't have value until they are in the hands of the customer at the time and place required. There are clearly many facets of customer service, ranging from on-time delivery through to after-sales support. Essentially the role of customer service should be to enhance 'value-in-use', meaning that the product becomes worth more in the eyes of the customer because service has added value to the core product. In this way significant differentiation of the total 'offer' (that is the core product plus the service package) can be achieved.

Those companies that have achieved recognition for service excellence, and thus have been able to establish a differential advantage over their competitors are typically also those companies where logistics management is a high priority. Companies like Rank Xerox, BMW and IBM are typical of such organizations. The achievement of competitive advantage through service comes not from slogans or expensive so-called customer-care programmes, but rather from a combination of a carefully thought out strategy for service, the development of appropriate delivery systems and commitment from people, from the chief executive down.

The attainment of service excellence in this broad sense can only be achieved through a closely integrated manufacturing and marketing strategy. In reality, the ability to become a world class supplier depends as much upon the effectiveness of our operating systems as it does upon the presentation of the product, the creation of images and the influencing of consumer perceptions. In other words, the success of McDonald's, British Airways, or any of the other frequently cited paragons of service excellence, is not due to their choice of advertising agency, but rather to their recognition that the logistics of service delivery on a consistent basis is the crucial source of differential advantage.

STRATEGIC LEAD-TIME MANAGEMENT

A recent international report on new product introductions found that the elapsed time from the drawing board to the market place was actually getting longer, yet at the same time more and more companies are facing volatile markets where product and technology life cycles are getting shorter.

This paradox is forcing management to reappraise the traditional structures and strategies whereby innovation is brought to the market. Similarly the ability to respond to market changes by modifying the existing product portfolio is now a prerequisite for success in many industries.

Clearly there are many implications for management resulting from this reduction of the time 'window' in which profits may be made. Many commentators have focused upon the need to seek out novel forms of managing the new product development process; venture teams along the lines pioneered by DuPont and 3M being one such approach. Others have highlighted the need to improve the quality of the feedback from the market place and to link this more directly into the firm's research and development effort.

All of these initiatives are indeed necessary if the business is to stay alive into the next century. However, amidst all the concern with the process of creating and managing innovation there is one issue which perhaps is only now being given the attention it demands. That issue is the problem of extended lead times.

The concept of logistics lead time is simple: How long does it take to convert an order into cash? Whilst management has long recognized the competitive impact of shorter order cycles, this is only a part of the total process whereby working capital and resources are committed to an order.

From the moment when decisions are taken on the sourcing and procurement of materials and components through the manufacturing and assembly process to the final distribution and after-market support, there are a myriad of complex activities that must be managed if markets are to be gained and retained. This is the true scope of logistics lead-time management.

The articles I have selected to explore these issues are:

(1) Creating a competitive advantage through implementing JIT logistics strategy
    G.A. Isaac III
(2) Managing strategic lead times
    M. Christopher and A. Braithwaite
(3) Fast-cycle capability for competitive power
    J.L. Bower and T.M. Hout
(4) BMW logistics: a step into the future
    H.-U. Pretzsch

Between them they provide some valuable insights into the importance of lead-time management in logistics.

ORGANIZATIONAL INTEGRATION

Whilst the logic of taking a systems view of the business might be apparent, the reality of implementation is something else. The classical business organization is based upon strict functional divisions and hierarchies. It is difficult to achieve a closely integrated, customer focused, materials flow whilst the traditional territorial boundaries are jealously guarded by entrenched management with its outmoded priorities.

In these conventional organizations, materials managers manage materials, whilst production managers manage production and marketing managers manage marketing. Yet these functions are components of a system that needs some overall plan or guidance to fit together. Managing the organization under the traditional model is just like trying to complete a complex jigsaw puzzle without having the picture on the box cover in front of you.

The challenges that face the manufacturing organization in the environment of the 1980s and 1990s are quite different from those of the past. To achieve a position of sustainable competitive advantage, tomorrow's organization will be faced with the need to dispense with outmoded labels like 'marketing manager', 'manufacturing manager' or 'purchasing manager'. Instead we will need broad-based 'integrators' who are oriented towards the achievement of market-place success based upon managing systems and people that deliver service. The clarion call that will increasingly be heard in the last decade that separates us from the twenty-first century is **service superiority**. The ultimate role of the organization therefore is to facilitate the provision of cost-effective service. How else can any of us justify our place on the payroll if we do not have a role in the process of either winning or keeping customers?

Generalists rather than narrow specialists will increasingly be required to integrate materials management with operations management and delivery. Knowledge of systems theory and behaviour will become a prerequisite for this new type of manager. As important will be the orientation of these managers: they will be market-oriented with a sharp focus upon customer service as the primary source of competitive advantage.

There is a very close analogy between the logistics management concept and this flow-oriented notion of integration. Indeed, I would suggest that the logistics model is the appropriate framework which seeks to optimize decisions concerning materials flow across the firm. The goal of logistics management is the achievement of cost-effective service, which, as we have argued, should be the ultimate objective of any organization. Thus the logistics manager has to balance materials requirements with production schedules and with distribution plans.

Many companies who have adopted the logistics concept have also recognized the advantage of extending the philosophy of integration beyond the confines of the organization. This is the idea of **supply-chain management**.

Supply-chain management requires the various parties in the supplier/manufacturer/distributor chain to co-operate in the development of schedules and in the sharing of information. The rapid growth of JIT facilitated by the revolution in electronic data interchange (EDI) has made organizations aware of the great benefits to be obtained by this wider extension of the logistics concept. There is no longer any justification, if indeed there ever was, for the old adversorial buyer/ supplier relationship. Co-makership and joint marketing are the parallel trends of the future.

A major justification for such co-operation is the simple fact that the output efficiency of the supplier will be reflected in the customer's costs. Because material costs represent such a large proportion of the sales pound, perhaps as much as 40% for a typical manufacturer, anything that can be done to reduce those costs should be explored. A point that is sometimes neglected is that the costs of materials to the buyer will include all of the supplier's overheads, which themselves are influenced in part by their logistics costs. Since the supplier's overheads might be as high as 50% of their costs – of which perhaps a third are logistics costs, anything the buyer can do to reduce those costs will be to the advantage of both parties.

The most significant impact that the buyer can have upon the supplier's logistics costs is through the integration of planning systems to provide the supplier with improved visibility of the buyer's materials requirements and through **schedule stability** to enable suppliers to optimize their own production schedules and hence minimize their inventory and working capital investment.

To choose four papers that between them could provide detailed coverage of these issues was not easy but the ones that are included here might all be considered 'classics'. They are

(1) The evolution of the logistics concept
    C.J. Langley
(2) Marketing – logistics opportunities for the 1990s
    R.D. Voorhees and J.I. Coppett
(3) Materials logistics management
    D.J. Bowersox, P.L. Carter and R.M. Monczka
(4) Supply–chain management
    K. Oliver and M. Webber

THROUGHPUT MANAGEMENT

One of the major implications of the three issues already identified (i.e. the customer service explosion, strategic lead-time management and organization integration) is that the task of **throughput management** becomes of the highest priority.

Throughput management is the process whereby manufacturing and procurement lead times are linked to the needs of the market place. At the same time, throughput management seeks to meet the competitive challenge of increasing the speed of response to those market needs.

The goals of throughput management are as follows:

(1) Lower costs
(2) Higher quality
(3) Greater variety
(4) More flexibility
(5) Faster response-times

The achievement of these goals is dependent upon managing the supply chain as a pipeline and seeking to reduce the pipeline length and/or to speed up the flow through that pipeline. In examining the efficiency of supply chains it is often found that many of the activities that take place add more cost than they add value. For example, moving a pallet into a warehouse, re-positioning it, storing it and then moving it out in all likelihood has added no value but has added considerably to the total cost. In looking at its total order cycle from order to delivery, one firm found that only 10% of the time was spent in value-adding activities – the other 90% actually only added cost.

Throughput management is concerned to remove the blockages and the fractures that occur in the pipeline which lead to inventory build-ups and lengthened response times. The source of these blockages and fractures are such things as extended set-up and change-over times, bottlenecks, excessive inventory, sequential order processing and in-adequate pipeline visibility.

To achieve improvement in the throughput process requires a focus upon the lead time as a whole, rather than the individual components of that lead time. In particular the interfaces between the components must be examined in detail.

The greatest opportunity for throughput improvement will generally come from a better use of information regarding demand. Too often data on demand is obscured from view because the **order penetration point** is too far down the chain. In other words when an order hits the system it is passed sequentially from one node in the chain to another, its very existence being hidden by the presence of intermediate stock-holdings. Thus in a traditional system, inventory held by a distributor will hide demand until that distributor's reorder point is reached.

A classic example of a company that has gained competitive advantage though its management of total throughput time is Benetton, the Italian company that has built a global fashion business.

Benetton utilizes direct feedback from its franchised outlets to moni-tor sales trends. Linking this information into its CAD/CAM system and making use of its highly flexible manufacturing processes, it can rapidly produce very small quantities to order. The time from order to delivery is less than four weeks – a performance that is almost unheard of in the fashion business.

By focusing upon reducing throughput times, Benetton has not only increased its responsiveness to market trends, but also has minimized the investment in inventory across its global network.

The four articles I have selected to expand on these issues are as follows:

(1) The rediscovery of logistics
    G. Sharman
(2) Using inventory for competitive advantage through supply–chain management
    T.C. Jones and D.W. Riley
(3) Analytic tools for strategic planning
    W. Copacino and D.B. Rosenfield
(4) Reducing logistics costs at General Motors
    D.E. Blumenfeld et al.

GLOBALIZATION

The fifth of the strategic issues that provide a challenge for logistics management is the trend towards globalization.

There is no doubting that globalization has become a major issue in business. Articles in the business press, seminars and academic symposia have all focused upon the emerging global trend. The competitive pressures and challenges that have led to this upsurge in interest have been well documented. What are less well understood are the implications for operations management in general and specifically for logistics management.

It is important that we define the global business and recognize its distinctiveness from an international or multi-national business. A global business is one which does more than simply export. The global business will typically source its materials and components in more than one country. Similarly it will often have multiple assembly or manufacturing locations geographically dispersed. It will subsequently market its products worldwide. A classic example is the Singer Sewing Machine Company (SSMC). It buys its sewing machine shells from a subcontractor in the USA, the motors from Brazil, the drive shafts from Italy, and assembles the finished machine in Taiwan. It then markets the finished machines in most countries of the world.

The global corporation seems to achieve competitive advantage by identifying world markets for its products and then to develop a manufacturing and logistics strategy to support its marketing strategy.

So whilst a company such as Caterpillar Tractor has dispersed assembly facilities to key overseas markets, it uses tightly controlled logistics channels to supply parts to offshore assembly plants and aftermarkets. Where appropriate, Caterpillar will use 'third-party' companies to manage distribution and even final finishing. So, for example, in the USA a third-party company, Leaseway Transportation, in addition to providing parts inspection and warehousing, actually attaches options to forklift trucks. Wheels, counterweights, forks and masts are installed as specified by Caterpillar. Thus local market needs can be catered for from a standardized production process by working with logistics partners.

Even in a geographically compact area like the European Economic Community we find that there is still significant need for local customization. A frequently cited example is the different preferences for washing machines. The French prefer top-loading machines, the British go for front-loaders, the West Germans prefer high-speed spins, the Italians prefer a slower speed! In addition there are differences in electrical standards and differences in distribution channels. In the UK most washing machines are sold though national chains specializing in white goods. In Italy white goods are sold through a profusion of small retailers and customers bargain over price.

The challenge to a global company like Electrolux, manufacturing washing machines, is how to achieve the cost advantage of standardization whilst still catering for the local demand for variety. Electrolux is responding to that challenge by seeking to standardize on parts, components and modules and then through flexible manufacture and local assembly to provide the specific variants demanded by each market.

In a way, the problem facing Electrolux is the problem that faces every global business: how to structure logistics and operations networks that can provide local service and variety whilst at the same time seeking to achieve a position as a low-cost supplier. The way in which the pipeline from components through to finished product is managed can literally mean the difference between profit and loss for the global corporation. Hence the current emphasis in these businesses upon logistics management.

The four papers selected to address these issues are as follows:

(1) Manufacturing logistics systems for a competitive global strategy
    C. Gopal
(2) International supply–chain management
    J.B. Houlihan
(3) The single European market: optimizing logistics operations in post-1992 Europe
    J.H. Van der Hoop
(4) Formulating and implementing a global logistics strategy
    J.H. Roberts

The overall aim of this book is to provide an insight from a variety of angles into the contribution that logistics strategy can make to the achievement of competitive advantage. It was not easy to restrict my choice of articles to twenty or indeed to limit the strategic issues in the way I have. I have also deliberately not grouped them by their major focus but instead placed them in an order where they might enjoyably and usefully be read consecutively.

Since I first began to get excited about logistics over twenty years ago a lot of development has taken place both in the theory and in the practice. This is clearly a continuing process and hence the selection of material presented in this book can only be a snapshot of the current 'state of the art'. However, I feel fairly confident that in a further twenty years time the ideas presented in these papers will still be as valid as they are now.

CHAPTER ONE

The rediscovery of logistics

G. Sharman

Back when direct labour accounted for the lion's share of manufacturing costs – and manufacturing, in turn, for the lion's share of operating expense – overall competitive ability had little to do with the mastery of logistics. Managing the flow of materials, components, and finished goods was, of course, a responsibility not to be ignored, but it rarely spelled the difference between success and failure in the market place.

Today, in an era of shrinking product life cycles, proliferating product lines, shifting distribution chains, and changing technology, mastery of logistics has become an essential ingredient of competitive success. As the author makes clear, a poorly managed logistics system can create an endless variety of problems, but no one approach or solution will work for every company. The challenge for managers, then, is to understand the often conflicting demands being placed on each system and to decide whether the best response is to make the current system more efficient, rebalance it, or redesign it.

The symptoms vary. An important customer calls to complain again about stockouts or slow deliveries. The Chief Executive Officer (CEO), finally looking into the matter, discovers that inventories of finished products are higher than they've been for three years, or that throughput from raw materials to finished product takes hundreds of times longer than the sum of manufacturing and shipping times, or that a minor upturn in orders produces a convulsion in the factory, or that

Reprinted by permission of *Harvard Business Review*, 'The Rediscovery of Logistics', Graham Sharman, September / October 1984

the company is months behind the competition in getting new products into the market.

Even if the CEO has never lost sleep over logistics before (a safe bet), troubled nights are about to begin. Top managers are, of late, beginning to realize that as customers, wholesalers, and dealers have become more sophisticated and demanding, their dissatisfaction with service levels has increased – as has their willingness to make that dissatisfaction known. Forced to look carefully at logistics performance for the first time in years, these managers often find things gone awry.

The troubles with logistics systems have their roots in deeper and more general trends:

(1) In a wide range of industries, product life cycles are contracting. Life cycles of audio products like home music systems and car radios, for example, have declined over the last decade from years to months. At the extreme, they are shorter than the total throughput time of manufacturers' existing logistics systems. Companies that have gone all out to slash costs by turning to large-scale batch production regularly find themselves saddled with obsolete stocks and unable to keep pace with competitors' new-product introductions.

(2) Product lines are proliferating. As more and more product-line variety is needed to satisfy the growing range of customer tastes and requirements, stock levels in both field and factory inevitably rise. For the vast majority of production facilities that have not yet installed computer-aided manufacturing systems, the costs of assembly-line changes and small-batch production escalate in tandem.

During the 1970s, for example, technologies based on computer-assisted tomography, ultrasound, nuclear magnetic resonance, and digital radiography began to supplement and supplant older X-ray technology in medical diagnostic equipment. Late in 1981 one manufacturer discovered that, since 1976, the number of parts in his products had tripled, inventories as a percentage of sales had risen by half, installation delays and costs had grown, and even planning costs had risen sharply. It took a complete overhaul and redesign of the logistics system – and a reduction of inventory by almost $100 million – to stop the rot.

(3) The balance of power in the distribution chain is shifting from manufacturers to the trade. Consider the market for colour television sets: a decade ago brand image and product features largely governed purchases; now retailers are the dominant influence on the consumer's buying decision. Since retailers can switch buyers

from one brand to another with ease, they have been able to cut their stock levels with impunity, place small orders, and demand speedy delivery at short notice. Manufacturers must comply or face erosion of their market share, and compliance means better logistics performance.

(4) In many industries, the value added by manufacturing is declining as the cost of materials and distribution climbs. One European multinational electronics company discovered that circuit miniaturization in such products as visual display units and microcomputers, combined with explosive sales growth and more stringent delivery requirements, had driven logistics costs up from 9% to 15% of sales.

(5) Many companies are restructuring their production facilities on a global basis. Some manufacturers are centralizing production to gain economies of scale; others find it prudent to set up production facilities in countries like France or Brazil in order to ensure political acceptability in local markets. Either move entails massive changes in logistics arrangements.

(6) The advent of low-cost, high-volume data processing and transmission is revolutionizing logistics control systems. Thanks to these new technologies, managers can now update sales and inventory planning faster and more frequently, and factories can respond more flexibly to volatile market conditions.

Given these trends, many current logistics systems, which were designed for the relatively stable conditions of the 1960s and early 1970s, have grown dangerously obsolete. As Fig. 1.1 indicates, even within a single industry there are vast differences between best and worst practice. The laggards, wallowing in inventories, pay a considerable penalty at today's high levels of real interest rates. More significantly, they operate at a marked competitive disadvantage.

1.1 THE NEED FOR REDEFINITION

As a rule, it is late in the day when shocked top managers start paying attention to an ailing logistics system. This delayed reaction arises partly because the incremental nature of these problems masks their cumulative effect and partly because cross-functional activities like logistics normally lack a voice in top-management councils. The real culprit, however, is the blinkered view of the scope and significance of logistics that has long prevailed.

To most top managers, logistics is just a fancy name for physical distribution – that is, for everything that happens to a product from the

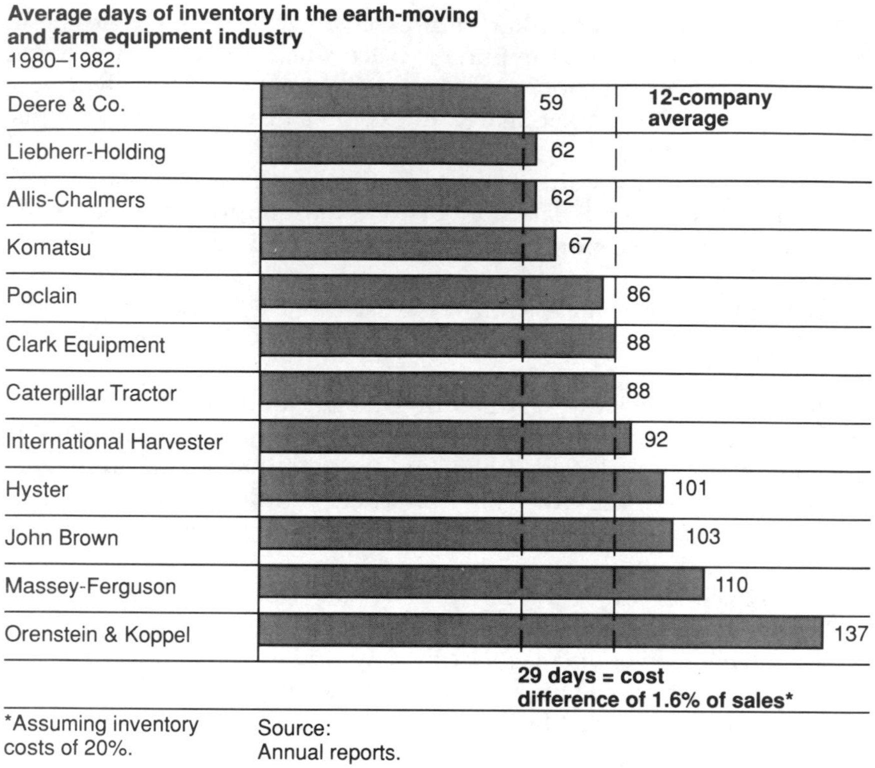

Average days of inventory in the earth-moving and farm equipment industry 1980–1982.

Company	Days	
Deere & Co.	59	12-company average
Liebherr-Holding	62	
Allis-Chalmers	62	
Komatsu	67	
Poclain	86	
Clark Equipment	88	
Caterpillar Tractor	88	
International Harvester	92	
Hyster	101	
John Brown	103	
Massey-Ferguson	110	
Orenstein & Koppel	137	

29 days = cost difference of 1.6% of sales*

*Assuming inventory costs of 20%.

Source: Annual reports.

Figure 1.1 Logistics performance.

time it leaves the factory until it arrives at the customer's premises. This view seriously underestimates the costs of moving and storing semifinished goods and altogether ignores the expense of necessary planning and computer systems. Worse, it obscures the reasons for poor delivery, high finished-goods inventory, and rising transport costs. True, managers who subscribe to the 'logistics = physical distribution' equation may succeed over the short term in cutting finished-goods inventory, but they will not address upstream structural problems until a rash of stockouts or late deliveries finally makes them pay attention.

1.1.1 An integrated view

Every make-and-sell business enterprise is a system for designing, producing, and delivering goods to customers. When properly defined as the total range of activities concerned with the movement of materials, including information and control systems, logistics constitutes a strand running through all the traditional functional responsibilities – from raw materials procurement to product delivery. Given the day-to-day pressures on functional managers to meet performance targets, it is impossible to manage logistics effectively unless its integrative nature is taken seriously.

Taking it seriously, however, does not mean appointing a vice-president for logistics, nor does it mean continuous top-level involvement in logistics decisions. On the contrary, in most companies there are good reasons why these decisions should remain the responsibility of functional managers. Indeed, precisely because logistics touches so wide a range of activities, taking it seriously means appreciating the subtle but powerful effects on logistics of the decisions made within and between the regular functional areas. Manufacturing and marketing people have to accept constraints on some day-to-day decisions. This may require senior management intervention in the beginning, but top-level involvement should be limited to periodic monitoring once the new approach is established.

Such an integrated view of logistics costs divides them into three roughly equal categories:

(1) Most visible and best controlled are transport and handling costs. Companies usually have a good idea of what these costs amount to, although the way companies allocate them to different products and customer groups is often largely guesswork.
(2) Often underestimated are the costs associated with inventory. At current interest rates the annual cost of holding stock in inventory can run as high as a third of its value.
(3) Least obvious and, hence, most often ignored are the staff and computer costs of running the logistics system, including the costs of forecasting demand, planning factory loading, procuring materials, and processing and dispatching orders.

In a manufacturing business, these logistics costs may run in total anywhere from 10% to 30% of sales – which is, as a rule, at least double the CEO's estimate.

Why so? In the first place, these costs are sensitive to factors that either lie beyond management's control or have proved especially hard to cut. Fuel and interest, for example, are more expensive than they were a decade ago, and indirect labour, which accounts for some 70% of logistics systems costs, has proved immune to most attempts to prune overload. In consequence, logistics costs have risen more sharply in the past ten years than have direct manufacturing costs.

More to the point, there is an internal mechanism driving this escalation of logistics costs. As functional managers strive to better their own performance, they tend to hedge lead times and build up buffer stocks. This process feeds on itself: the more determined the push for functional excellence, the costlier these protective measures are likely to become. In a 'make-to-order' business, for example, this vicious cycle frequently leads both engineering and production to hedge lead times and so stretch delivery periods beyond those offered by competitors.

Consider the relation of marketing to production in a 'make-to-stock' business. Marketers often find it difficult or impossible to forecast sales accurately for individual product models. Errors here inevitably lead to stockouts of some models and stock surpluses of others. As a result, production people are constantly besieged by requests from the field for changes in production volume and mix – requests that take little account of lead-time constraints on the factory's ability to respond. In the absence of disciplined short-term planning and control systems, crash changes in production schedules and expediting of suppliers become a way of life.

If, in such a situation, manufacturing performance is measured partly or wholly against a factory 'bogey' or standard of so many units a month, the factory will naturally turn out the model mix for which it has parts and materials. Because this mix is not likely to match the most recent requests from the field, stockouts and surpluses will grow worse. Marketing, of course, reacts by expanding buffer inventories as a shield against the risk of stockouts, while the factory piles up semi-finished parts so that the next flurry of change requests will not set off another factory-floor crisis.

Managers can bring this kind of escalation under effective control only if they are prepared to tackle logistics issues in an integrated way. A co-ordinated approach may well produce a quantum-leap improvement in logistics performance. Without degrading their customer service levels in any way, a number of companies have achieved cost reductions of anything from 1% to 3% of sales.

1.2 ROUTES TO IMPROVEMENT

Implicit in an integrated approach to logistics are important choices between continuous and batch production, between automated and manual warehousing, and between central and decentralized stocking. Taken together, these choices establish a given level of customer service for a given level of cost. With an optimal system, boosting service means raising costs, and reducing costs means cutting service. Most systems, however, are so far from optimal that substantial opportunities do exist for improvement in both costs and service. There are three main routes to such improvement: straightforward reduction of costs, system redesign, and system rebalancing.

1.2.1 Efficiency

Because inefficiencies drive inventories and logistics costs higher than necessary for a given level of service, the most obvious route to better logistics performance is traditional cost reduction. Disposing of dead stocks, policing minimum order-size rules, and cutting warehouse costs, for example, can enhance efficiency without the need for altering a company's logistics system.

Some managers have even begun to follow the Japanese in questioning the need for any inventory at all. The visible ill effects of holding stock – tied-up capital and higher interest costs among them – are only the tip of the iceberg. Excess work-in-process covers up underlying imbalances in equipment capacity and masks chronic manufacturing problems. Finished stocks can deteriorate, be damaged, or become obsolete. Equally important, making to stock delays the recognition of quality problems and, by relaxing the tension in the production process, encourages sloppy work practices.

1.2.2 Redesign

A more radical route to superior performance is through redesign of the logistics system. Although the possible combinations of ways to manage the flow of materials are virtually infinite, the one key variable in every logistics configuration is the point at which a product becomes earmarked for a particular customer. Downstream of this order-penetration (OP) point, customer orders drive the systems that control materials flow; upstream, forecasts and plans do the driving. In most cases, the OP point is where product specifications get frozen. More important, it is also the last point at which inventory is held.

Businesses making products like packaged foods and small appliances, in which the OP point is located at the field warehouse, design logistics systems to facilitate the sale of standard products from local stock. At the other extreme, builders of oil refineries make or adapt all components (pumps, compressors, and so on) to final customer specification. Consequently, the OP point for a refinery producer is located upstream at the design stage. As Fig. 1.2 indicates, OP points vary from industry to industry, as does the location of intermediate stocks.

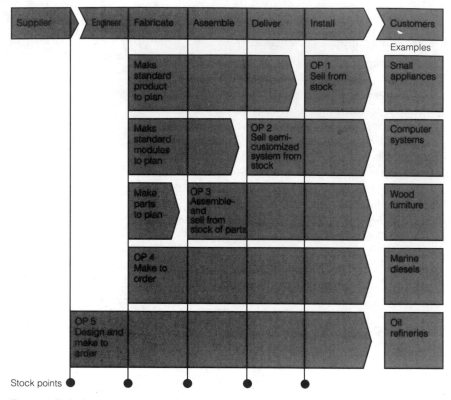

Figure 1.2 Order penetration points.

In some industries, product design and customer segmentation determine the OP point. The purchaser of a Mercedes, for example, specifies optional features two to six months before delivery, and production earmarks each vehicle for its eventual owner before it rolls off the assembly line. By contrast, Toyota supplies most extras as standard equipment and so confines a buyer's options to the choice of colour – a choice that gets made when the car reaches a dealer's showroom or a distributor's lot. Differences in product design and marketing philosophy set the OP point for Toyota at the dealer; for Mercedes, it occurs at the factory.

Thus, for every product design, the optimum logistics configuration, including the OP point, depends on a balance between competitive pressure, product cost and complexity. The stronger the pressure, the greater a manufacturer's incentive to provide better service by moving the OP point downstream and increasing the range of models available

from stock. The greater the cost and complexity, however, the stronger
a manufacturer's incentive to move the OP point upstream. Makers of
industrial fasteners cannot afford frequent stockouts of standard items;
aircraft manufacturers cannot supply commercial passenger planes off
the shelf.

Moreover, a company's optimal OP point will change as market and
industry conditions change. If retailers and wholesalers increase their
leverage within a distribution chain, manufacturers who once forced
distributors to place large orders two or three months in advance may
find themselves compelled to hold local or even consignment stock for
small overnight deliveries. Faced with such challenges, manufacturers
often need to redesign their logistics systems so as to shift their OP
points. They sometimes have to redesign their products as well for
easier handling or more economical storage.

Such redesign can move a company's OP point upstream. One
approach – reducing lead times through shorter planning cycles,
smaller batch sizes, and faster model changeovers – can enable a
manufacturer to eliminate costly finished goods inventory without
compromising service levels. Indeed, making products to order from
stocks of intermediate components saves money and heightens flexibility. Another approach is to change the flow of materials through the
system. Using computer-to-computer ordering may allow a reduction
in safety stock costs if shorter order acceptance and processing times
permit deliveries to be made from a central warehouse.

As any consumer knows, deregulation of the telecommunications
industry has led to a spectacular proliferation of telephone models and
colours. Galled by the heavy cost of stocking a full line in retail phone
boutiques, one manufacturer decided not to assemble each phone in
the factory and ship it to retail shops in ready-to-install form. Instead,
he redesigned the product so that the costly internal mechanisms could
be fabricated and shipped separately from the inexpensive covers.
With a full range of covers but only a few mechanisms in stock, a
retailer could assemble a customer's choice in minutes. Customers
could immediately get any colour of phone, and the number of
mechanisms held at retail locations fell by three-quarters, cutting the
cost of stock by 40%.

Remember, though, that few companies have the same OP points in
all their businesses. The optimum configuration for a company often
includes two or more discrete (or partially discrete) logistics systems,
which are tailored to the requirements of different customer or product
segments. To take an overly simplified example, a broad-line computer
company would use different logistics systems to serve microcomputer
and mainframe customers. In practice, of course, logistics segmenta-

tion is considerably more subtle than this, but the general point stands: there is an appropriate OP point for each separate market segment.

1.2.3 Rebalance

By itself, redesigning a logistics system will seldom prevent the inflation of buffer stocks at the various points of linkage between functions in a company's business. Rectifying this problem is, instead, a matter of rebalancing the system: identifying the key trade-offs in logistics system design, adjusting the priorities of the functions involved, and then changing the planning and control systems as necessary to lock the new trade-offs into place.

For example, in a make-to-stock business the percentage of orders deliverable from stock is usually the best measure of customer service levels. The costs of providing a given service level include the tangible cost of holding safety stock to meet variations in demand and the opportunity cost of losing a sale when the product is out of stock. Only after calculating the optimum cost/service trade-off can managers rebalance the level of local stocks to arrive at the best trade-off between marketing's objective (maximizing inventories to avoid lost sales due to stockouts) and finance's objective (minimizing inventories to reduce capital and related costs).

Similar cost/service trade-offs – and a similar need to rebalance conflicting functional objectives – occur elsewhere in a company's business system. To optimize a rush order procedure, for example, managers must first understand the value of rush delivery to various categories of customers. A rush shipment of printing ink is, after all, likely to be worth more to a newspaper than to a monthly magazine. Depending on the value of the service and the nature of the competition, managers can then either discount prices or add a price premium.

A still more complex logistics-related trade-off is the decision on how much commonality of parts is appropriate in the design of a typical product line. Achieving maximum product performance and value would require that each model be designed from scratch with parts uniquely suited to its requirements. In practice, of course, the need to keep control over parts and work-in-process inventories, to say nothing of the downstream costs of spare parts and service engineers' training, forces managers to settle for less.

Trade-offs can be hard to live with. If, for example, the optimum service level for a given product is 95%, managers must be prepared to accept 5% stockouts and the customer complaints that come with them. Reacting to stockouts for this product by forcing up service levels would disrupt service for other products and compromise the company's ability to respond in a balanced way to all its customers.

Throughout a company's activities, such trade-offs between value and cost are inevitable and will be made either by default or by reasoned analysis. Managers must know, therefore, which trade-offs are critical, must ensure that the information on which to base them is available, and must see to it that the functional managers responsible for implementation adjust objectives and priorities as required. Unless managers bring product development plans, material procurement plans, master production schedules, goods movement plans, and sales plans into harmony, no logistics system can function effectively.

1.3 FIRST STEPS

Suppose a chief executive has recognized symptoms of a logistics problem and wishes to explore the potential for improvement. Where should he or she begin? Because the purpose of an integrated logistics system is to serve customers as well as or better than competitors do, the CEO can start the ball rolling by asking customers for their assessment of the company's delivery times and reliability. Meanwhile, marketing can undertake customer interviews to determine the value customers put on – and the quality of – the company's logistics performance vis-à-vis its competition.

Compared with other elements of the 'product package' (price, characteristics, brand name, technical support, and the like), customers often rank logistics performance surprisingly high in terms of perceived value. Distributors and retailers are increasingly alert to the effect of reliable deliveries in reducing their costs and in enabling them to give their customers more responsive service. In a recent European survey of 11 industries, ranging from semiconductor manufacturing equipment to consumer white goods, customers rated delivery service on a par with product characteristics – and somewhat ahead of both price and brand name – as a determinant of their buying decisions.

To measure a company's logistics service against those of its competitors, managers must find out what parameters of service performance count most heavily with the customer. Figure 1.3 illustrates a not unusual situation in which retail customers rated a company below its competitors on the aspects of service they valued most but above competitors on less-valued aspects. Streamlining the company's order processing and setting new priorities and performance standards in shipping led within three months in this case to increased sales and market share and, eventually, to some improvement in pricing.

Along with this kind of outside-in assessment of logistics performance, an internal assessment, based on measures such as percentage of orders delivered from stock or on time, is likely to turn up some

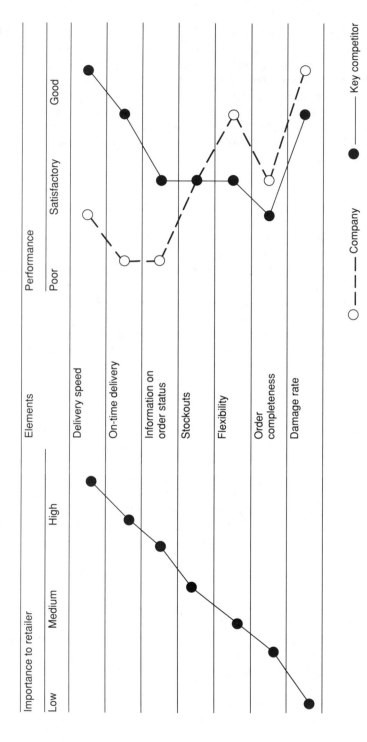

Figure 1.3 Customer service analysis for a consumer durable product.

surprises for senior managers. Indeed, most companies do not track these measures. Other relevant data include the costs and lead times associated with stocking and moving materials through the company's business system and, as shown in Fig. 1.4, the capital and time delays tied up in inventory at all stages of the logistics chain. These assessments should also consider the inventories held by key suppliers and by representative customers, for opportunities may exist to reduce costs and time delays by sharing inventories.

Nor ought managers overlook the number of different items stocked at each stage of the logistics chain. Speeding up lead times through shorter planning cycles or smaller production batches can often reduce finished-goods inventories or even replace them entirely with smaller stocks of less costly subassemblies.

Finally, the decision-making processes that control materials flow are well worth careful review. When, as in the case illustrated by Fig. 1.5, more than one function is involved, the resulting fragmentation of logistics decisions can make the allocation of responsibilities ambiguous. In fact, a poll of this company's middle managers revealed great confusion about who was responsible for each type of decision, and who had to be consulted along the way. The inevitable result of such confusion: inferior customer service and high logistics costs.

After analysing customer needs, current performance levels, costs, lead times, and decision-making processes, managers can accurately identify the level of service their company should provide, the improvement required to reach that level, and the cost of reaching it. Implementing these changes requires, in turn, both careful planning and genuine commitment. Simple cost reduction activities may pay off in a matter of weeks, but it may take months to test and revise control procedures after a system redesign and rebalance. The monitoring of customer service levels and reliability of factory product mix, not just sales trends and factory performance against budget, will be essential. The commitment must be there to carry through – if these changes are to prove worthwhile.

1.4 THE CHALLENGE AT HAND

The discovery of logistics as a senior management concern dates back at least to the rationalization of fragmented warehouse networks, the introduction of formal materials management, and the appearance of systematic inventory planning and control during the 1960s. So marked were the improvements in most companies at that time that logistics dropped to the bottom of managers' priority lists of problem areas.

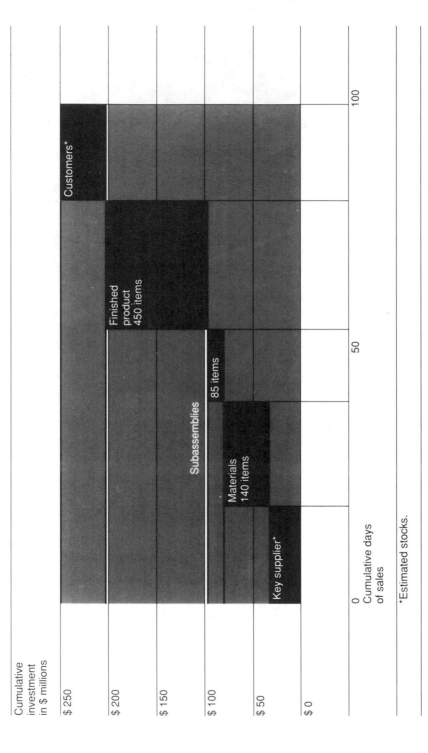

Cumulative
investment
in $ millions

$ 250

$ 200

$ 150

$ 100

$ 50

$ 0

Customers*

Finished
product
450 items

Subassemblies

85 items

Materials
140 items

Key supplier*

0

50

100

Cumulative days
of sales

*Estimated stocks.

Figure 1.4 System-wide dollar and time costs of inventories in a manufacturing company.

| Typical logistics decisions | Factories — Department | | | | Product divisions | | | | Country marketing organizations | | |
	A Factory manager	B Production	C Materials management	D Factory controller	E Marketing	F Product management	G Central planning	H Finance	I Country management	J Product management	K Country controller
Medium term											
Number of product types per country					●					●	
Annual country sales plans (totals and by type)					●		●		●	●	
Monthly country sales pattern by country					●		●			●	
Finished goods inventory per country					●		●		●	●	●
Production level (total by product family and type)	●				●	●	●		●		
Production allocation	●				●	●	●		●		
Component make/buy decisions			●		●		●				
Short term											
Monthly production plan per factory	●	●	●				●			●	
Materials stock level per factory	●	●	●	●		●	●	●	●		●
Allocation of output	●						●		●		

● Significant departmental involvement

Figure 1.5 Decision fragmentation in a multinational company.

Only now is the critical relationship between logistics and business performance once again becoming a focus of management attention.

One symptom of this renewed concern, documented in annual surveys carried out for the National Council of Physical Distribution Management, is the increased responsibility of logistics managers at both the business and the corporate level. True, such middle-management concern can help raise a company's awareness of logistics issues, but it cannot trigger the type of top-down, comprehensive review of the whole logistics chain suggested above. Top-management initiative and sponsorship are needed too – not least because these issues have become too far-reaching in their effects for any simple 'fix' within the logistics function.

Leading companies, for example, are already testing and installing computer-aided design, production, and scheduling technology that requires the integration of all operations and information systems within the factory, permitting radical increases in product customization and production flexibility that can confer important competitive advantages. These advantages will, however, be realized only if the companies can effectively manage this increase in product variety, traditionally the bane of logistics control.

As computer-integrated manufacturing penetrates an industry, the survivors will be the companies that master the structure and control of materials flow – not only within the factory but also with suppliers and customers. The Kanban or 'just-in-time' inventory systems in the Japanese automobile industry provide a taste of things to come in relations between OEMs and suppliers. It is the link with customers, however, that offers the greatest potential for computer-integrated logistics. In the food industry, which has often in the past been a logistics pioneer, the emergence of computer-to-computer ordering, the widespread use of a common bar-code labelling system, and the availability of direct product costing now permit integration and optimization of the whole manufacturer–retailer logistics system.

To today's managers, preoccupied as they are with more immediate challenges, logistics may seem an unlikely battleground in the contest for future competitive advantage. But it is, indeed, where much of that battle will be fought. The rediscovery of logistics is occurring not a moment too soon.

CHAPTER TWO

The evolution of the logistics concept

C. John Langley Jr.

INTRODUCTION*

The logistics concept has undergone many significant changes over the past two decades, and is likely to be on the cutting edge of innovation and creativity in the years ahead. This article provides a commentary on the evolution of the logistics concept, and in so doing, highlights a number of significant accomplishments which have been made to date. In addition, a number of key areas where future change is likely and needed will be identified and discussed.

The overall approach of this article is to cast the evolution of logistics into three specific contexts: logistics past, logistics present and logistics future. By understanding where we have come from and where we are at present, we will be in a better position to understand and anticipate the likely priorities and directions of the future. There is no question that unbelievable opportunities and challenges still lie ahead.

Also, the discussion will draw liberally upon the rich background of commentary and experience which relates extensively to a number of historical perspectives on logistics. The topic of 'evolution of logistics' is not a new one, and there are many people who already have made assessments and evaluations of where we were in the past and what they regarded as the priorities of those days.[†] Following acknowledgement of

---

* An earlier version of this manuscript was delivered as the keynote address at the European International Logistics Workshop, conducted by the Council of Logistics Management and held in Brussels, Belgium, June 9, 1986.
† Although the contributions of a number of authors could be cited here, an exceptionally interesting sequence of three articles appeared in Vol. 4, No. 1 of the *Journal of Business Logistics*. Included were the following: La Londe, Bernard

Source: Langley, C.J. (1986) *Journal of Business Logistics*, 7(2), 1–13

several of these contributions, an editorial commentary will be provided on the topics of where we are and where we are headed.

One preliminary issue is that of terminology, and specifically the meaning of terms such as logistics, materials management, and physical distribution. While many authors go to great lengths to provide concise definitions of each of these terms, the fact is that in actual business practice these terms are often used interchangeably. Each professional in this field has at least a slightly different interpretation of what each of these terms means, as does each and every individual business or enterprise in existence. For this reason, terminology will not be an issue here if it is assumed that there is some common understanding that any or all of these terms refer generally to a comprehensive set of activities relating to the movement and storage of product and information. These activities are all undertaken to achieve two common goals, namely, providing an acceptable level of customer service, and operating a logistics system to provide overall conformity to customer requirements.

2.1 LOGISTICS PAST

One would think that an activity as large as logistics would be as well known as the marketing, sales, finance, legal, or engineering professions. Surprisingly, it is not. Because movement does not really change the appearance of an item, many people seldom think of packaging, material handling, warehousing, or transportation as adding value to a product. And yet, a piece of industrial equipment manufactured in

---

J., 'A reconfiguration of logistics systems in the 80s: strategies and challenges', pp. 1–11; Heskett, James L., 'Challenges and opportunities for logistics executives in the 1980's', pp. 13–19, and Bowersox, Donald J., 'Emerging from the Recession: The Role of Logistical Management', pp. 21–33. Also relevant and insightful are: La Londe, Bernard J., Grabner, John R. Jr. and Robeson, James F., 'Integrated distribution systems: past, present, and future', appearing as Chapter 2 in *The Distribution Handbook* (New York, NY: The Free Press, 1985), pp. 15–27; Langley, C. John Jr., 'Physical distribution management: a strategic perspective', *Proceedings – 1982 Annual Conference of the National Council of Physical Distribution Management* (Oak Brook, IL: National Council of Physical Distribution Management, 1982); and Stewart, Wendell N., La Londe, Bernard J., Heskett, James L. and Bowersox, Donald J., 'A Look to the Future', appearing as Chapter 4 in *The Distribution Handbook* (New York, NY: The Free Press, 1985), pp. 44–72.

Germany, but destined for Chicago, Illinois, is of little value until it is available at the right time, at the right place, and in the right condition. The logistical requirements which ensure the necessary unique combination of packaging, handling, storage, and transportation – that is, logistics – in many cases double the value of a product from the time it is manufactured or grown until it is consumed or used in a further industrial process.

In terms of historical development leading to today's contemporary physical distribution and logistics functions, Donald J. Bowersox analysed the development of the distribution and logistics function in three stages.* The first was the stage from 1950 to 1964 titled 'Origination and a new direction'. In the post-war years, product proliferation and scrambled merchandising, two basic marketing trends, forced the need for managers to look for new ways to help control distribution costs. Physical distribution management was born in a reactive posture, with the original impetus being to react to marketing problems. Although physical distribution costs range from 10 to 30% of sales and even more in some firms, very few companies have the organizational structure in place to take advantage of the wide range of trade-offs in the area of logistics or physical distribution management. For example, most management people in physical distribution during the 1950–64 period did not have responsibility for inventory control, and so there was no mechanism to justify larger inventories, for example, in order to realize transportation costs savings. The greatest challenge of this era was to gain top management's awareness of the concept of physical distribution.

However, such generalizations must be viewed in the proper perspective. The first issue is to keep in mind the fact that logistics and distribution were not entirely new concepts, even in the era 1950–64, and that even some of the trade-off decisions which are being highly touted today are actually far from what could referred to as 'contemporary'. For example, a readings book prepared a number of years ago by Norm Daniel and Dick Jones recited a very interesting passage which was published in the year 1844 by Jules Dupuit, a French engineer, in explaining how a shipper might choose between road and water carriage. The text of his statement reads as follows:†

> The fact is that carriage by road being quicker, more reliable and less subject to loss or damage, it possesses advantages to which business-

---

* Bowersox, Donald J., 'Emerging from the Recession: The Role of Logistical Management', pp. 21–24.
† Daniel, Norman E. and Jones, J. Richard. *Business Logistics Concepts and Viewpoints* (Boston, MA: Allyn and Bacon, Inc., 1969), p. xi.

men often attach a considerable value. However, it may well be that the saving of 0 fr.87 induces the merchant to use the canal; he can buy warehouses and increase his floating capital in order to have sufficient supply of goods on hand to protect himself against the slowness and irregularity of the canal, and if all told the savings of 0 fr.87 in transport cost gives him an advantage of a few centimes, he will decide in favor of the new route ...

Thus, the concept of trading off transportation and inventory costs was recognized formally at least as early as the mid-1880s, and exploitation of this basic trade-off surely goes even farther back in time.

In the early 1960s Peter Drucker, the often quoted management guru, identified the problem and focused attention on the challenges and opportunities in the field of logistics and distribution. Quoting Drucker from his 1962 landmark article titled 'The economy's dark continent':[†]

We know little more about distribution today than Napoleon's contemporaries knew about the interior of Africa. We know it is there, and we know it is big; and that's about all. There are plenty of experts on individual phases: on transportation and warehousing, on retailing and consumer buying habits, on labeling and packaging, on factoring and insurance. But when a major government department recently looked for two or three men to advise it on distribution, none of the many people consulted in industry, government, and even the universities could name even one qualified candidate ...

Professor Drucker identified the challenge, and then left it for others to accept it and resolve it. For this reason, the years which have intervened since the early 1960s have seen significant advances and progress made in the fields of logistics and distribution, and part of the responsibility for this progress should be attributed to the relatively stern and forthright evaluation made by Peter Drucker in those early years.

2.2 LOGISTICS PRESENT

The 20-year period leading up to the present has been one of the most exciting and intense eras in the history of logistics and physical distribution. It was during this period of time that business people and educators made a firm commitment to themselves and to their pro-

---

[†] Drucker, Peter F., 'The economy's dark continent', *Fortune*, April, 1962.

fession to 'accept the challenge', and to do whatever it would take to improve the professionalism and effectiveness of the logistics function within today's modern business firm.

A number of significant accomplishments were made during this time period, and it is important to consider the key areas in which progress has been made. 'Logistics present' is the culmination of many exhaustive and effective efforts.

Bowersox refers to the era beginning in 1965 as 'the years of maturity for physical distribution and materials management.'* An emphasis on customer service during this period was a significant factor in the maturing of physical distribution and logistics management. In addition to the fact that the physical distribution manager began to have a significant say in inventory decision-making, it was recognized that a well-managed logistics operation could have a positive effect on cash flow by reducing the length of the order cycle, and hence by reducing accounts receivable. Physical distribution executives could feel comfortable taking a 'proactive' rather than a 'reactive' approach to decision-making.

Also in this time period, an integration of physical distribution and materials management took place. This recognized the need to coordinate both the inbound and the outbound movements of product and information, and as a result produced a far more effective and responsive organizational structure.

Coupled with the contemporary capabilities of state-of-the-art computers and management information systems, the top management people in the areas of physical distribution and materials management began to be recognized as truly executive level decision-makers. Thus, perhaps a meaningful way to look at this era and its results is to identify and discuss a number of milestone accomplishments which were made.

The first is that we have finally succeeded in achieving some consensus as to what we mean by logistics management. While terminology is unique to each and every individual and business, there appears to be some general agreement that the term 'logistics' actually combines the individual concepts of materials management and physical distribution. As a result, and in coordination with its recent name change, the Council of Logistics Management has restated its definition of logistics:

---

* Bowersox, Donald J., 'Emerging from the Recession: The Role of Logistical Management', pp. 24–27.

Logistics is the process of planning, implementing, and controlling the efficient, cost-effective flow and storage of raw materials, in-process inventory, finished goods and related information from point of origin to point of consumption for the purpose of conforming to customer requirements.

It is important to note that this definition includes inbound as well as outbound material flows. It includes in-plant as well as dock-to-dock movements. It stresses co-ordination and control of storage and movement systems.

Although the Council's earlier definition of 'physical distribution management' placed emphasis on the specific activities contained within the function, the current definition does not provide such a listing, but by implication suggests that the range is actually quite broad. Depending upon what is moving and where it is moving, the functions could easily be interpreted to include activities such as: transportation, order processing and related distribution center operations, inventory control, purchasing, production, and customer and sales services. While the term 'logistics' can have exceptionally broad implications, the true focus of the logistics function will vary from firm to firm.

Finally on the topic of what we mean by logistics, there appears to be a high sense of agreement that logistics activities are performed for the purpose of conforming to customer requirements, whether these requirements take the form of customer service needs or manufacturing facility needs. By incorporating the generic term 'conformity to requirements', the goal of any logistical effort may be communicated accurately and successfully.

Second, the alternative roles of logistics within the business firm have been identified and analysed. The four stages in the development of a logistics function range from stage one, which is the least sophisticated, to stage four, which is the most advanced.*

There is a disconcertingly large number of firms which have advanced no further than stage one, in which physical distribution or logistics is viewed only as an area for cost control. Unfortunately, while some of these firms have designated certain people in the area of logistics to hold important-sounding titles, the fact is that logistics is not viewed necessarily as a key element of the firm's overall strategic activity. Stage two companies have recognized the fact that logistics capabilities can have a positive, or revenue-enhancing impact on sales,

---

* For a more detailed explanation of the various stages in the development of the logistics function, see Langley, C. John Jr., 'Emerging from the Recession: The Role of Logistical Management', pp. 837–839.

and they have been able to justify a profit-centre orientation. The fact that many firms have not been fully successful in measuring the precise impacts of physical distribution capabilities on sales should not cause us to relegate their position from stage two back to stage one. While credit should be given here for at least trying, it is hoped that a continued effort will produce results before too long. Stage three is reserved for those firms which have advanced beyond the profit-centre concept itself, and which view logistics as a key way in which a firm can differentiate its product and service offerings from its competitors. In this way, the firm's logistics capabilities can be considered a key input to strategy formulation in the area of market segmentation. Finally, there are certain instances in which a firm's principal strategic advantage revolves around its logistics activity, and thus the designation of stage four is warranted. While this stage certainly represents the highest level of importance for the logistics function within the firm, aspiration to this level seems less appropriate for certain industries than for others. As a general goal, each individual business firm should exploit every opportunity to rise to at least stage two, and preferably stage three.

Also related to the present status of logistics within the firm is an increasingly high level of visibility for this important function, and a recognition by executive level management of its true strategic importance. Actually, the fact is that logistics is being used more frequently as a means to develop a competitive advantage, whether it be in the form of helping to lower the unit cost of doing business, or as an added means of achieving differentiation in the market place. At any rate, the obvious trend is that companies are expecting more from their logistics function, and they are not being disappointed. Last, today's logistics functions are far more comprehensive than those of yesteryear, and they generally include more activities. While managers in other areas of the business firm are sometimes concerned about the apparent desire of logistics managers to increase the scope of their responsibility, a true understanding of the definition of logistics will actually justify such expansion in most cases.

Another major area of accomplishment during the past twenty years is that we have identified the need to integrate our logistics systems, and we have made significant progress toward accomplishing this goal. Specifically, we have begun to measure our logistics costs, understand trade-offs, and make integrated logistics decisions. We have adopted an emphasis on the order cycle as a basis for the evaluation of customer service levels, and have made significant progress in the area of formal systems for accounting and control. Thus, we have demonstrated an ability to be far more effective in the co-ordination and management of a number of logistics activities in a simultaneous fashion.

In addition, it is encouraging to see the ability of the logistics function to co-ordinate and work closely with other major functional areas of the firm. Meaningful interrelationships with areas such as marketing, finance, and corporate management are essential to the continuing responsiveness of logistics to the priorities of the day.

One other way in which logistics systems have become more integrated is evidenced by the trend toward development of partnership arrangements with vendors, customers, and external third parties. This trend is clearly defined and supported by the fact that more and more firms have adopted a 'total channel' perspective on their businesses, and have developed linkages with vendors and customers in an effort to make more 'win–win' logistical decisions which benefit both parties. Also, efforts have been successful at developing effective customer service policies, and redefining sources and procurement strategies so as to effectively link in with channel partners. Last, we have begun to take advantage of the capabilities offered by third-party suppliers of essential logistical services, and this trend appears to be a growing one.

A fourth area of significant accomplishment in recent years is that we have seen the development and emergence of a number of fine academic programmes which have focused squarely on issues and approaches which are most central to logistics management. We have succeeded in legitimizing logistics at the university level, and as a profession, are now able to direct our best and brightest career prospects to any one of a number of fine university programmes in this area. We have seen significant upgrading in recent years in the quality and quantity of entry level positions for degree candidates who have chosen logistics management as an area of concentration, and there is no question that industry has attached a priority to seeking people who have an interest and background in logistics management. The academic community must continue to turn out graduates who have knowledge and insight in areas which will be most valuable to the business world. It will take a continued closeness of thinking and planning between the academic community and the business world in order to meet this challenge in the future.

Fifth, it is accurate to categorize or characterize the past twenty years as a period of time during which we have made considerable progress in terms of professionalizing the logistics function in the business firm and positioning ourselves to take even greater advantage of our logistical strengths in the future. Although the factors will change from one part of the world to the next, in the USA we have seen a recent significant reduction in the nation's logistics bill expressed as a percentage of our gross national product. While there are a number of ways to interpret this change, the most popular one is that we have become more effective at managing our logistics activities, and as a result, have been able to achieve conformity to customer requirements at generally lower levels of unit costs.

2.3 LOGISTICS FUTURE

There are several specific areas wherein 'logistics future' will succeed in distinguishing itself from logistics present and logistics past.

The first is that we are seeing a tremendous contemporary interest in the topic of 'quality' and the importance of quality management to the overall logistics effort. Just as many of our top corporations have made a commitment to quality, we are seeing firms attach a priority to the development of innovative programs to achieve quality in the logistics area. Whether quality is defined in general terms such as 'doing it right the first time', or 'zero defects', or perhaps even 'statistical process control', these efforts are all designed to produce conformity to customer requirements. Given the fact that the logistics area of the firm is very activity-oriented, there is ample opportunity to develop logistical systems and capabilities which will lead to the desired levels of conformity.

Second, significant advances are being made in terms of our ability to integrate the concepts of 'time' and 'space'. Logistics decisions have traditionally been made with regard to these two concepts, but in general they have been treated separately, rather than jointly. For example, we frequently speak of time in terms of minutes, hours, or days; and space in terms of miles or kilometres. The fact is that we have been reminded by a number of authors about the importance of combining these two concepts, and there is no question that we will make significant advances in this area during the years ahead.

The third area where logistics future will distinguish itself relates to the tremendous opportunities in international logistics. While international marketing may be viewed largely as a matter of choice, international sourcing and procurement in many instances should be regarded as a matter of economic necessity. As companies in various industries expand their ability to procure needed raw materials, component parts, and goods for resale from off-shore and third-world vendors, this places significant pressure on competitor firms to at least investigate the acquisition of similar capabilities. To choose not to respond to this type of challenge can very quickly manifest itself as economic suicide for the firm which refuses to change the time-honoured ways of doing business. As a result, progressive firms are looking for additional ways to increase their business strengths through appropriate international business relationships. This trend will not only continue, but there will be an increasing interest of firms desiring to compete and operate in the international arena.

Fourth, there will be changing emphasis toward the consideration of logistical 'attributes', rather than continually making direct reference to 'specific logistical services'.* Perhaps the transportation activity is the best example, in that in the USA we have traditionally relied upon characterizing transportation activity in very specific terms such as truckload, less-than-truckload, rail-car load, small package, etc. The wave of the future will be to unbundle these specific terms into their key underlying 'attributes', and to procure transportation services which most closely match the set of attributes which are desirable, and which may or may not exactly match the capabilities of a mode or carrier which is presently available. In this way, we will not only receive what we are asking for in greater measure, but for all practical purposes will encourage the development of innovative and progressive forms of transportation to help meet those needs.

Fifth, is the emergence of the 'ultimate' third part. While under the logistics present scenario third parties were becoming more and more involved in the logistics function, increasing attention is being directed to the use of third parties literally to take over the entire distribution and/or logistics function within a firm. We have some excellent examples of this at present in the domestic USA, and our level of sophistication regarding third party and dedicated contract services is surpassed significantly by what has occurred to date in Europe. While this approach to doing business may be somewhat alien to traditionally oriented managers, there is a critical need to understand exactly what needs to be done, and then to identify and develop the best approach to accomplish those goals.

The sixth area distinct to logistics future is the possibility that many of today's top logistics managers are actually in the process of working themselves out of a job.† While at first glance this may appear to be a somewhat austere statement, the fact is that a well-rounded logistics

---

* Usage of the word 'attribute' in this section is analogous to the fact that many marketers define a product in terms of its attributes, or services it provides, rather than its specific physical characteristics.
† The notion that logistics managers may be 'working themselves out of a job' was first noted and discussed by Heskett, James L., 'Challenges and opportunities for logistics executives in the 1980's', *Journal of Business Logistics*, **4**(1), 18–19.

organization may be regarded internally as so important to the company's overall direction, that it sometimes becomes difficult to tell the difference between logistics management and corporate management. What has really happened in this type of situation is that the logistics concept has succeeded in permeating activities throughout the firm, and the loss of its separate identity in no way indicates a diminishing of the importance of logistics. Also, logistics managers who have succeeded in developing those systems which are effective, may very well have established a track record of performance which will qualify them for higher-level positions in corporate management or in the management of other functional areas. Such promotions should not only be viewed as reflective of the contribution of the individual, but also awareness and tacit approval of the importance of logistics to the overall goals of the firm. Success stories such as these are occurring at an increasing rate today.

Seventh, and finally, there is a tremendous need for all of us to educate others regarding the logistics concept, and to assist in communicating and marketing it to other functional areas of business and to other sectors of industry. It is incumbent upon each of us to do whatever we can to 'sell' the logistics concept, and to make others aware of the benefits which can accrue from attaching a priority to responsible management in this area of the firm. Since there are various ways in which the logistics function can help to lower costs and differentiate a firm from its competitors, there is ample opportunity to use logistics as a tool to help make other functional areas of the firm look better. To the extent that this occurs, the internal credibility and concern for the logistics function will unquestionably accelerate.

2.4 CONCLUSION

There are two quotes which come to mind regarding the path which logistics has taken through the past, present and the future. While they are not overly complementary, we sometimes make the most progress when someone has succeeded in irritating us. For example, to paraphrase another portion of Peter Drucker's earlier essay,*

> To a technically oriented man, most of the work in distribution is donkey work and the technical man tends to put a donkey in charge – more often than not a man of proved incompetence for more 'demanding' work as a manufacturing supervisor.

---

* Drucker, Peter F. 'The economy's dark continent, *Fortune*, April, 1962.

Bernard J. La Londe has made an interesting observation in that American management's philosophy (toward distribution) for some time had been: 'If you're smart enough to make it, aggressive enough to sell – then any dummy can get it there!'[†]

Comments like these have encouraged many of us to 'accept the challenge' with an even greater vigour and to push the forefront of logistics thinking and innovation to the highest levels possible. While there are a number of areas in which progress needs to be made, we should be exceptionally proud of the level of accomplishment which has been exhibited to date. The priorities of the future have been identified, however, and the next step is to move forward in these directions.

[†] Shapiro, Roy D. (1984) 'Get leverage from logistics', *Harvard Business Review*, 119–126.

CHAPTER THREE

Marketing-logistics opportunities for the 1990s

Roy Dale Voorhees and John I. Coppett

Technological advancements and deregulation in the transportation and communications industries have opened a host of new opportunities for nearly any business to improve its techniques for delivering products and services to customers. As a result, logistics, or the delivery of goods, is moving to the forefront as a way to reap dramatic profits.

Logistics has become separated from the marketing function in many companies. This separation poses a serious problem for management in its efforts to formulate viable strategies for the 1990s. It is the purpose of this article to examine why the functions have separated and why they should be put back together to form the basis for a business strategy for the 1990s.

3.1 THE SEPARATION OF MARKETING AND LOGISTICS

New marketing problems developing at the beginning of this century did not of themselves produce a marketing concept. They impelled thought, resulting in the gradual evolution (from 1900 to 1980) of a marketing concept (Bartels 1976). During the first part of the evolution, marketing became the business discipline concerned with the complete distribution of goods and services. This included both the negotiations

Source: Voorhees, R.D. and Coppett, J.I. (1986) *Journal of Business Strategy*, **7**(2), 33–8
Reprinted by permission

leading to the transfer of ownership and also the physical storage and delivery of goods. However, during the 1930s more emphasis was placed on selling and sales management and less attention was devoted to logistics. In the 1950s, Wroe Alderson broadened the marketing concept with the new term 'marketing management'. This concept focused on creating new demands, taking the action needed to satisfy them, and paying less attention to purely physical exchanges (Alderson 1982). Alderson was followed by Kotler and McCarthy in the 1960s and 1970s. They popularized the concept of the '4 Ps' in marketing – price, promotion, product, and place (logistics or physical distribution). During this period, marketing emphasized its transaction, promotion, and product negotiation functions and neglected logistics. As a result, logistics gradually received separate management attention and became increasingly separated from marketing. At present, marketing and logistics are managed separately in more than 50% of the Fortune 500 companies. According to Bartels, the separation can be attributed to three basic reasons (Bartels 1982).

(1) During the post-World War II years, the logistics costs of business rose, and these increased costs created a profit sequeeze for US businesses. The significance of theses costs for business was highlighted in Drucker's classic article, 'The dark continent', in which he compared business executives' ignorance of logistics costs to the ignorance of Napoleon about 'the large dark continent of Africa' (Drucker 1962, p. 103). To treat this ignorance, in the 1960s management began paying more attention to the costs of storing and distributing goods. This increased focus on storage and transportation costs contributed to the separation of marketing and logistics.
(2) Conceptual voids in marketing thought hastened the separation of marketing and logistics. For example, the marketing literature of the 1950s did not include transportation and storage institutions as marketing institutions.
(3) Separation was also caused by confusion about delivery responsibilities in marketing channels. Logistics gradually assumed primary responsibility for transportation and warehousing actions within traditional marketing channels. This left marketing with the primary responsibility for negotiating, promoting, and selling rather than the overall responsibility for all aspects of channel management.

3.2 THE LOGISTICS–SEGMENTATION PROBLEM FOR THE 1990s

With business, the fundamental problem has always centred on the relationship with the customer. This relationship needs to be managed

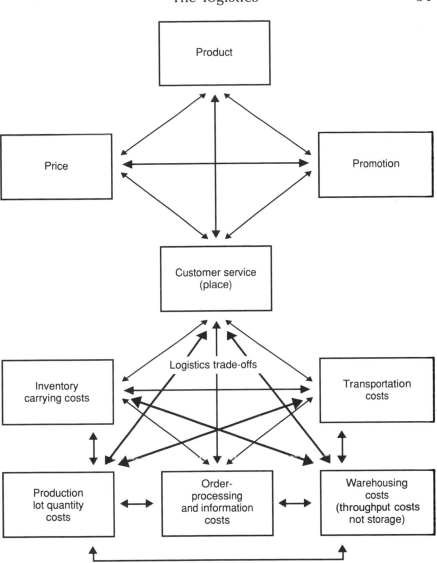

Figure 3.1 The four Ps and customer service (Source: Lambert 1976, p. 7).

for profit. Profitability is determined largely by the difference in the selling price of a product and the cost of providing it to a customer. In fact, the marketing functions of product, price, and promotion are highly dependent on the cost of making a product available to a customer. In Fig. 3.1, this availability is called customer service (place). The exhibit shows the function of customer service as fundamental to other marketing functions and central to logistics cost trade-offs.

Although market segmentation is a foundation stone for marketing, the segmentation of logistics into individualized services for specific customer needs is just emerging. The traditional negotiation over product and price with a customer is well understood; the negotiation for logistics services is not so well known. Increased logistics options for customers mean that profit or loss is now dependent not only on negotiations over products and prices but also on negotiated logistics services stemming from the trade-offs illustrated in Fig. 3.1. Some examples of logistics services that can be negotiated and tailored to fit individual customer needs are described below.

(1) A wide choice of transportation costs can be based on the use of different transportation modes and combinations of modes, such as piggyback, air truck, and others, stimulated by transportation deregulation. For example, CSX, one of the nation's largest railways, provides an intermodal transportation solution to citrus growers with its Orange Blossom Special. By combining its high-speed Seaboard System with truck pickups and delivery, it is offering a logistic service, or fast delivery option, which can be integrated into the marketing programme serving citrus growers – its customers.

(2) Different logistics prices and services can be tailored to different elasticities of product demand. This could mean higher distribution prices for products with inelastic demands and lower prices for products with higher elasticities of demand. For example, the Burlington Northern Railroad, the nation's largest railroad, uses a hub strategy, which focuses on the market needs of shippers in their major markets. This strategy integrates local service into long-distance rail service and is co-ordinated by a single management sensitive to the transportation needs, products, prices, and markets of shippers in hub areas.

(3) Negotiable prices can be based on the consistency or reliability of logistics services. Safety stocks can be reduced through careful planning and reliable transportation. Reducing safety stocks, which protect against variations in demand and resupply times, can reduce inventory carrying costs and improve efficiency. An example of this strategy is the Ryder–Ford Motor Company relationship. Ryder distributes most of Ford's parts on the East Coast with a guaranteed second-day delivery. This consistency of delivery reduces the need for safety stock inventory. The reduction translates into savings for the customer.

(4) Shipping more often but in smaller quantities can mean savings on high-value inventory. For example, use of premium transportation, such as airlines or dedicated truck loads, can reduce inventory in

transit but transportation costs will be higher. For high-value commodities, the extra cost of a fast, reliable carrier may mean an overall logistics saving by reducing inventory in transit costs. The use of air transport to supply more shopping malls in Hawaii is an example of this application.

(5) The ability to buy transport service on a large scale through contracts is perhaps the most important change from the previous practice of using common carrier transportation. For example, General Motors has negotiated more than eighty-five transportation contracts covering 35% of its rail costs. Contract transportation can be more closely tailored to fit the unique logistics needs of customers than could the use of traditional common carriage (Schneider 1985, pp. 118–26).

(6) Flexible deals can be made for special customers under transportation deregulation. New strategies based on the new services offered by rail contracts, which can vary widely in price and service, are both possible and popular. For example, the Chicago and Northwestern Railroad has developed an advanced program of negotiating contracts with more than 100 separate customers; each contract is tailored to the customer's specific needs. The contracts differ widely and can last from less than a year up to 35 years. In all cases, the new objectives of the contracts are to negotiate around customers' needs instead of around standard services available from the fixed schedules of common carriers. Before deregulation, these flexible deals were not available for special customers.

(7) Transport costs can be lowered by holding shipments for consolidation or by granting the carrier authority to defer shipments within guaranteed delivery-time limits. This method has become widespread in air cargo shipments. Air carriers have lower prices available for shipments that can be deferred, if necessary, to flights that are not fully loaded. By keeping shipments in a standby status, airlines can make better use of their capacity and share some of these savings with shippers.

(8) Alternative levels of services can be established under contract pricing for different cities or territories. For example, Roadway Express, one of the nation's largest truckers, used few contract rates before motor carrier deregulation in 1980, but between 1982 and early 1984 it negotiated 35 contracts with individual shippers for nearly $200 million in revenues (Schneider 1985, pp. 118–26).

Although the foregoing examples are by no means a listing of all possibilities, they are a sample of what is available. As a result, the co-ordination of the new flexible logistics services with traditional

Table 3.1 Capabilities and costs of communications

Year	1958	1965	1972	1980
Technology	Vacuum tube	Transistor	Integrated circuit	Large-scale integrated circuit
Cost per unit	$ 8.00	$ 0.25	$0.02	$0.001
Cost per calculation using a computer	$160.00	$12.00	$2.00	$0.05

Source: McKenney and McFarlow (1982, pp. 109–21)

marketing functions has become a major business opportunity for the 1990s. Before transportation deregulation, the costs of these services were fixed and known to everyone. Now they are flexible, frequently uncertain, usually unknown, and generally negotiable around customer preferences. As a result, the typical market transaction of the past, with a single negotiation over the price of the product or service, is being replaced with the transaction of the future, which has two negotiating dimensions – one for marketing and one for logistics. Indeed, the addition of negotiations for the logistics function is increasing the possibilities for different prices and services. These increased possibilities are making both marketing and logistic decisions more inseparable and, as a result, the two functions now need to be integrated and managed together.

3.3 TECHNOLOGY AND THE DEREGULATION OF COMMUNICATIONS

The technological improvements in the industry and the recent deregulation of communications are also having a synergistic effect on logistics and marketing options. Table 3.1 indicates the basic technological improvements, along with their capabilities, that are available in the current market.

Because of the increased performance and decreased costs indicated in Table 3.1 as well as the new market flexibility available under communications deregulation, many business firms are purchasing new electronics capabilities and applying them to their logistics and marketing activities. For example, the use of advanced electronic order entry communications technology by Crown Zellerbach has integrated its marketing and distribution functions with its customers. It enables customers to order directly and to obtain the price and distribution

Table 3.2 Impact of Communications and Data Processing on Logistics and Marketing Activities*

		Results reported (%)	No impact (%)
A	Order cycle length	78 decreased	15
B	Inventory requirements	72 decreased	22
C	Customer service (place)	86 improved	10
D	Frequency of stockouts	77 decreased	20
E	Reorders (to correct delivery failures)	36 decreased	46
F	Bad credit	43 decreased	54

* By percentage of firms reporting.
Source: Voorhees and Snyder (1982)

information for all of its products, including forest products, pulp, paper, containers, packaging, and oil and gas. Another integrated system is found in American Hospital Supply (AHS), which has placed 3000 terminals in client hospitals to manage 30 000 critical items. These items include everything needed for hospital operations from surgical equipment to bedpans. At the time an order is placed, the integrated order system instantly informs the purchasing agent in the client hospital of the distribution centre where the order item is stored, the date it will be shipped, and the expected date the hospital will receive it. This information is in addition to normal invoice information. The wider use of communications is indicated by a survey conducted at Iowa State University. The survey shows that increased communications and data-processing terminals have been adopted for logistics and marketing activities by 94% of the 200 major (more than $1 billion in annual sales) firms surveyed. The firms were from a cross-section of US industries. Table 3.2 summarizes the results of the increased use of communications in logistics and marketing activities.

The increased use of communications services is not appropriate for all firms; some companies can benefit more from increased communications use than others. Figure 3.2 illustrates varying degrees of communications sensitivity for different types of firms and products. Important criteria for determining distribution needs are the criticality of time, service, and distribution costs to the firm. Where these are critical, the potential is great for the increased use of communications for telelogistics-oriented services. Frequently, communications services of all types, including voice and data transmission, can be shared by distribution and marketing. The communications services can be used for people-oriented marketing activities during business hours, and for distribution activities during the night.

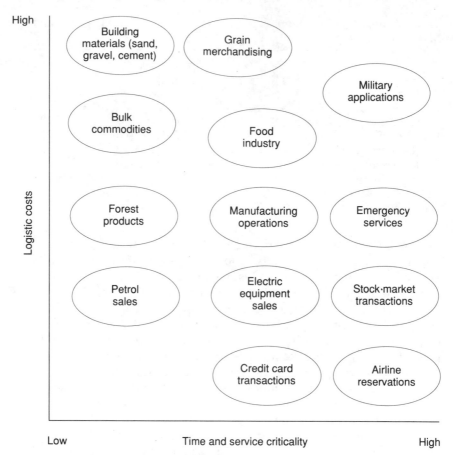

Figure 3.2 Teleologistics sensitivity.

Many of the firms using increased communications services are experiencing the benefits of a unified strategy – but that has not usually been the original objective. The objective has usually been economic in nature, stemming from the old idea of the substitution of communications service, such as the use of the telephone, television, teletype, telegraph, or computers for transportation. Past substitutions have been telegraph service for the Pony Express, and satellite transmission for air transportation of information and data. Today, it involves substituting the telephone and computer for the expensive salesperson on the road. Although the current objectives for substitution vary widely, the results are usually improved management of marketing and logistics as shown by the study summarized in Table 3.2.

3.4 STRATEGY FOR THE 1990s

The current separation of logistics and marketing inhibits business strategy for the 1990s. As a result of the new logistics segmentation, leading scholars from both disciplines recognize the need to co-ordinate logistics and marketing more closely. For example, LaLonde terms the 1990s as the 'decade of distribution integration' and he calls for 'distribution managers to develop new ways of thinking' and for 'different distribution strategies for different markets'. Bartels also calls for integration and observes that 'the need is greater than ever for integration, rather than separation, of thought and effort in the coordination of physical and exchange functions' (LaLonde and McGinnis 1981, p. 48).

It would appear that both disciplines see the need for coordination but that neither has a solution. So far, each has concentrated on de-fending its own conceptual turf. Returning to previous organizational arrangements or continuing the present separation do not appear to meet future strategic needs. Transportation deregulation, technological improvements in communications, and communications deregulation have created the foundation for new strategic business opportunities in the 1990s.

REFERENCES

W. Alderson (1957) *Marketing Behavior and Executive Action*, Homewood, Ill., Richard D. Irwin, Inc.

R. Bartels (1976) *The History of Marketing Thought*, Ohio State University.

R. Bartels (1982) Marketing and distribution are not separate, *International Journal of Physical Distribution and Materials Management*, **12**(3).

P.F. Drucker (1962) The economy's dark continent, *Fortune* 65, No. 4, April.

B.J.A. LaLonde and M.A. McGinnis (1981) Strategic distribution for the 1980s, *Distribution*, December.

D.M. Lambert (1976) The development of an inventory costing methodology, *A Study of the Costs Associated With Holding Inventory* (National Council of Physical Distribution Management, 1976).

J.L. McKenney and F.W. McFarlow (1982) The information archipelago – maps and bridges, *Harvard Business Review*, **60**(5).

L.F. Schneider (1985) New era in transportation strategy, *Harvard Business Review*, **63**(2).

R.D. Voorhees and R. Snyder (1982) Iowa State University Graduate School of Business, Survey, September.

CHAPTER FOUR

Materials logistics management

Donald J. Bowersox, Phillip L. Carter and Robert M. Monczka

A few years ago the faculty of the Graduate School of Business Administration at Michigan State University responded to a developing industry need for young people trained with an understanding of the interfaces between physical distribution, manufacturing and purchasing. In 1980 the Materials Logistics Management Programme (MLM) was established to meet this industry requirement. Students of the MLM programme have been in great demand by industry since the programme's inception. For the past two years MLM graduates have received the highest starting salaries of all MSU business graduates. This article presents an overview of the MLM philosophy that has emerged as the programme matured.

Figure 4.1 provides an overview of the MLM concept. It is a process chart of the significant value-added activities included in MLM. In the centre of the chart an industrial enterprise is represented. The prototype enterprise is one that procures materials, component parts, and products destined for resale from suppliers. The MLM process physically transports items that have been procured through a manufacturing complex during which form-value is added and then through a physical distribution network during which time-value is added. In a broad sense the MLM process incorporates two flows. The flow from customers to suppliers illustrated at the bottom of the prototype enter-

Source: Bowersox, D.J., Carter, P.L. and Monczka, R.M. (1984) *IJPD & MM*, **15**(5), 27–35

First presented to the *National Council for Physical Distribution Management Conference* (1984) Dallas, USA, under the title 'Computer-aided purchasing, manufacturing and physical distribution co-ordination in materials logistics management'

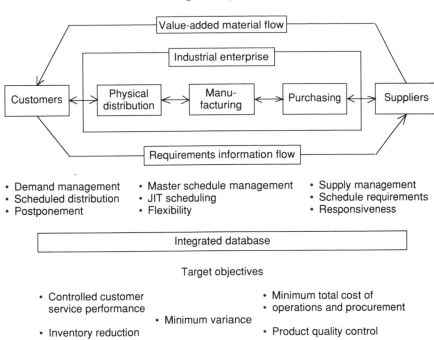

• Demand management   • Master schedule management   • Supply management
• Scheduled distribution   • JIT scheduling   • Schedule requirements
• Postponement   • Flexibility   • Responsiveness

Integrated database

Target objectives

• Controlled customer   • Minimum total cost of
  service performance   • operations and procurement
                   • Minimum variance
• Inventory reduction   • Product quality control

Figure 4.1 Materials logistics management process.

prise represents information. The flow illustrated across the top reflects
value added by the MLM process. The change in form and location of
inventory is the primary MLM value-added process. An integrated
database capability as illustrated near the bottom of the figure highlights the need to capitalize upon the modern-day computer power to
guide the MLM process. Thus, the MLM concept is properly viewed as
an integrated logic to guide the allocation and control of human and
financial resources committed to physical distribution, manufacturing
and purchasing operations. MLM represents a single system to manage
assets committed to the materials logistics process. It consists of the
co-ordinated performance of forecasting, order processing, transportation, inventory management and warehousing as they are planned and
co-ordinated in the performance of physical distribution, manufacturing and purchasing.

4.1 TARGET OBJECTIVES

In a generic sense, MLM seeks the balanced achievement of five target
objectives. These are illustrated at the bottom of Figure 4.1. The overall

goal is a system solution and control mechanism that achieves these five objectives. Each of the five objectives is briefly discussed prior to a detailed discussion of the interfaces between physical distribution, manufacturing and purchasing.

First is the objective of controlled customer service performance. Controlled customer service requires the right combination of availability, dependability and speed for each different operational situation supported by the MLM system. Customer service requirements are quite different if the system is serving industrial customers as contrasted to consumer remarketers. The maze of 2.2 million retailers and 350 000 wholesalers that are serviced by physical distribution systems within the Unites States means that any given MLM system cannot be all things to all customers. It means that the MLM system must be geared to provide customer service differentiated by geography, target markets, and specific customers. Manufacturing is a major customer of purchasing. Physical distribution is a customer of manufacturing. Controlling customer service performance requires that the MLM system seek to satisfy desired goals by a highly co-ordinated effort across all operational areas.

Second is the objective of inventory reduction. It is not always clear why inventories develop in a given business situation. If large inventories exist in an organization, it serves to cover up problems. In such situations, the MLM system may appear to operate well day in and day out. The real system defects do not appear until inventories are leaned to the lowest level possible. Concepts like 'zero inventory' are becoming increasingly popular to reflect a desire to eliminate all unnecessary inventory. It is important to remember that inventory performs some essential functions in an MLM system. Inventories offer a sound return on investment when they permit economies of scale in manufacturing or other operating efficiencies. The key objective is to reduce and control inventory to the maximum extent possible while simultaneously achieving operating objectives.

Minimum variance is the third MLM objective. Variance in a systems context is represented by any uncertainty that causes disruption in planned operations. Whether it is order cycle uncertainty, a surprise in the manufacturing run, goods arriving at the right location damaged, or at the wrong location ready to use, the result is variance which must be accommodated. To the degree that variance can be controlled throughout the MLM system, inessential costs can be eliminated.

The fourth objective is minimum total cost of operations and procurement. The total cost concept has been discussed for years. Logistical managers are well aware that it may be cheaper under selected situations to ship very high-priced transportation and offset the higher expenditure with cost savings realized from other operational areas. Manufacturing executives understand total cost trade-off analysis and so do purchasing professionals. In the last decade it has become increasingly obvious that through the interface and interrelationship of the total MLM process, higher-level cost trade-offs can be achieved than are possible within each functional area. Trade-offs that cut across physical distribution, manufacturing and purchasing, if properly balanced, offer more significant pay-offs than are attainable within each of the individual areas. An objective of the MLM system is the realization of such higher-level trade-offs.

Finally, the objective of product quality control. The MLM concept has an implicit obligation to achieve and maintain high levels of product quality. In today's world, product quality has become critical because attention has been directed to the high cost of failure. If a product is defective after the entire MLM process is complete, no value has been added. In fact, the total process often must be recalled and repeated. Some experts estimate that the cost of satisfying a customer order that must be reworked as a result of incorrect shipment or damaged arrival is more than eight times the cost of a correct customer shipment. The realization of quality control starts with zero defect purchasing and extends throughout the MLM process.

The MLM process represents a complex conglomeration of cost areas that can be moulded into a strategic system capable of achieving competitive superiority. As a result of the varied activities included in MLM it is, from an organizational perspective, a boundary spanning process. Traditionally, organizations have not been structured to manage MLM as a single integrated process. There are different schools of management involved in physical distribution, manufacturing and purchasing which have traditionally exploited different mentalities. The challenge is to bring all of these viewpoints together into a broader perspective. Such a broad perspective requires a commitment from top management. More and more top managers understand the strategic importance of MLM and are willing to do what is necessary to put state-of-the-art information systems in place to make it happen. With this background, attention is now directed to the critical interfaces within the MLM system.

4.2 THE PHYSICAL DISTRIBUTION INTERFACES

The critical interfaces of physical distribution are with customers and manufacturing. The interfaces between customers, physical distribution and manufacturing are inherently conflictive. On the one hand, you have marketing which is reluctant to deny customers. This reluctance is illustrated by: (1) how difficult it is to get away from gross sales volume as a measure of marketing success, and (2) the general reluctance of marketing managers to implement principles of selectivity in terms of servicing customers and selecting product offerings. On the other side is manufacturing that traditionally desires to keep things simple. Manufacturing likes to start up machines and keep them running. To the extent possible, steady manufacturing processes result in lowest production cost. The traditional method of solving these marketing–manufacturing conflicts is to build up inventory. The standard practice of managing stockpiled inventory is to move it forward in the physical distribution system in anticipation of future sale. Thus, products are transported at the risk of being shipped to the wrong market at the wrong time. They often end up completely out of position to support customer service requirements.

This form of conflict must be resolved to realize the benefits attainable from integrated MLM. From the viewpoint of physical distribution management, three concepts are capable of contributing to MLM productivity. They are illustrated in the middle of the left side of Fig. 4.1 as demand management, scheduled distribution and postponement.

The concept of demand management requires that managers think proactively about what can be done regarding the way customers act and react of an MLM system. The objective of demand management is to co-ordinate and modify how customers order products in an effort to reduce uncertainty and simplify transactions. First, every effort should be made to realize the best forecasting accuracy possible. Perhaps an easier accomplishment is a programme of advanced order substitution. When customers have made a commitment to purchase a specific item, they often will accept substitutions as long as they are informed in advance and are not surprised. When an order is in hand, it often makes sense to service the order from a different warehouse rather than cutting product lines. If a firm is cutting ten per cent of line items due to stockouts, it should ask: 'What would it take to increase our total sales volume by ten per cent in terms of sales effort and promotional expenditure?' Conceptually, a firm can afford to spend up to the last penny of gross margin contribution to service an order and still make a profit contribution. In such situations, firms could afford to cross ship warehouse territories to protect order revenue. By aggressive programmes of demand management companies are capturing more and more revenue that traditionally has been achieved by sales only to be lost as a result of ineffective MLM operations.

Scheduled distribution is an important concept related to minimum operational variance. Scheduled distribution means that delivery of a customer order can be specified and controlled to occur within a narrow time window. In today's world, a requirement to provide plus or minus one hour delivery of a component or part may be specified in the purchase contract. Carried to its ultimate, distribution may need to arrange for any authorized size shipment to arrive at a specified time at any authorized customer facility. The challenge is to satisfy such demanding customer service standards while maintaining physical distribution efficiency. To realize least-cost scheduled distribution, it is necessary to have a high degree of manufacturing flexibility. It is necessary to understand what degree of flexibility is feasible and understand the associated trade-offs. To control physical distribution cost it is necessary to consolidate transportation. The economy of scale of transportation cost has not changed as a result of deregulation and it is not going to change just because a customer wants 'just-in-time' delivery. It is necessary to establish more ingenious consolidation programmes. To consolidate properly it is necessary to know both current and planned inventory status. It is desirable to be able to mortgage future production runs. To whatever extent practical, consolidations should be planned prior to order processing. All aspects of scheduled distribution require timely and relevant information concerning order-cycle variances.

A third concept important to MLM system design is postponement. Postponement means planned delay of the scheduled performance of an activity as long as possible in the overall MLM process. For example, not shipping an order until absolutely necessary to meet customer service requirements (geographical postponement). Another example is to refrain from final assembly of a product until a customer commitment has been received (form postponement). While the idea of postponement has been around for over 50 years, examples within MLM systems are difficult to find. In order to incorporate postponement in MLM operations, it is necessary to have timely and relevant information regarding customers, coupled with the cost and risk of forward movement or assembly. It is also necessary to maintain quality control across a vast geographical area, perhaps all the way down to the dealer or retail level, as opposed to controlling quality at a centralized manufacturing plant.

From the viewpoint of the physical distribution system there are many potential trade-offs that can reduce commitment to forward inventories. The customer-based commitments to demand management, scheduled distribution and postponement must interface into the manufacturing environment.

4.3 THE MANUFACTURING INTERFACES

Manufacturing must interface between physical distribution and purchasing. There are three concepts that are of critical importance if manufacturing is going to fulfill its role in the MLM process. They are identified in the middle of Fig. 4.1 as master schedule management, 'just-in-time' scheduling (JIT); and flexibility.

Master schedule management, broadly defined, is the interface concept between manufacturing and physical distribution. That is, master scheduling is the point where overall requirements, as determined from forecasts, customer orders, back orders and physical distribution replenishments are brought together. In addition to overall requirements, current inventories and manufacturing capacities must be considered in master production schedule (MPS) development. The MPS can be used to resolve conflicts between manufacturing and marketing. The end result is viewed as a contract which states what manufacturing agrees to produce and what marketing agrees to sell or inventory. The master schedule must be well managed if the organization is to meet its cost, service, quality and other profit goals.

A good MPS has several characteristics. First, it is complete in that all requirements are considered, including customer orders, forecasts, service requirements, inter-plant orders and physical distribution replenishment. Secondly, the MPS should be as stable as possible. A schedule which manufacturing has a chance of meeting may conflict with one that is maximally responsive to the market place. It must be realized that this conflict exists and must be managed from a total organizational perspective. How can stability be built into the schedule to obtain manufacturing goals without shutting out marketing? Several techniques are available. Firm planned orders can be used to establish stability. Further, people should manage the master production schedule instead of computers. Finally, time fences can be utilized. A third characteristic of a good MPS is that it is feasible with respect to the overall production or business plan. If the MPS is totalled for all products in dollar terms, the total should be compatible in an upward sense with the financial plans for the organization. The MPS should also be feasible in a downward sense with respect to timing and utilization of manufacturing capacity and key resources such as material or people. A fourth characteristic is that a good MPS should represent the manufacturing game plan and be used for driving the capacity planning system and the material requirements planning system for suppliers. Lastly, a firm has good material and capacity plans if manufacturing can live up to the contract. If state-of-the-art computer systems and data bases are available 'what if' simulations can be performed regarding the MPS. This permits an evaluation of the capability to satisfy market demand prior to resource commitment and, if necessary, what trade-offs are available.

Just-in-time scheduling (JIT), also called zero inventory and Kanban, is a second concept of great importance to manufacturing. The Japanese have become the experts in inventory reduction and US managers are observing their operations to determine what aspects can be applied in this country. The basic philosophy of JIT is that inventories only exist to cover problems. By reducing inventories, problems are exposed which then must be solved before inventories can be further reduced.

One way to lower work-in-process inventory is by reducing lot sizes. To do this economically, set-up costs and times must be reduced. Dramatic reductions have been accomplished in Japan as well as in the USA. Load levelling is another part of the JIT strategy. Balancing the work schedule to the maximum extent possible permits fine tuning of manufacturing operations at all levels. The MPS is the key to balancing the work load. Quality control is another important element of JIT. Poor quality requires the consumption of more capacity for a given level of output and results in more inventory. Techniques such as statistical process control and quality circles can be utilized to help improve quality performance. Preventive maintenance is also important in JIT. Safety stock has traditionally been used to cover breakdowns. If breakdowns can be reduced as a source of variance, it will help achieve flow management and reduce inventory.

Flexibility is the final concept important to manufacturing. Flexibility is best achieved through the usage of 'pull' systems. Using a pull system of manufacturing a firm will not produce a product unless specifically required. In contrast, a push system of manufacturing permits the production of any authorized product if the necessary parts are available. The closer a firm can operate to a pull system, the greater the overall opportunity to achieve the MLM target objectives. Computer-based planning and control systems are the key to increased flexibility. These include traditional time-phased material scheduling and capacity planning programmes. United States industry is just beginning to see the applications of computer-aided manufacturing integrated with computer-aided design, computer-controlled processes, flexible manufacturing systems and robotics. The main gains are still ahead. Development over the next five to ten years will be amazing. All of these computer applications will enhance manufacturing flexibility.

In summary, manufacturing needs to be viewed in a new light. Manufacturing is not an isolated area of activity, but is one step in the

MLM process. Thus, the objectives of manufacturing must also include the objectives of physical distribution and purchasing.

4.4 PURCHASING INTERFACES

Purchasing can be thought of as a boundary-spanning activity that acts as the primary interface between manufacturing and the external supplier network. The significant contributions of purchasing are the form, place and time utility it provides by obtaining products or raw materials from outside suppliers. Purchasing impacts MLM target objectives by improving product quality, minimizing the total cost of outside purchases and reducing inventories, thus influencing overall profitability. The three concepts of supply management, schedule requirements and responsiveness are essential to integrating purchasing into the overall MLM process. These are illustrated on the right side of the middle of Fig. 4.1.

The supply management concept is that buying firms seek to identify and implement opportunities for longer-term competitive advantage through effective purchasing. Supply management is based on the careful specification of current and future manufacturing requirements as the foundation for designing a supplier network. Supply management requires a more comprehensive view of requirements than has traditionally been required by purchasing. It is necessary to obtain accurate data regarding supplier availability, purchase lead times, historical performance, and quality management. It is also important to understand the relationship between productivity, cost and price. By knowing the percentage relationship of a supplier's fixed cost to purchase price, the buyer can better assess the impact of volume changes on cost and profit.

Information is required about specific supplier capacity and business volume. A supplier's overall capability and resources to provide manufacturing and engineering technology should be assessed. Data about the logistical system is necessary. Where are the producing locations? How do they ship? Who owns the modes of transportation? A full understanding of such capability is required to make decisions regarding the appropriate number of suppliers or how to minimize total cost of inbound freight. All of the above data is needed to take a proactive approach to purchasing.

Supply management differs from the traditional purchasing philosophy which was focused on buying what was needed to support a rather inflexible MPS. Supply management requires that the buying organization determine which suppliers are best positioned to provide long-term competitive advantage, how many suppliers are most appropriate and when orders should be established with the supplier(s) and for how long. The supply network must be 'managed' using the buying companies' resources to co-ordinate the external and internal requirements for the highest level of performance. Since 40–60% of the cost of goods sold is accounted for by external payments to suppliers, purchasing provides a key opportunity to realize competitive advantage. It is also a key interface both organizationally and for information transfer between the buying firm and the outside supplier network. The supply management concept is a key ingredient to achieving competitive advantage through effective use of suppliers.

Another key purchasing concept is schedule requirements. The JIT philosophy requires more frequent deliveries to user locations, not only to the plant, but to the exact place in the plant where the product will be used. This requires more exact information concerning quantity, delivery time and location. Both buyer and seller, therefore, need to manage the communication interface more closely than in the past. Suppliers need to provide exact lead-time information and purchasers must provide accurate requirements information to the supply network as early as possible. To realize scheduled requirements, there must be increased openness in the business relationship between buyer and seller. This requires two-way exchange of information between buyers and suppliers. Buyers and suppliers tied together by data-processing systems will increasingly exchange information about their respective business situations.

Increased responsiveness of the supply network is required to meet overall MLM objectives. The premium on supply network responsiveness is due to frequent changes in customer requirements and shorter product life cycles. These factors, along with advertising promotions, require more frequent product and quantity changes. Suppliers need to be able to accommodate buying firms' changing requirements through their JIT distribution methods or through change-control systems which permit modification in design or specification.

Suppliers will be increasingly evaluated on their ability to react to the need for productivity enhancements. Reductions in cost through productivity can lead to reductions in price which in turn increase profit margins. Fewer suppliers will probably be chosen by a specific firm in the future as a result of the need to build up inter-organization communications. Suppliers selected will have the financial and management resources to stay abreast of changes in technology, manufacturing, communications and business practices.

4.5 CONCLUSIONS

This article has focused on the benefits and challenges involved in establishing an integrated MLM system. The overall MLM system includes the functional areas of physical distribution, manufacturing, and purchasing. It is becoming increasingly clear that for firms to gain competitive advantage, co-ordination and appropriate cost trade-off analysis must occur throughout all aspects of the supply, manufacturing and distribution network. This article has identified target objectives and key interface concepts associated with integrated MLM.

Increased use of computer-based information systems will be required to achieve co-ordination and improved performance toward simultaneous attainment of the 'target objectives'. The information system required to manage the totality of the MLM process is becoming increasingly sophisticated and is based upon the power of an integrated database. As they evolve, these transaction systems will be on-line and provide accurate and timely information about materials and logistics actions and decisions.

The databases created to guide MLM systems will also be used for decision support and management control purposes. Decision-support models are available to assist in developing distribution networks, making inventory policy decisions, deciding on appropriate production schedules, evaluating long-term contracts and establishing lowest total-cost supplier networks. The 1980s and 1990s will require that firms use today's rapidly changing computer technology to manage effectively the materials and logistics system.

CHAPTER FIVE

Get leverage from logistics

Roy D. Shapiro

As the industrial battlefield has grown steadily more dangerous for American companies, managers have once again begun to look to logistics systems as a potential source of competitive advantage – and not merely as a necessary but uninspiring collection of apparatus. This refocusing of attention comes none too soon, for the potential of a well-designed system to advance a company's strategic goals – and of a poorly designed system to retard their accomplishment – is enormous. As the author demonstrates, strategies based on innovation, customer service, and low-cost place different and often contradictory demands on a company's logistical infrastructure. Subordinating other considerations to the need for rapid product delivery may, for example, work wonders for one company but be ruinous for another. The responsibility of managers is, as always, to understand precisely what their companies are trying to do and then to bring logistical capabilities in line with corporate purpose.

(1) After watching both its competitive position and profits erode steadily for several years, a manufacturer of consumer durables restructured its logistics system. This restructuring included a consolidation of distribution centres, a 50% reduction of investment in finished goods inventory, a centralization of the purchasing and materials management functions, a switch to intermodal truck and rail transport combinations, and a change in pricing policy to encourage customers to order full truckload shipments.

These changes prompted a shift in the company's customer base from dealers who ordered in small quantities and required 'when

Source: Shapiro, R.D. (1984) *Harvard Business Review*, May–June, 119–126
Reprinted by permission of *Harvard Business Review*, 'Get Leverage from Logistics', Roy D. Shapiro, May / June 1984

needed' delivery to dealers for whom larger orders at lower cost made sense. At first, market share decreased as short-term profits rose. Within two years, however, increased order volumes started to raise market share while profits remained strong.

(2) During the mid-1970s, a multifacility metals service centre came under mounting competitive pressure from smaller local companies as well as from a large outfit that served the entire region with a narrow product line from one central site. Reacting aggressively, the multifacility centre achieved a better record of on-time deliveries by boosting its number of branch warehouses and the level of finished goods inventory while cutting the market area served by each warehouse. In addition, the company extended its product lines to ensure full-line availability to its customers.

These logistics choices were expensive, but they led to a higher market share among those customers who ordered frequently and in small quantities and who were willing to pay premium prices because the steel they ordered was a small percentage of their costs.

(3) Also in the mid-1970s, a broad-line producer of disposable medical supplies like catheters began to fall behind the industry's rapid growth. Product proliferation and waning control over its far-flung network of more than 20 distribution centres lay at the heart of the company's problem. Excess inventories played havoc with margins, and frequent stockouts pushed irate customers into the arms of competitors. Management consolidated operations in four distribution centres, an action that cut both total finished goods inventory and the likelihood of future stockouts. Simultaneously, management turned to air freight for most deliveries so as to ensure rapid response to customer orders.

Management viewed this consolidation not only as a way of reducing costs and gaining efficiency but also as a way of gaining control over a rapidly changing product line in a market characterized by fluctuating demand. Customers agreed. Growth got quickly back on track.

Each of these companies used its logistics system to gain competitive advantage, yet each chose a different way of doing so – by designing its logistics system and operating policies to fit carefully a chosen competitive strategy. That 'fit' is the subject of this article.

Much as with Wickham Skinner's notion of the 'focused factory', no single logistics system can do everything well.* Trade-offs are inevit-

---

* See Wickham Skinner, 'The Focused Factory', HBR, May–June, 1974, p. 113.

able, for example, among considerations of low cost, range of services, and flexibility to changes in product specifications, volume, and customer preferences. Thus, the crucial question for managers is, 'What must our logistics system do particularly well?'

These important logistical tasks, where a little effort can generate a lot of return, create opportunities for leverage. Identifying such key leverage points is, of course, part and parcel of the broader effort to fit logistics systems to a company's competitive strategy. The choice of an overall competitive focus – product innovation, for example, or superior customer service or cost leadership – sets logistical requirements that, if not explicitly considered in designing the system's trade-offs, can do much to undercut the prior choice of competitive focus. There is, then, much to be gained from successfully applying leverage through logistics – and much to be lost from applying that leverage incorrectly.

5.1 PRODUCT INNOVATION

An innovation-based strategy puts a premium on avoiding market saturation and on serving high-income markets with a flow of new, different, and high-performance products. Such a strategy need not be limited to companies in high-technology industries, as the success of consumer goods companies like Gillette or Procter and Gamble attests. What matters is the ability of management to develop the market – first by creating an awareness of the product among potential customers and then by ensuring product availability. The newer the product, the more important it is for customers to have a favourable first experience with it.

As a result, well-run distribution systems, especially those for consumer goods, become critical. If the product is not available, customers cannot make that crucial first purchase. At the same time, of course, retailers and wholesalers invest cautiously in new stock. Their typical orders are small and erratic, and this preference for thin stocks increases the demand for rapid delivery and so puts further strain on the distribution system.

To meet these requirements, a logistics system must ensure continuity of supply from vendors; keep high safety stocks to prevent stockouts, rely on air freight, where possible, to guarantee rapid and consistent delivery, and be able to handle small orders and erratic order frequencies. An innovation-based strategy, however, also entails rapid product change, uncertainty about volumes, low density of demand, and possible shifts in customer preferences. These requirements argue for flexibility in supplier contracts (because raw material spe-cifications may change) and for low levels of investment in inventory (to minimize obsolescence) and in bricks and mortar (at least until stable demand patterns evolve).

Setting inventory policy in this strategic context is especially difficult. Concern for product availability and rapid delivery argues that large stocks be kept near the customer, but rapid product change and fear of obsolescence argue for minimizing inventories. Not surprisingly, this tension necessitates a compromise appropriate to the particular charac-teristics of both industry and product. The hard part is defining the compromise correctly.

Consider, for example, the gramophone record industry, in which all companies compete through innovation in products with built-in obsolescence. Only one new release in 50 is successful, yet in so fragmented and competitive an industry, product availability is truly essential. Because stockouts during the short period when a record is 'hot' can spell failure, most record companies view obsolescence as an unavoidable cost of doing business and provide high safety-stock coverage during the time a release is being heavily promoted.

Figure 5.1 outlines the policy implication of the most important determinants of such inventory compromises – rate of product change and level of competitive intensity. As described previously, the record industry belongs in the upper right-hand quadrant. In the early 1960s, Xerox – to cite a different example – faced rapid product change yet enjoyed a patent position in its basic technology that guaranteed high entry barriers. Its centralized inventory policy for spare parts fits well in the lower right-hand quadrant. As the expiration of its patent in 1973 approached, however, Xerox foresaw increasing competition. Consequently, it rapidly started to expand its local and regional ware-houses in order to build an unassailable nationwide service network.

Recall, if you will, the case of the manufacturer of medical supplies described at the beginning of this article. Management viewed product innovation as the key to success in a high-growth and hotly competit-ive industry. In an attempt to get its new disposable catheters quickly to a nationwide customer base, the company had established more than 20 warehouses, but new product proliferation and demand uncer-tainty turned this network of warehouses into a corporate millstone. Inventory carrying costs grew in part due to unanticipated product obsolescence. Nonetheless, demand fluctuations created stockouts that could be filled only by disrupting the plant's production schedule so often that effective capacity plummeted and shipments fell further and further behind.

At last, management realized that fast transport by air could guaran-

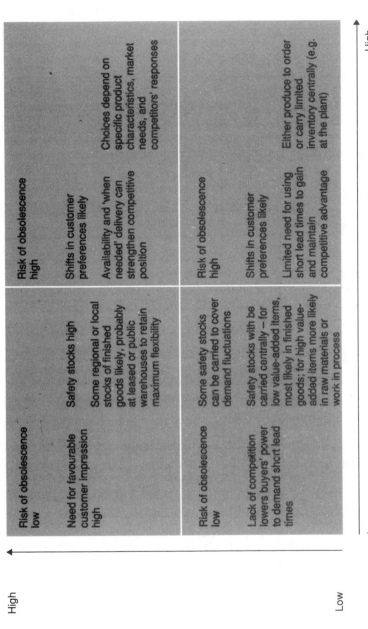

Figure 5.1 Inventory policies.

tee timely delivery. Local inventories were unnecessary in all markets; in fact, when the dust had settled, only four warehouses remained. Reduced inventory carrying costs more than offset increases in transport costs, and both obsolescence and local demand fluctuations became easier to handle.

Far too often, managers think an effective logistics system can provide benefits only through cost cutting. For companies following a strategy of innovation, however, other factors are often more important than straight cost reduction. Still, in their preoccupation with research and development, marketing and sales, and production – 'getting the product out the door' once orders come in – managers commonly forget the real leverage in logistics. Worse, they approach logistics in a purely tactical, cost-minimizing fashion.

Listen, instead, to what Daniel T. Carroll, then president of Gould, told a 1978 meeting of the company's division general managers:

> If [you] really want to get scared, . . . remember that we spen[d] $12 million a year on new product R&D. Do you know the easiest way to bomb a new product? Poor materials management – you can't get the right materials or the quality is off or you can't get the product through the factory or you can't coordinate transportation and distribution to get the product into the hands of the customer. I would be willing to bet that substantially greater than half of all new product failures are not because the technology or market strategy is deficient, they're because people don't pay enough attention to materials management.*

5.2 CUSTOMER SERVICE

All differentiation-based strategies involve providing the market with a bundle of products and related services that is – or appears to the market – unique. One common differentiation strategy, followed by Coca-Cola and Colgate-Palmolive, relies on heavy advertising and other marketing expenditures to develop brand identification. Another, followed by Braun in small appliances and Mercedes-Benz in automobiles, emphasizes product performance. A third, exemplified by Xerox's response to the approaching expiration of its patent, uses logistics to provide superior customer service.

In practice, of course, the problem is that service can mean many different things. Before managers can answer the question, 'What does

---

* See Gould, A., *Harvard Business School Case Services*, 9–678–184, Boston, Mass. 1978, p. 1.

our logistics system have to do especially well?' they must first decide what service is to be delivered – short delivery lead times, for example, or broad-line availability or consistent performance or responsiveness and flexibility to buyer need.

How can managers use the structure and operating policies of a logistics system to support the needs of their customers? In the first place, they can do business with suppliers who themselves provide consistent delivery, product availability, and fast response. They can also employ local inventories (for example, by using public ware-houses) to provide market presence and rapid delivery, even though such inventories need not imply excessive investment in an elaborate network of facilities. And they can establish a two- or three-tiered transport system, with short-haul arrangements for transport from local warehouses to customers, long-haul arrangements (in efficient full truckload or carload quantities) for restocking the local warehouses from regional or national facilities, and a network for emergency ship-ments.

Rather than pay the price for such a wide range of logistics-based services, many companies choose to focus their differentiation strate-gies on a more cost-effective subset of services. One key choice of focus is that between providing full-line availability and quick, consistent delivery. As illustrated schematically by Fig. 5.2, this choice has major implications for both inventory and product line policy.

5.2.1 Dimensions of service

The vertical axis of Fig. 5.2 captures where in the logistics pipeline inventory is to be carried. In general, the spectrum of approaches included here involves different degrees of postponement (make to order) and 'speculation' (make to stock). The horizontal axis speaks to product-line breadth: Do we focus our resources on a narrow line or serve the entire market with a full line? All too commonly, managers decide on a product line or inventory location policy without paying adequate attention to how the interaction of the two is crucial to the effectiveness of a logistics system.

That interaction gives rise to the four generic modes of operation illustrated by Fig. 5.2.

(1) *Full service* Two factors combine to drive costs here above those in any other quadrant: one, a broad product line requires more fre-quent changeovers and shorter production runs, both of which raise production costs; and two, higher levels of finished goods inventory, especially when coupled with product proliferation, boost inventory carrying costs. Still, for companies following a full-service strategy, these are necessary costs of doing business.

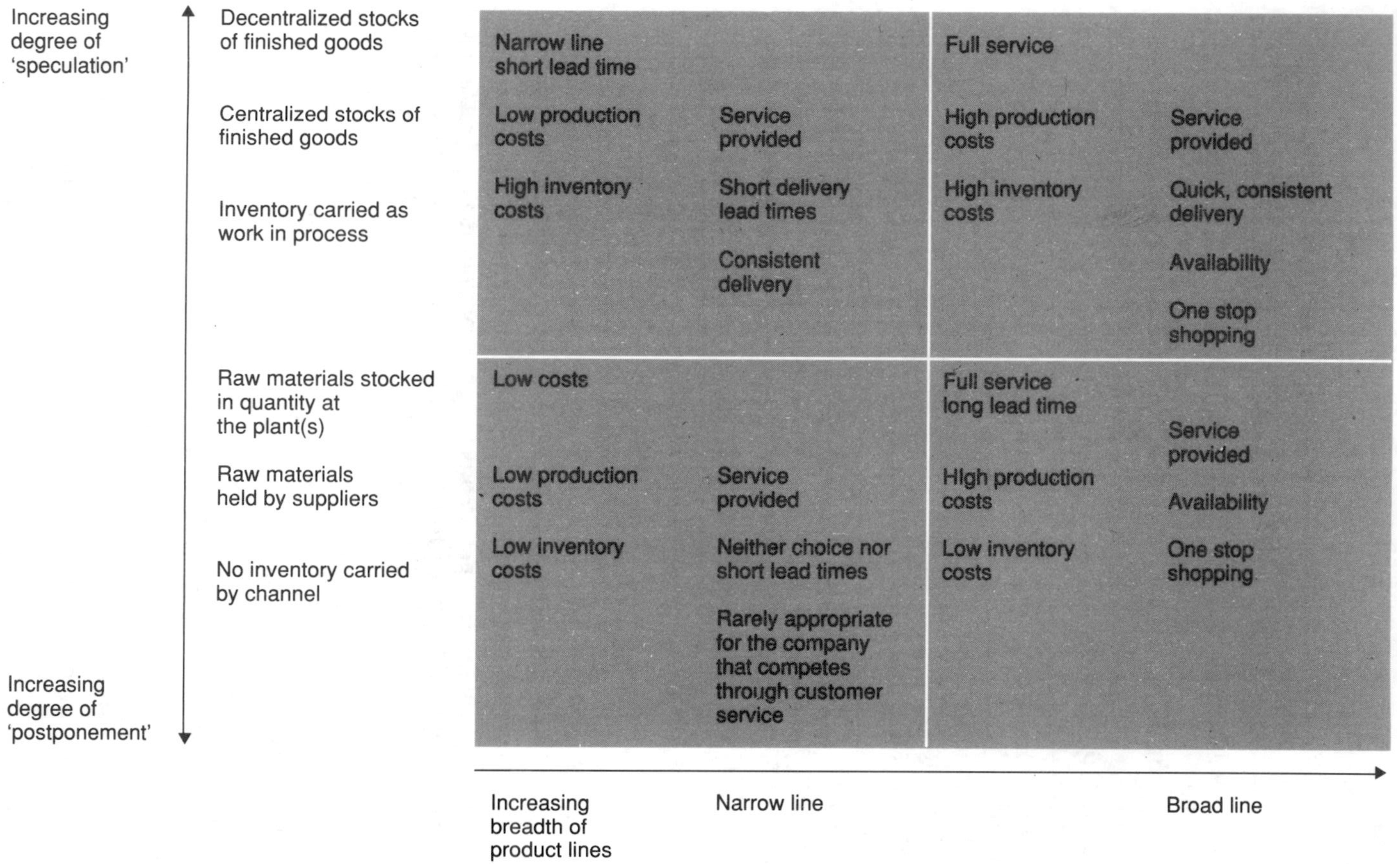

Increasing degree of 'speculation'

Decentralized stocks of finished goods
Centralized stocks of finished goods
Inventory carried as work in process
Raw materials stocked in quantity at the plant(s)
Raw materials held by suppliers
No inventory carried by channel

Increasing degree of 'postponement'

	Narrow line	Broad line
	Narrow line short lead time Low production costs High inventory costs Service provided Short delivery lead times Consistent delivery	Full service High production costs High inventory costs Service provided Quick, consistent delivery Availability One stop shopping
	Low costs Low production costs Low inventory costs Service provided Neither choice nor short lead times Rarely appropriate for the company that competes through customer service	Full service long lead time High production costs Low inventory costs Service provided Availability One stop shopping

Increasing breadth of product lines

Figure 5.2 Where in the logistics pipeline is inventory carried?

As an executive of a major appliance manufacturer observed, 'Think about the emergency replacement market [for refrigerators]. If your refrigerator goes, you need a new one, and you need it *now*. And, if your kitchen is done in flamingo decor, you want a flamingo refrigerator. If we don't have one, you'll go somewhere else'.

(2) *Low cost* A strategy of offering neither product customization nor rapid delivery is, obviously, inappropriate for a company wishing to differentiate itself or its product in terms of service. It is, however, appropriate when the strategy is to be the low-cost producer, where differentiation of other than service dimensions is possible (for example, providing applications engineering consultation). It is also appropriate where – as in the old days of the telephone industry – the intensity of competition is sufficiently low and barriers to entry sufficiently high that offering limited service does not provoke fear of retaliation.

(3) *Narrow line* Companies following a low-cost strategy rely much less on logistics systems than on efficient production for competitive leverage. Those following a strategy of focused service, however, usually seek a moderate cost position while emphasizing a particular aspect of service. A narrow-line strategy trades off product-line breadth for low cost and rapid delivery, much as Ford rather emphatically did with the Model T in the early 1920s.

A less extreme example of this strategy is provided by the sound profitability and fast growth of Martin-Brower, now the third largest food distributor in the USA. Unlike most food distributors, which compete on the basis of full-line service and rapid delivery, Martin-Brower has restricted its customer list to eight large fast-food chains and stocks only their narrow product lines.

(4) *Full line* By contrast, some companies choose to sacrifice quick delivery capability for product customization. Good examples here are mail-order operations like that of Sears and highly customized job shop operations like Avery Label's custom-printing business, National Lead's oil well products and services, and the commercial telephone systems industry.

Some batch manufacturers follow an important variant of this strategy. Rather than incur the exorbitant costs associated with production of each order as it comes in, these companies often batch incoming orders (by model, size, or type) until enough have accumulated to warrant an efficient production run. This approach requires some inventory of raw materials. Alternatively, a company may carry standardized work-in-process inventory 'upstream' – as US carmakers have done for years – and wait until orders come before assembling components into customized end products.

The metals service centre described earlier successfully used logistics to pursue a strategy based on customer service. In the mid-1970s, McKinley Metals (not its real name) served a ten-state region of the western USA with four warehouses. Its largest competitor served the same region with a narrow line from a single large warehouse. Competition also came from several small local centres, each operating a single facility serving a single metropolitan area. McKinley was caught in the middle: its logistics system could not achieve the cost position of its prime competitor, nor could it boast the market presence or rapid delivery of the local centres.

McKinley acted to differentiate itself by providing both rapid delivery and broad-line availability – that is, by placing itself firmly in the 'full-service' quadrant of Fig. 5.2. It opened four additional warehouses to make overnight deliveries possible for a larger part of its market and expanded its product line. Because a logistics system of this sort was expensive, McKinley aimed its services at end-users, especially those in high-tech industries, for whom steel was a small percentage of overall costs. The company kept costs in line by centralizing procurement and carefully coordinating its transport fleet.

The strategy worked. During the recession of 1981–82, McKinley prospered while its major competitor suffered losses and several of the local service centres went under. With interest rates breaking 20%, steel users cut both inventories and order sizes. A company able to cope with frequent small orders and the need for immediate delivery was in great demand. McKinley had built its logistics system so that it was such a company.

5.3 COST LEADERSHIP

From the mid-1970s on, soaring costs of energy, raw materials, transportation, and capital have made an overall strategy of cost leadership increasingly attractive. As a result, managers have turned to logistics in the fight against eroding margins. And it is right to do so – on average, logistics costs eat up more than 21¢ of every US sales dollar.

How can a company design its logistics system and associated operating policies to minimize cost while keeping service at an acceptable level? Most obviously, by making use of scale economies that arise from high production volumes, volume discounts in purchasing, and shipping full truckloads or rail-carloads of goods. One major car maker, for example, has established 14 centres across the USA to consolidate small shipments of raw materials and components from its more than 2000 suppliers into full truckloads or carloads for transport to its various assembly plants.

Then, too, companies can centralize inventories as much as possible, especially for low-volume items, in a manner that is consistent with required levels of service. Montgomery Ward recognized that nation-wide inventory reductions could be achieved by consolidating all slower moving items into one central warehouse seven miles from Chicago's O'Hare Airport. Lower carrying costs far outweigh higher transport charges from air-freighting items when rapid delivery is essential.

Another relevant tactic is to strive for the lowest cost routeing of products from plants to warehouse to customers. This tactic is often of great importance to large companies late in their life cycles, when service has grown spotty and geographic expansion and multiple levels of warehouses have created a logistics nightmare.

In 1978 International Paper had 20 million acres of woodland and operated 124 manufacturing facilities and some 100 storage and trans-fer facilities in North America, France, Italy, and Brazil. Its network of raw materials suppliers and customers was world-wide in scope. An optimization-based system allowed it to rationalize this multifacility operational structure to ensure cost efficiency – a task that would have been impossible without such a logistics-based decision aid.

Finally, companies can automate materials handling and order pro-cessing as much as is consistent with customer needs and the physical characteristics of the product.

True, the kind of cost-efficient system just detailed is rationalized, centralized, tightly co-ordinated, and inflexible. But since the choice of a low-cost strategy position is typically made late in a product's life cycle, customer preferences and product specifications have stabilized, and there is little uncertainty about overall volumes or demand pat-terns. Flexibility is, therefore, of less value than it would be earlier in the life cycle.

As the consumer durables manufacturer discussed earlier matured, it failed to become cost effective in a market where sophisticated buyers increasingly demanded lower prices. Management had tried to achieve a low-cost position by integrating vertically into metal fabrication and plastic-injection moulding and by automating much of its production process. The resulting high quality and lower production costs should have given the company a competitive advantage, but its distribution system, which had been designed to provide short lead times, no longer suited a market that now prized low cost.

Market share and profitability continued to erode, as larger dealers, for whom cost was important, took their business elsewhere. With a manufacturing system and a distribution system pulling in different

Table 5.1 Leverage through logistics

Chosen modes of competition	Product innovation	Customer service	Cost leadership
Goals of logistics system	Availability Flexibility of volume shifts Flexibility to product changes Ability to handle small orders Ability to handle erratic order frequencies	Rapid delivery Consistent delivery Availability Flexibility to customer changes	Minimum cost with an 'acceptable' service level
Locus of planning	Line management	Line management	Staff
Procurement	Seek vendors who can ensure: Supply continuity Quality Flexibility to changes in specifications	Seek vendors who can ensure: Consistent delivery Full-line availability Responsiveness	Make maximum use of volume purchase economies Centralized purchasing organization Seek vendors offering low prices
Inventory policy	Tension between the need for high safety stocks kept locally to ensure availability and the need to keep inventories low to retain flexibility and guard against obsolescence: a compromise between these two extremes is required: the form of that	For the company that produces to inventory, local inventories will be required for 'market presence' and rapid, consistent delivery	Investment in inventory at minimal levels that ensure 'acceptable' service

compromise will depend on a variety of technological, physical, economic, and competitive factors; most important are pace of product change and competitive intensity

Transport policy	Premium, rapid transport (air freight if sensible) Use of common carrier rather than investment in private fleet LTL* shipments common	For normal supply, a mix of short-haul LTL* (for customer delivery) and long-haul TL† or CL‡ (for warehouse restocking) Emergency shipment network planned and available when needed Private fleet may be necessary for service (especially short-haul)	Low-cost transport (rail and/or piggyback) High utilization (full TL† or rail-carload shipments) Volume discounts to encourage direct-from-the-plant, full carload shipments Private fleet may be desirable for better control, lower transport costs
Facilities network	Almost non-existent in most cases – delivery from plant to customer When warehouses required, public or leased warehouses used	For the company that produces to inventory, a multi-echelon system (plant or national warehouses, regional warehouses, local warehouses) will be likely	Centralized Consolidated (minimize number of local facilities) Rationalized (number, size, scale) and sourcing decisions made to minimize costs Automated as much as is sensible

* LTL = less-than-truckload
† TL = truckload
‡ CL = carload

directions – the first toward a position of cost leadership, the second toward excellent, but high-cost, service – conditions rapidly deteriorated. As described earlier, management finally restructured the logistics system to achieve as low a cost as possible at a 'reasonable' level of service. This new, coherent strategy paid off.

For logistics systems designed to support a strategy of overall cost leadership, the key management task is not just to get the elements of the system right. It is also to locate logistics planning in the appropriate organizational context. A low-cost strategy, for example, requires that such planning be designed, controlled, and administered as a centralized staff function. By contrast, innovation- and differentiation-based strategies, for which cost minimization is not a primary goal, require that line management be involved in the design and administration of the logistics system.

5.4 THE RIGHT FIT

In the preceding pages I have tried to show how a company might gain leverage by ensuring a good fit between its logistics system and its competitive strategy. Table 5.1 summarizes the operational details of that fit. The three major examples cited illustrate the practical value such leverage can have.

But these companies are the successes. For much of US industry, logistics remains a second-class citizen and a logistics strategy at best an afterthought. In today's competitive environment, such neglect is no longer tolerable. As Bernard LaLonde of Ohio State University has remarked, 'American management's philosophy has typically been: "If you're smart enough to make it, aggressive enough to sell it – then any dummy can get it there!" And now we're paying for [that philosophy].'*

---

* As quoted by James C. Johnson and Donald F. Wood, in *Contemporary Physical Distribution and Logistics*, Pennwell Books, Tulsa, Oklahoma, 1982, p. 3.

CHAPTER SIX

Supply-chain management: logistics catches up with strategy

R. Keith Oliver and Michael D. Webber

In the world of the logistics manager ten years ago – another era altogether in terms of business economics – the mission, while perhaps not always readily achieved, was at least clear: balancing-inventories between both production capacity and the demands of customer service. While the manager might have understood intellectually that assets should be employed to make the most of both factors, it was also accepted that hidden costs were bound to creep into even the best-managed system – and that these could be borne.

Now all that has changed. The job of the logistics manager has begun not only to overwhelm him or her, but also to have an increasing significance for overall corporate health. What were once simple trade-offs seem to result, with increasing frequency, in what is not merely a suboptimal utilization of assets, but, in the worst cases, a no-win materials management policy. Companies are faced with the prospect of incurring double or even triple costs in order to build up inventories to support marginal increases in customer service. But at the same time, more intensive competition in slow-growth markets, combined with the rising costs of other production and supply factors, means that many firms can't afford not to supply a level of service that results in a competitive edge.

Over the last few years, our analyses of the particular problems of multinational companies in the context of today's more challenging

Source: Oliver, R.K. and Webber, M.D. (1982) *Outlook*

economic environment resulted in a fundamental shift in our own perceptions about materials management. What were hitherto considered 'mere' logistics problems have now emerged as much more significant issues of **strategic management**. Through our study of firms in a variety of industries in the USA, Japan, and western Europe, we found that the traditional approach of seeking trade-offs among the various conflicting objectives of key functions – purchasing , production, distribution, and sales – along the supply chain no longer worked very well. We needed a new perspective and, following from it, a new approach: **supply-chain management**.

6.1 CHALLENGES OF THE MARKETPLACE

To appreciate the urgency in the move toward adoption of new approaches to logistics, executives need look no further than the current economic and competitive environment. Within the macroeconomic sphere, the cost of capital alone stands out as a major concern. Between 1977 and 1981, the prime rate tripled in the United States and the relevance of that to European financial health is seen not just in parallel high European rates but in the acrimonious international debates surrounding the issue. This factor, coupled with generally slower growth and uncertainty in demand, makes investment decisions all along the supply chain – whether in capacity, systems, or inventories – riskier than ever before.

Economic uncertainty and, in particular, the swings in and out of recession are, by themselves, problematic from the viewpoint of materials planning. The natural inertia of the supply chain itself and of its decision-making mechanisms magnifies the impact of such changes, producing major inventory surpluses or shortages in sharp succession. so wrenching are these swings that even politicians have started to monitor national inventory trends. Add to this problem the tendency of management to overreact to these ups and downs in the hope of providing a safety net for the next swing, and the incurring of still further costs and risks is almost guaranteed.

Evidence of such behaviour can be found in various functions all along the supply chain. Marketing, for example, may boost its forecasts in order to secure large allocations from manufacturing so as not to be caught short in a potential upswing. In response, the manufacturing and distribution functions may develop their own independent forecasts or try to second-guess actual sales and inventories. Functions all along the supply chain tend to exhibit a certain possessiveness, and as a result inventories accumulate like snowdrifts at organizational fences. Finally, both short-term and long-term decisions on capacity, lagging

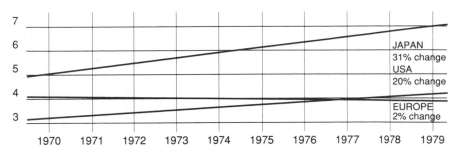

Figure 6.1 Comparative ratios of total costs to inventory (total costs of goods divided by inventory = inventory turnover).

as they do behind the market and inevitably reflecting the tendency to build in a safety net, as described above, very often make the firm even more vulnerable to subsequent changes in demand – if not actually influencing the market.

To a large extent, the driving force behind these conflicts and responses is another reality of the current business environment: increased competition in slower growth markets. Higher investment and operating costs cry out for increased market share as a means of assuring high (or at least adequate) return on investment. But as ever-stronger competitors vie for a larger part of the same (and in some cases shrinking) pie, the overall cost implications of increased performance in the distribution and marketing functions may be overshadowed by the desire to enhance the firm's competitive position through greatly increased customer service.

The trouble is, certain competitors out there are doing a better job of not only providing a high level of customer service, but also simultaneously keeping inventory costs down. Evidence of such performance showed up in a Booz·Allen survey, completed in mid-1980, in which inventory turnover and facility utilization in some 1100 companies representing 18 industries were examined. The study showed that inventory turnover among Japanese firms had increased 31% over a nine-year period, compared with an increase of only 20% in the USA and a drop of 2% for European firms (see Fig. 6.1). And because the Japanese were starting from a higher base, they came out the undisputed winner. This study showed, quite tangibly, why the 'Japanese challenge' should not be discounted merely because it has, by now, become a cliché.

It is not feasible, of course, to suggest that Western firms slavishly emulate the Japanese, either in terms of the particular features of their production operation (de-integration, smaller plants, narrowly focused facilities, etc.) or in terms of their particular managerial style (consensus and 'bottom-up' decision making). Nor is it logical to suggest that the historical and environmental factors that have shaped Japanese industry – almost complete dependence on imported raw materials, a limited domestic market, and as a consequence of the two , the need to build a strong presence internationally – have much relevance for the majority of Western firms today. However, the study does indicate certain characteristics that American and European firms successful in supply chain management have in common with Japanese firms; these can, and probably should, be emulated. The strategic balance of supply and demand, based on firmwide objectives, and more particularly, its support by a systems approach that places a premium on the fast transfer and accessibility of information across functional barriers are all highly relevant. While 'natural' conflicts between functions may be inevitable, common and shared data encourage the development of a broader perspective on supply-chain management and foster decision making that is more likely to be keyed to the overall objectives of a business rather than to the local or parochial functional objectives that have tended to dominate in the past.

6.2 FUNDAMENTALS OF SUPPLY-CHAIN MANAGEMENT

Supply-chain management differs significantly from classic materials and manufacturing control in four respects. First, it views the supply chain as a single entity rather than relegating fragmented responsibility for various segments in the supply chain to functional areas such as purchasing, manufacturing, distribution, and sales (see Fig. 6.2). The second distinctive feature of supply-chain management flows directly from the first: It calls for – and in the end, depends upon – strategic decision making. 'Supply' is a shared objective of practically every function on the chain and is of particular strategic significance because of its impact on overall costs and market share. Third, supply-chain management provides a different perspective on inventories, which are used as a balancing mechanism of last, not first, resort. Finally, supply-chain management requires a new approach to systems: Integration, not simply interface, is the key.

All of these features, and all of the challenges of the business environment that lie behind the move towards supply-chain management, point in one direction: to the top. Only top management can assure that conflicting functional objectives along the supply chain are reconciled and balanced, that inventories assume their proper role as a mechanism for dealing with inevitable residual imbalances, and finally, that an integrated systems strategy that reduces the level of business vulnerability is developed and implemented. Logistics and materials

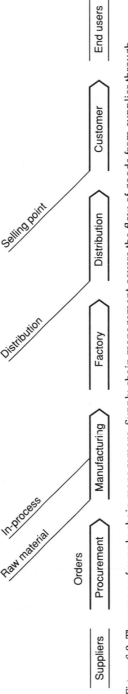

Figure 6.2 The scope of supply-chain management. Supply-chain management covers the flow of goods from supplier through manufacturing and distribution chains to the end user.

managers will continue to play important roles, but only top management can be expected to have the perspective to recognize the significance of supply-chain management, and only top management can provide the impetus for adopting this new approach.

6.3 BALANCING FUNCTIONAL OBJECTIVES

The conflicting objectives of marketing, sales, manufacturing, and distribution are a fact of business life. The imbalances resulting from these conflicts have become almost structural in nature and traditionally have been bridged by inventory. It is not necessary to challenge the direction of the individual strategies of each of those functions. What is needed, rather, is a critical evaluation of the opportunities for trade-offs between the key elements of these strategies with significant cross-functional implications, such as:

(1) The demand characteristics, lead time, reliability, and responsiveness implications of the marketing strategy;
(2) The lead time, flexibility, minimum run size, and changeover implications of the manufacturing strategy;
(3) The variety, range, and likely demand implications of the product strategy.

Some companies tend to resist the notion that a better balance can indeed be achieved, claiming to be victims of their own structures, culture, and environment. Many companies also find it difficult to articulate their objectives at this level, particularly in manufacturing, where traditionally reactive positioning precludes 'objectives' and where management tends to talk in terms of 'constraints', in sharp contrast to the Japanese view of manufacturing as a 'competitive weapon'. Customer service objectives are frequently taken as givens, and the utilization of certain supply points and lead times are considered rigid. So, the traditional approach to managing these imbalances is via inventory and sophisticated control systems.

Supply-chain management suggests a quite different approach, however: addressing the imbalances directly and evaluating opportunities for minimizing them. In our diagnostic studies for international companies, we found – sometimes to management's genuine surprise – that key functional strategies affecting logistics are indeed negotiable. It may be possible, for example, that delivery reliability to customers can, in some instances, be traded against lead times: A 99% reliability on a four-week lead time is frequently more acceptable to customers than 85–90% reliability on a two-week lead time. Moreover, such supply policies are usually negotiable by individual item based on relative volume or price.

In addition, the tendency of manufacturing executives to use the longest procurement time for materials as the basis for quoting standard lead times can be challenged – as can many attempts to protect manufacturing costs via batch sizes, particularly in times of low demand. We can see that decisions at these levels do have a fundamental and significant impact on inventory requirements. And as a consequence, the failure to achieve a balance of objectives at the strategic level will tend to put the burden on inventories alone, inevitably resulting in greater working capital requirements and increased costs.

6.4 OPTIMIZATION OF INVENTORY

This kind of approach – analysing in detail the individual functional strategies and attempting to reduce structural imbalance to a minimum – leads to a whole new role for inventory and supply policies. They become the mechanisms by which the inevitable residual imbalances are bridged, rather than the primary tool for managing the supply chain. The deployment of inventory as an asset, however, remains a strategic rather than an operational issue. At this level it should not focus on planning and batching rules or on systems tools, but on sourcing and supply policies, customer service and delivery performance objectives, and demand and supply decisions. This is the only way in which structural reductions in inventory requirements are likely to be achieved. The superior performance of Japanese industry – five and even ten times that of Western firms – highlights the opportunities for reducing the dependence of high inventory levels in the logistics systems of most European and US companies. This performance does not emanate from knowing how much is where but from why is it there? How many so-called inventory control systems in Europe and the USA today advance beyond mere 'status' into the areas of simulation and goal setting?

6.5 CONTROL SYSTEMS STRATEGY

Once this strategic framework has been established, then management and control mechanisms can be developed. It is only at this point that the issues of organization, tools, techniques and support systems should be addressed. The basic architecture of most systems today follows the traditional functional and organizational divisions of the supply chain – purchasing systems, production control systems, distribution systems, and sales order processing systems. This structure may do a fine job of supporting the hierarchical upward flow of data within any single function, but it is not very effective in the context of cross-functional or total supply-chain communication. The same holds true for 'interfaces' (frequently a synonym for time-consuming meetings), which by now have become a commonly accepted means of providing the necessary cross-functional communications.

The systems interface approach has several shortcomings, not the least of which is its hidden cost in terms of indirect manpower, and the related delay and distortion in the transfer of information. In addition, this approach frequently results in strategic and directional decision-making at too low a level. Further, systems groups either directly or indirectly 'sell' their services separately to functional vice-presidents or directors. Typically, there is no one 'client' for cross-functional communications, although the information-processing technology needed to support supply-chain management has been available for some time. The end result is that systems modules have tended to reflect organization segmentation with little or no emphasis on integration across the total chain.

Probably the best example of this problem is the master scheduling or master production planning 'interface' – actually one of the most critical tactical activities in any manufacturing business. Until very recently, the level of systems support available to this function was minimal. To be sure, materials requirement planning (MRP), which assumes the availability of a master schedule, has been around for some 15 years. Real-time order processing and sophisticated sales-forecasting systems for the front end of the chain are equally mature. However, the conversion process involving orders and forecasts and MRP occurs at a functional interface, and those conversions have been almost devoid of systems support. What is lacking here is a unified, overall perspective on the entire supply chain: who takes responsibility for systems interface in a predominantly functional organization structure?

Here, again, management must lead the way, laying the groundwork for integration of the various systems throughout the organization's supply chain rather than simply accepting the traditional forms of interaction among them.

There can be no doubt that the supply-chain management approach places additional burdens on top management: it requires the incorporation of a logistics focus into the strategic decision-making mechanisms of the business. It demands the rejection of inventory as the easy 'buy-out' option to many of the troublesome balancing and trade-off decisions. It implies an approach to control systems which supersedes the traditional functional divisions and which is likely to have significant organizational implications in the longer term. None of these are easy challenges, but the competitive environment of the 1980s for Europe and for the USA puts a high premium on meeting them.

6.6 MAKING SUPPLY-CHAIN MANAGEMENT WORK – TWO EXAMPLES

Supply-chain management opens up new vistas when it comes to both diagnosing and correcting inefficiencies. Most important, top management is heavily involved in supply-chain management; what previously were merely logistical issues are now strategic ones. Then, too, the broader view provided by supply-chain management makes it possible to find solutions that directly reflect the concerns of the customer and the technological boundaries within which a firm operates.

This is evident from the example of two companies, one in the United States and one in the United Kingdom, that Booz·Allen has counselled in the implementation of supply-chain management. In both cases, the application of traditional techniques might well have resulted in an all too familiar no-win trade-off: a cost premium for higher capacity or inventory investment versus shortfalls in customer service, with real costs showing up eventually as lost business. With the broader perspective of supply-chain management, however, it became evident that these were two quite different problems requiring two quite different solutions.

6.6.1 Alternatives to improved customer service

A US-based multinational pharmaceutical company faced market-growth problems in several divisions; these were exacerbated by customers demanding better service than they were receiving. Each division defined its problems somewhat differently, but it was clear that no one functional manager could solve the problem independently. Eventually the supply-chain management concept was used in four divisions, but its application in two of them highlights the effectiveness of the approach.

One division produced a highly specialized pharmaceutical product whose lead time had grown to three years and whose delivery performance was so poor that senior management was handling customer complaints. Only 30–35% of the orders were being delivered on time. As a result, customers were forced to stockpile inventory at a time when interest rates were rising and square foot costs were increasing. Manufacturing responded by blaming unreliable forecasts and long purchasing lead times. While these were partially to blame, this explanation ignored the internal scheduling problems that compounded that of poor delivery performance.

A traditional approach to solving these problems might have started with an attempt to reduce total lead time by eliminating capacity bottlenecks. However, the supply chain management method called for a different first step: analysing the benefits that would result from shorter lead times or improved delivery reliability. Once it was demonstrated to management that the market really wanted greater reliability – not necessarily shorter lead times – and that increased reliability could result in increased volume, then the decision to invest in alternative solutions was considerably easier to make.

The primary recommendation arising from our approach involved the development of an improved manufacturing system – one that was tied to forecasting and that incorporated a mechanism which offered a certain level of protection against forecast deviations. On-time reliability increased to more than 95% within two to three months. Reducing work-in-process inventory via smaller in-process buffer stocks resulted in a 15% decrease in overall inventory investment in the first year and a 30% decrease in the following year, as market volume increased.

The second division was coping with another set of problems. Externally, it faced a retail and wholesale trade group that was becoming increasingly sophisticated in its inventory management policies. As a result, the group was operating with less inventory, ordering more frequently, and demanding that orders be filled completely from regional distribution centres. Internally, the division was faced with conflicting views on its performance. According to marketing and sales, management had three problems: a stagnant market, stiff competition, and uncompetitive service levels. Manufacturing, on the other hand, believed that poor forecasting and antiquated distribution methods were to blame and that no one had demonstrated that improved service would sell more products. In the meantime, management was being evaluated on return on assets and was therefore reluctant to do much more than squeeze inventories.

A traditional logistics approach would have tried to reduce raw material and work-in-progress inventory to allow some incremental investment in finished goods. However, with the supply-chain management approach, management agreed to involve all the functional groups in solving the problem and not to assume that improved service was the answer until it could evaluate its cost implications.

A customer services survey of the trade indicated that service was becoming an important criterion in the purchasing decision and that there was a correlation between increased market share and high levels of service. As a result, programmes aimed at improved sales forecasting, new distribution policies, and plant scheduling methods were developed and cost implications were weighed against the service targets.

Implementation proceeded on all the programmes and within six months, service levels rose from 60% order fill to 75%, management's target. At the same time, inventory turnover did not change and in fact is expected to improve by 10% in the first full year of implementation. Finally, management was left with a system that could respond quickly to market demands for service as well as internal pressures to minimize inventory investment at certain points during the year.

6.6.2 Complementing manufacturing and marketing strategies

At the confectionery division of a UK-based food and beverage producer we found a vastly different operating environment and different market requirements. Not surprisingly, the application of supply-chain management here resulted in a radically different solution.

When we began our diagnostic study, the firm was almost three years into a major overhaul designed to strengthen its competitive position. The effects of this ambitious programme – which included modernizing and rationalizing production facilities, restructuring the product range, and refocusing marketing programmes – were already visible at that time. Market share was rising, manufacturing productivity was improving, and inventory levels had been reduced. In addition, rationalization of the new product line, coupled with the introduction of new size ranges, had provided a strong foundation for an upgraded advertising programme that capitalized on the brand franchise. All this showed up in the bottom line: Sales, profits, and return on assets were all improving.

Despite that obvious success, management sensed that fundamental structural issues had not been faced squarely. Their particular concern was one which supply chain management addresses: the balance between manufacturing strategy and inventory investment as a means of meeting the challenges of the marketplace.

Booz·Allen's diagnostic study led to a more precise identification of supply-chain management issues that validated management's concern:

(1) High customer service and product availability ex-stock were givens, not open to significant negotiation;
(2) Forecast accurary at the item level on a month-to-month basis was inaccurate (not unusual for consumer products businesses).

The new manufacturing strategy, focusing on four principal manufacturing lines, had succeeded in reducing costs, but was considerably less flexible than the previous system which had been built around 18 different lines.

The results of the three-year programme thus carried a certain irony. The company had succeeded both in rationalizing product lines and manufacturing and in streamlining inventories, yet these successes worked against each other. All 'stack' or flexibility had been removed from the system.

One obvious area for potential improvement was forecasting accuracy; a more traditional approach might have focused on this, probably without success, given the challenges of consumer product market places. Perhaps an even more obvious response might have been to reinstall the inventory buffers that had so recently been eliminated. But in this case, quite aside from the issue of carrying costs, this option was particularly unappealing for several reasons. First, brand franchise depended largely upon quality, and chocolate and candy plainly and simply taste better if they have not spent excessive time in a warehouse. Second, EEC regulations requiring open-date coding were imminent, and could be expected to draw consumer attention to the product age – yet another reason not to adopt a strategy that would have added a month of finished inventory to the supply-chain time frame.

Strategically, management faced the challenge of absorbing the high level of forecast error and seasonality while providing the desired level of customer service through an appropriate, cost-effective mix of capacity, flexibility, and inventory. That challenge was made even more formidable by an ever-changing environment – in particular, by continuing shifts in overall volume levels and in product mix coupled with changes in interest rates and hence investment or carrying costs. A one-time exercise would not be sufficient; the firm needed a framework within which periodic reappraisal of capacity and inventory costs could be measured and adjustments made. Working with management, we developed a model in which all the relevant elements – including forecast error and inventory costs – could be converted to standard hour equivalents. Using this model, management could determine the appropriate method for meeting the demands of the market place, e.g. high inventory/less capacity, greater capacity/less inventory.

The initial appraisal exercise showed that the environment at that time militated against inventory build-up: the inventory investment would have to double in order to reach the desired level of customer service. The solution lay in stretching production capacity – specifically, by investing more in the packaging process. This basic strategic decision was complemented by the introduction of a new, capacity-oriented approach to production scheduling. Installation of tighter controls over the total number of changeovers and associated down-time were built into the scheduling system, allowing a limited number of product-mix decisions to be made over a short horizon. As a result, the impact of near-term forecast error was considerably softened in terms of manufacturing economics while allowing customer service and supply objectives to be maintained.

These two examples provide only a small window on the benefits that flow from effective supply-chain management. Still, it is evident that such management is a far cry from simple manipulation of inventories and more than improved materials management, both of which may be inadequate – not inappropriate – responses to an unstated economic environment. Unlike these approaches, supply-chain management requires an underlying strategic focus, along with the involvement and commitment of top management. And because supply-chain management can provide the framework needed to meet the demands of today's uncertain economy, top management is likely to find that commitment worthwhile.

CHAPTER SEVEN

Creating a competitive advantage through implementing just-in-time logistics strategies

George A. Isaac III

To compete effectively in today's world economy, businesses must develop and implement strategies to differentiate themselves from local and overseas competitors – typically, by being a low-cost producer or providing high value to customers in terms of product quality, distribution, and customer support.

Just-in-time (JIT) logistics strategies is the vehicle for providing high-value customer service to the many companies that are currently requiring this level of support from their suppliers. The implementation of a JIT logistics strategy, however, has a tremendous impact on a company's organization and overall culture. Few new management concepts in the past decade have had as much effect on companies as JIT and this makes implementation of JIT logistics strategies difficult.

This article outlines how a company can create a strategic competitive advantage through implementing JIT concepts in the logistics area. The logistics functions addressed are purchasing, distribution, transportation, and warehousing. Specifically, the strategic, organizational, operational, and systems-related issues associated with implementing JIT will be discussed.

Source: Isaac, G.A. *Touche Ross Series*
© 1985 Touche Ross, Chicago, USA

Just-in-time (JIT) is a company-wide philosophy or culture oriented towards the elimination of waste throughout the entire logistics and manufacturing functions. It is symbolized by low inventories and the highest levels of quality and customer service.

JIT affects all of the basic business functions, including manufacturing, marketing, logistics, and finance/administration (see chart below). For example, under JIT, design engineering in the manufacturing function must challenge product designs to ensure that quality assurance has been designed into the product. Production scheduling must alter traditional run sizes to support small, economic lot sizes that can meet JIT distribution and inventory management objectives.

JIT brings the marketing organization new standards in customer service/support. Improvements in computer communication to support short-order lead times and increased order volumes resulting from small order sizes are also required.

In logistics, JIT creates totally new relationships with both vendors and carriers. In addition, the location of distribution centres and the management of inventories require new approaches.

The finance/administrative functions must respond to significant increases in customer and purchase order volumes resulting from the smaller order sizes associated with JIT. The MIS function should also address integrated logistics system needs, including both internal and external telecommunication requirements.

From a culture perspective, many of the fundamental business management practices that were common during the past two decades require significant change, as Table 7.1 suggests.

Given the impact of JIT on both the organization and culture of a company (Fig. 7.1), implementation must focus on training and emphasizing new values in quality and customer service.

This article addresses how your company can either gain market share or protect its markets by implementing JIT logistics strategies. The successful implementation of JIT can be organized into four phases:

(1) Preparing logistics for JIT;
(2) Operations 'clean up';
(3) Phased JIT implementation;
(4) Post-implementation review and ongoing support.

7.1 PHASE I – PREPARING LOGISTICS FOR JIT

In preparing the logistics function for implementing JIT, issues relating to strategy, organization, operations, and systems must be addressed.

Table 7.1 The effect of JIT on a company's culture

Issue	Conventional wisdom	JIT strategic thinking
Quality vs. cost	Least cost with 'Acceptable quality'	Top, consistent quality 'zero defects'
Inventories	Large inventories from Quantity purchase discounts Manufacturing economies of scale Safety stock protection	Low inventories with reliable 'continuous' flow' delivery
Flexibility	Long 'minimum' lead times; minimal flexibility	Short lead times; customer-service driven, much flexibility
Transportation	Least cost within 'Acceptable service levels'	Totally reliable Service levels
Vendor/carrier negotiations	Tough 'adversarial' negotiations	Joint venture 'Partnerships'
Number of suppliers/carriers	Many: avoid sole Source – no leverage and dependency exposure	Few: long-term Open relationship
Vendor/carrier communications	Minimal: many secrets; tightly controlled	Open: sharing of information; Joint problem solving; multiple relationships
General	Business is cost driven	Business is customer-service driven

This section outlines a step-by-step approach for planning a successful implementation.

7.1.1 Strategic issues

To address the strategic issues associated with JIT, company executives should ask themselves four fundamental questions:

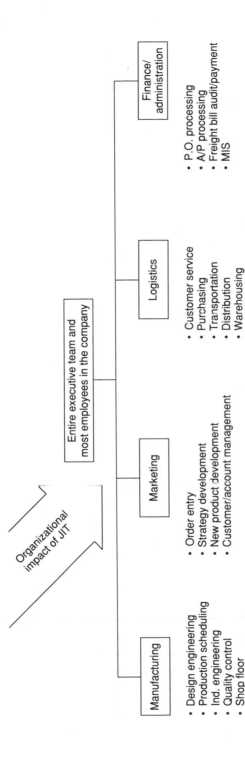

Figure 7.1 The impact of JIT on the organization.

(1) Is JIT an appropriate business strategy for your market place?
(2) In which business segments should JIT logistics be implemented?
(3) What service levels should JIT logistics provide (by business segment)?
(4) How will JIT benefits and performance be measured?

To answer the first question requires an understanding of the competitive trends in your industry and the JIT strategies of your primary competitors. In addition, since JIT can often increase a company's costs, particularly in the short-term because of high service levels, it is important that the basic economics of the business and market place be understood. Another factor that should be considered is how JIT will fit into the company's overall business strategies and plans.

To determine in which business segments JIT logistics should be implemented, remember that the key benefit from JIT should be sustained company profitability. An analysis of the company's market segments, product lines, distribution channels, and customers will provide the information necessary to determine where JIT will have the greatest impact on profits.

The third question requires analysis of desirable service levels for each business segment in which JIT will be implemented. JIT calls for different strategies for various business segments. Issues such as quality standards, frequency and timing of deliveries, modes of transportation, customer communications, inspection responsibilities, return goods replacement, containerization and product sequencing programmes, and order entry and billing processes must all be addressed when planning for JIT implementation.

The fourth question should be addressed during the first stage of planning, because it will specify the programme's business objectives. Specific performance measures (e.g. on-time delivery indicators, order-fill rates, etc.) in addition to benefit targets (e.g. customer profitability, incremental sales, inventory turns, etc.) should be defined.

Once the strategic issues have been resolved, it is time to outline plans for implementing JIT in the various business functions. The first issue to address is organization.

7.1.2 Organizational issues

To meet the rigorous service level demands of JIT, it is critical that the logistics functions be integrated and well directed. The first step is to combine the related logistics functions into one organization that can develop cohesive strategies and plans. In addition, the development of integrated logistics performance measures and open communication channels is critical for success. During this step, care should be taken to identify any additional training requirements for the organization.

7.1.3 Operational issues

Once the organizational issues have been resolved, the next step is to review each operational area (purchasing, distribution, transportation, and warehousing) and develop specific implementation plans for each.

(1) *Purchasing* There are several issues to address in preparing the purchasing function to implement JIT. These issues include the following:

  (a) *Vendor performance evaluation* The first step is to evaluate your current vendors. Examples of areas in which to evaluate historical performance include fill rates, reject rates, on-time deliveries, co-operativeness, and stability/reliability. The next step is to review the vendors' business plans and JIT/customer service strategies and determine if there is a good 'operational fit' between the vendor and your company.

  (b) *Selection criteria and sourcing strategies* The objective of this critical step is to reduce the number of suppliers for a specific commodity/item to one or two. Some of the key issues to consider include the vendor's proximity to your receiving sites, the vendor's willingness to be a sole source supplier (and accept the responsibilities associated with sole sourcing), the vendor's willingness to customize delivery systems to meet your needs, and an overall willingness to maintain flexibility and open communications between both organizations. Under a JIT arrangement, the vendor and the purchaser basically become vertically integrated: operational fit, systems, business direction, and JIT customer service philosophies must be in sync.

  (c) *Quality management* The key to JIT is quality; one can never achieve JIT with only 95% quality. Mechanisms must be in place to assure, detect and control quality throughout the material-flow pipeline. These mechanisms include insisting on statistical process control, requiring the vendor to inspect shipments so you can eventually eliminate your receiving inspection function, challenging your engineering designs to facilitate quality, and modifying stated tolerances/specs to true requirements.

  (d) *Order processing* Given the importance of short lead times and emergency requirements fulfilment, systems must be in place to provide real-time communications capabilities between key suppliers, your business and at times the transportation carrier. Analysis of your vendors and your own order-processing work flows may identify options to reduce the combined lead times. Another concern is the vendor's and your company's ability to process the large number of orders resulting from smaller daily deliveries.

(e) *Vendor communications/relations*   Your selected JIT vendors must be willing to establish a unique vendor–buyer relationship. The relationship must be structured around the long term and be viewed by both parties as a joint venture. Both multilevel and multifunctional communications must be established based on honesty, candour, and a sharing of information that typically has never before been attempted or achieved. As a buyer, you must have first-hand knowledge of your vendor's capabilities and limitations.

(2) *Distribution*   The distribution function must address some 'structural' issues that are difficult to change in the short term. As a result, distribution executives have exercised a great deal of innovation and creativity in developing plans to support JIT. Some of the key ways to prepare distribution for JIT include the following:

(a) *Network redesign*   The traditional objective in network design is usually cost minimization within some acceptable service level constraint. Under JIT, the service levels are significantly higher than historical levels, which requires total redesign of most traditional networks.

(b) *Improving customer service*   The first step is to define the service levels for each business segment. Next, real-time monitoring and performance tracking systems must be established to measure customer service performance. In addition, communications systems must be established to provide performance results to both management and customers.

(c) *Improving inventory management*   Strategies must be established for inventory stockkeeping locations, safety stock levels, etc. In addition, a 'pull' inventory system must be in place to support JIT.

(d) *Implementing assembly and distribution carrier services*   A and D services are an innovative alternative to consider when custom designing a distribution network. The advantage of A and D is that physical facilities of the company are not required to support the network. A and D carrier services are typically custom designed to meet your specific needs, and are flexible and easily implemented.

(e) *Implementing flow-through warehousing*   Another innovative way to consolidate multiple sourcing spots is to create a 'flow-through' warehouse strategically located to support JIT distribution. The warehouse can support multiple deliveries per day and may provide final assembly, kitting, or staging services.

(3) *Transportation*   Preparing the transportation function for JIT is similar to preparing purchasing. JIT calls for purchasing transportation carrier services on a long-term, open basis rather than short term. Some of the key issues to address are the following:

   (a) *Carrier performance evaluation*   First, evaluate carrier historical performance in terms of on-time deliveries, co-operativeness, reliability and stability. Next, review the carrier's business plans and JIT/customer service strategies and determine if there is a good 'operational fit' between the carrier and your company.

   (b) *Selection criteria*   The objective is to reduce the number of carriers utilized by the company by contracting dedicated transportation services with a few carriers. Some of the key issues to consider include the carrier's ability to customize routeings, the carrier's willingness to dedicate a portion of its fleet to your account, the carrier's telecommunication capabilities, and the carrier's overall willingness to maintain flexibility and provide innovative value-added services (e.g. packing, inspection, consolidation, warehousing, and A and D services).

   (c) *Communications*   A key function of a JIT carrier is to provide real-time visibility on the status of your shipments, both inbound and outbound. Early warning communication systems and back-up provisions are critical in a JIT transportation system. Computerized scheduling capabilities are also essential to manage the increased number of receipts and shipments resulting from smaller order sizes.

(4) *Warehousing*   Like the distribution function, warehousing must address some 'structural' issues that are difficult to change in the short term. The major issues centre around facilities and material-handling systems:

   (a) *Facilities*   One key issue is the number and location of docks. The basic facilities must support a significantly increased number of receipts and shipments. Ideally, the docks should be located adjacent to the work areas needing the materials (e.g. the shop floor for receipts) or adjacent to the work areas producing the finished goods (for shipments). When evaluating external warehousing, consideration should be given to innovative, value-added services such as kitting, final assembly, in-sequence loading, flow-through, and others.

   (b) *Material handling systems*   Automated material-handling systems (e.g. automated guided vehicles, automated storage and retrieval systems, and high-speed sorters) should be considered for certain high-volume operations. In addition, customized containers can facilitate undamaged product movement, aid in item counting, and eliminate waste of costly disposable containers.

7.1.4 Systems issues

A key component of JIT logistics is systems integration and communications. The systems foundation needed to provide high levels of JIT service typically include customer-linked computer order entry systems, real-time order and inventory management systems, and integrated performance measurement systems. In addition, because of the importance of close communications and co-ordination among all of the logistics functions, integrated logistics systems for order entry, invoicing, warehouse picking, receiving, shipping, and purchasing are critical.

Other areas for systems support could include bar coding and radio remote data-collection systems.

7.2 PHASE II – OPERATIONS 'CLEAN-UP'

Most companies' operating practices do not support a JIT logistics strategy. Prior to initiating JIT, several unconventional operating policies and practices addressing organization, operations and systems must be in place. Without strong policies in these areas, implementation of JIT could hinder corporate profitability and customer relations/service.

7.2.1 Organization problems

While logistics has become a separate organization reporting to the chief operating officer in several companies, in most companies the logistics function is still fragmented among three organizations: manufacturing, marketing, and distribution/transportation. The problem with the latter structure is that each function has conflicting objectives. In addition, there are typically tight territorial boundaries associated with this organizational structure that inhibit good communications. The problem often is compounded by the absence of overall logistics performance measures

7.2.2 Operating problems

Careful review of your operating practices in purchasing, distribution, transportation, and warehousing should be completed and addressed prior to JIT. The purpose is to resolve operating problems that are too significant to address during JIT implementation.

Examples of problems in purchasing include too many vendors to adequately manage under a JIT environment; having excessive lead times; or unsatisfactory product quality. Problems in distribution include poor inventory management and control practices or an inadequate distribution network. Problems in transportation include unreliable service levels and poor communication among carriers, shippers, and consignees. In addition, the shippers' market created by the Motor Carrier Act of 1980 has resulted in high carrier turnover and somewhat adversarial carrier–shipper relations.

Problems in warehousing often include facility constraints such as the number and location of receiving and shipping docks. Other problems may include inadequate picking and material-handling systems.

7.2.3 Systems problems

From a systems perspective, major issues requiring attention include the overall integration of existing logistics systems in addition to telecommunications capabilities with vendors, customers and carriers.

7.3 PHASE III – PHASED JIT IMPLEMENTATION

Once implementation plans have been completed and the necessary advance work has been addressed, the next step is to begin the actual implementation of JIT. While there is no blueprint for installing JIT, successful implementation typically requires a company to:

(1) Implement JIT in phases and monitor the implementation to ensure early successes in terms of organizational acceptance, customer satisfaction, and company benefits.
(2) Require top management support/involvement throughout the entire implementation;
(3) Initiate the implementation phase with training programmes/ materials and continue training to reinforce the culture changes necessitated by JIT;
(4) Establish fully integrated communications with everyone involved with JIT, including vendors, carriers, customers and internal company employees;
(5) Where possible, simplify your operations.

7.4 PHASE IV – POST-IMPLEMENTATION REVIEW AND ONGOING SUPPORT

Given the significance of the organizational and culture changes associated with implementing JIT, It is important that close tracking and reinforcement of company objectives are provided. Suggestions for this stage of implementation include:

(1) Continuously monitor and report on performance against original goals;
(2) Systematically track-integrated logistics performance measures;
(3) Establish regular, company-wide communication programmes to reinforce progress and results; and
(4) Keep senior logistics management 'close to the materials flow pipeline' to identify any problems with respect to quality, delivery, etc.

7.5 SUMMARY

US manufacturers and distributors have been forced into the JIT race to assure their survival. The USA's ability to compete in world and domestic markets depends on businesses' ability to differentiate their products with respect to quality, delivery, price, and customer support. These attributes are the cornerstone of JIT.

Two things to remember are:

(1) JIT is extremely difficult to implement successfully because of the company-wide culture change this approach requires; and
(2) Open, honest communications/relationships with vendors, carriers, customers, and internal management are essential to provide an appropriate foundation for JIT.

CHAPTER EIGHT

Using inventory for competitive advantage through supply-chain management

Thomas C. Jones and Daniel W. Riley

Competitive pressures will force major changes in inventory management in the next few years. Changes will result from businesses identifying and capitalizing on the opportunities to manage their entire supply chains as single entities. Supply chain management techniques deal with the planning and control of total materials flow from suppliers through end-users (see Fig. 8.1).

These techniques will probably destroy many of the myths of the past. This article covers four areas:

(1) Inventory myths versus realities;
(2) How to gain competitive advantage through supply chain management;
(3) Case studies of supply-chain techniques;
(4) Barriers to a supply-chain approach.

8.1 INVENTORY MYTHS VERSUS REALITIES

In our practice we have been exposed to a number of inventory myths – some new, some as old as business.

(1) Sophisticated techniques and organizational discipline will provide more accurate sales forecasts.

Source: Jones, T.C. and Riley, D.W. (1984) *IJPD & MM*, **15**(5), 16–26
© 1984 Council of Logistics Management, USA
First presented to *National Council for Physical Distribution Management Conference* (1984), Dallas, USA

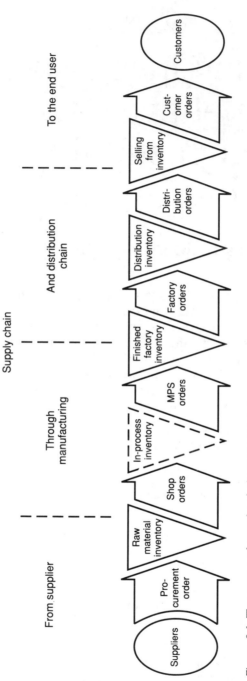

Figure 8.1 The scope of supply-chain management.

(2) Japanese techniques, such as just-in-time, will all but eliminate inventory problems.
(3) Inventory provides the necessary buffer to protect manufacturing from seasonal and business cycle variations.
(4) Local presence is a key element of our service – you can't sell from an empty wagon.
(5) Distributors, as independent businessmen, provide local availability and entrepreneurial inventory management.
(6) Local dealers need to be backed up by readily available regional stocks.
(7) Modern information systems and control methods will all but eliminate obsolete and slow-moving inventories.

Myth 1: Sophisticated techniques and organizational discipline will provide more accurate sales forecasts All too often highly sophisticated techniques exacerbate the situation – no one understands them or they are misapplied. Forecast accuracy increases as the forecast horizon is shortened; further, problems created by inaccurate forecasts become easier to deal with as response time is shortened. There are often major opportunities to reduce the forecast horizon by shortening supply chain response time. Response time has usually never been directly attacked and we find that the application of manufacturing technology coupled with well-thought-out semi-finished inventory policies can often shorten lead times dramatically.

Myth 2: Japanese techniques, such as just-in-time, will all but eliminate inventory problems 'Just-in-time', at this point, is largely a dream in most industries. In the automotive industry, for example, from a vendor perspective, little has changed in recent years: requirements still change at short notice, printed releases have little bearing on near-term requirements, and crises and phone calls are often the real drivers of shipments. It is obvious that these costs must wind up in final vehicle cost. In order for 'just-in-time' to work, significant investments in basic building blocks are required and, to date, few US firms have progressed very far. These investments usually include changes in manufacturing process and layout and personnel practices. New working relationships must be developed which foster teamwork, high morale, and flexibility. Finally, implementation requires a level of understanding and support from top management which is all too often unavailable.

Myth 3: Inventory provides the necessary buffer to protect manufacturing from seasonal and business cycle variations Our experience indicates that inventory more often aggravates the problem. An analysis of sales and production fluctuations usually shows more variation in production than sales. Inventory overhang and resultant management indecision can result in panic decisions to 'correct' inventory levels, usually at high penalties in terms of both costs and customer service.

Myth 4: Local presence is a key element of our service – you can't sell from an empty wagon The reality is that local stock offerings are usually limited and more out-of-balance than centralized inventories. Further, local order entry to shipment cycle times are often excessive, thereby precluding the benefits of local presence. Experience has shown that demand uncertainty is much higher at the local market level than at the national level and, as a result, local market inventories inevitably require much greater safety stock investment for a given service level than central stocks. This reality with weak controls leads to local warehouse systems characterized by limited offerings, slow response, and imbalanced inventories.

Myth 5: Distributors, as independent businessmen, provide local availability and entrepreneurial inventory management Our experience has been that independent distributors would often rather act as sales agents than wholesalers, and often lack basic inventory management skills. We frequently find the manufacturer performing the basic inventory control functions for the independent distributor. An additional problem is that in many industries, independent distributors/dealers are financially incapable of stocking a full line. The key here is a thorough understanding of the economics of the total supply chain and the real requirements of the segments served.

Myth 6: Local dealers need to be backed up by readily available regional stocks In numerous industries, large retailers have vertically integrated backwards, thereby duplicating and overlapping levels of the manufacturers' supply chains. These large local businesses are usually embarked on strategies of using their scale advantages in warehousing, inventories, and advertising cost to take share from smaller outlets. Elaborate warehousing networks provided by manufacturers can therefore interfere with the business strategy of the large local retailers who, in many industries, are increasing their share rapidly.

Myth 7: Modern information systems and control methods will all but eliminate obsolete and slow-moving inventories Unfortunately, obsolete inventory, like the poor, will always be with us. Securing competitive advantage will require that these costs be minimized through sound inventory deployment strategies. Information systems will continue to play a major role in planning and controlling inventories along supply chains but are far from a panacea.

Beyond 1984, using inventory for competitive advantage will require dealing with inventory realities rather than myths. An integrated approach to overall supply chain management is a proven method of obtaining competitive advantage.

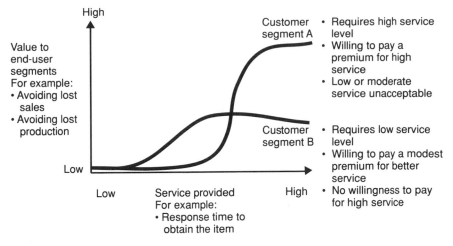

Figure 8.2 Differential response to customer service.

8.2 HOW TO GAIN COMPETITIVE ADVANTAGE
THROUGH SUPPLY CHAIN MANAGEMENT

Supply-chain management deals with the total flow of materials from suppliers through end-users – see Fig. 8.1. The key to efficiency managing a supply chain is to plan and control the inventories and activities as an integrated single entity. Three elements must come together for integrating the supply chain to operate effectively:

(1) recognizing end-user customer service level requirements;
(2) defining where to position inventories along the supply chain, and how much to stock at each point;
(3) developing the appropriate policies and procedures for managing the supply chain as a single entity.

In today's markets, inventory and distribution must satisfy key customer needs of time and place utility (item availability, delivery response time). Customers place value on their service needs and frequently these needs vary substantially from segment to segment and even customer to customer (see Fig. 8.2).

Further, a supply chain will utilize increasing amounts of resources to satisfy higher service levels and customer needs. The resources comprise inventory, transportation expense, facilities and people. The objective of integrating the supply chain is to lower the total amount of resources required to provide the necessary level of customer service to a specific segment (see Fig. 8.3).

The second step in integrating the supply chain is to consider and

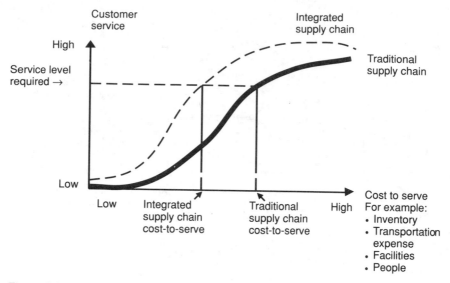

Figure 8.3 Reducing the cost-to-serve through supply–chain management.

evaluate alternative inventory stocking points along the supply chain that will provide acceptable customer service without unfavourably impacting overall cost-to-serve. Obviously, this evaluation must also deal with the impact on manufacturing costs and efficiencies.

A final step in supply-chain integration is to develop and install the necessary policies, organizational relationships, systems, and controls to manage the supply chain as a whole.

8.3 CASE STUDIES OF SUPPLY-CHAIN TECHNIQUES

Application of the basic techniques varies widely from situation to situation. The cases below were selected from client situations in a variety of industries.

8.3.1 Case 1: Recognizing customer service requirements

The company is a large manufacturer of a line of consumer durables shipped through a captive network of regional distribution centres. These centres received products both from the manufacturer's plants and outside suppliers. The key functions performed within the region-al centres included the following:

(1) Providing a mixed product offering to all customers;
(2) Performing order entry and status functions;
(3) Planning for and controlling transportation modes and carriers;
(4) Planning and controlling inventories to meet target service levels;
(5) Processing incoming materials and order-picking and shipping activities.

The distribution operations were well disciplined and provided 95% off-the-shelf service and delivery within three or four days of order receipt. Products were sold through various retail channels to the ultimate end-consumer.

The costs to operate the distribution network and provide the level of service offered were substantial, and amounted to close to 20% of landed cost. Management questioned whether the service offered was cost effective, and whether it should be the same for all segments.

Under analysis, it was determined that customer segments had quite different service level needs (see Fig. 8.4).

As shown, the exclusive dealers' segment's characteristics include the following:

(1) Only one manufacturer's brand;
(2) Little inventory to support their selling efforts;
(3) Customers sold on the basis of features and quality of specific brands.

Clearly, exclusive dealers of this product were highly dependent upon the manufacturer's supply chain and its performance.

At the other extreme were large, dominant dealers with completely different characteristics:

(1) most were multi-branded with products from several manufacturers;
(2) floor sales techniques often involved switching customers between brands to either improve margin or sell available stock;
(3) inventories were held and replenished with spot buys when products were on special promotion at attractive prices;
(4) little interest in fast response from manufacturers' supply chains; low acquisition price the primary driver.

Clearly, some segments were being over-served, but other channels were highly dependent upon the high-cost, captive supply chain. Recommendations here were to modify the service offering to each channel appropriately. For example, offer a unique limited line of make-to-order products, shipped direct from plants with relatively long response time which would be more attractive to large outlets.

Segments

Factor	Exclusive dealers	Small dealers	Sears/ Pennys/ Wards/K-Mart	Rural dealers	Non-exclusive dealers	Dominant dealers
Product delivery requirements	●	●	◐	◐	◐	○
Delivery order size	●	●	●	◐	●	◐
Product availability	●	●	●	◐	◐	◐
Delivery time	○	◐	○	○	○	○
Post delivery service	◐	◐	◐	◐	◐	◐
Information requirements						
Sales counsellor/order entry	◐	◐	◐	◐	◐	◐
Stock availability information	◐	◐	◐	◐	◐	◐
Overall relative importance of a distribution system	●	●	●	◐	◐	○

Legend: ● Very important ◐ Important ○ Not important

Figure 8.4 Inventory/distribution service requirements by segments.

8.3.2 Case 2: Defining where to position inventories along the supply chain and how much to stock at each point

A manufacturer of component parts sold its products in both the aftermarket and to original equipment manufacturing companies. The supply chain was highly integrated, beginning with steel coils and ending with a network of sixteen captive warehouses serving the aftermarket. OEM accounts were shipped direct from the manufacturing plant. The manufacturing process was relatively complex, beginning with extensive materials processing and proceeding through primary forming and machining operations. The aftermarket customers being served were full-line, automotive parts wholesalers and a number of repackagers.

Management had watched finished goods inventories grow significantly over a two- or three-year period. Not only was the investment very large, but turns were low, and many of the most popular items were in chronic short supply.

Initial efforts were focused on gaining a sound understanding of the entire supply chain, including:

(1) Lead times through the manufacturing process, transportation times between facilities, and required customer delivery times;
(2) Manufacturing process characteristics: set-up and changeover times, costs, and cycle times;
(3) Inventory management policies and procedures, forecasting techniques, and horizons.

The conclusion of the study was to make dramatic reductions in finished goods inventories and create a semi-finished inventory point at the plant (see Fig. 8.5).

Creation of this stock, coupled with the addition of finishing capacity, became the foundation of shorter response time, reduced set-up costs, improved service and lower inventory investment.

(1) Inventory is now stocked at a more flexible stage, as shown by the complexity index.
(2) Less value has been added at the semi-finished state.
(3) Forecast error, and therefore safety stocks, could be reduced since demand variability was much lower at the semi-finished stage.

8.3.3 Case 3: Using just-in-time techniques to manage the supply chain

Japanese just-in-time manufacturing techniques, when successfully implemented, are an excellent approach for reducing supply-chain

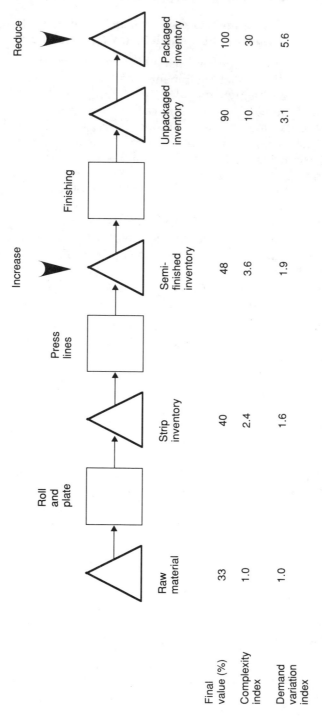

	Raw material	Strip inventory	Semi-finished inventory	Unpackaged inventory	Packaged inventory
Final value (%)	33	40	48	90	100
Complexity index	1.0	2.4	3.6	10	30
Demand variation index	1.0	1.6	1.9	3.1	5.6

Figure 8.5 Reducing complexity by re-positioning inventory in supply chain.

inventory. These techniques require, in many cases, a high level of manufacturing flexibility. As indicated earlier, just-in-time, at this point, is not widely adopted in the USA. There are, however, several highly successful implementations in 'green-field' sites. There are several success stories in small personal computers manufacturing.

Just-in-time will work – at one manufacturer the programme is well under way, and sub-assembly and final assembly operations have been achieving an inventory turn of 32. One key to its success is a high level of top management commitment and understanding. This understanding was developed through thorough educational programmes involving all levels of personnel – top management down through the shop floor. In several areas, unique materials-handling and revised layouts were installed to minimize queue time between operations. A number of changes were made in personnel practices:

(1) All levels became involved in scheduling and line balance problems.
(2) Performance measures were changed to reward flexibility and adherence to schedule.

A full quality programme was installed featuring visual control and statistical techniques. The next step for this manufacturer will be to involve key suppliers in the overall programme.

8.3.4 Case 4: Managing the supply chain as a single entity in a seasonal business

This company manufactures refrigeration products which have a seasonal pattern of heavy demand during the first half of the calendar year. The company was building a new facility in the south, and decided to review and challenge existing operating policies. A key element in operating strategy for this business was the policy for planning operating levels and inventories to meet the seasonal business characteristics. An analysis of the cost trade-offs between maintaining seasonal inventories and adjusting output levels resulted in a unique approach to using temporary, seasonal employees (see Fig. 8.6).

This substantially reduced the cost penalties associated with adjusting manufacturing capacity utilization during peak periods. The planning process was built around two key decision points: when to add the seasonal workers and when to cut back. The existence of the seasonal work force shortened the normal forecast horizon for making a major change in output levels, and thereby simplified the forecasting

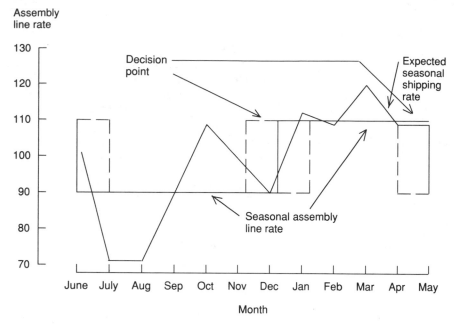

Figure 8.6 Production decisions in a seasonal business.

problem. Further, the risks, costs and time period necessary to carry seasonal inventories were all greatly reduced.

8.3.5 Case 5: Dealing with independent distributors

This company manufactured a line of industrial products that were sold to original equipment manufacturers. An independent distributor network was responsible for providing aftermarket service parts to the OEM products installations in the field. Many of these distributors were maintaining insufficient supplies of aftermarket parts to guarantee availability in the event of a field emergency breakdown. A decision was made to develop basic inventory guidelines for the distributors. An aggressive approach was taken by preparing a comprehensive inventory management programme:

(1) The independent distributors were provided with extensive training in management and offered a systems package.
(2) A standardized national stock list of specific items and minimum inventory levels was developed for each item for each distributor.
(3) Distributors were given the opportunity to customize and tailor local stocks.

Functional objectives	Impact of objectives on ...		
	Inventory	Customer service	Total costs
• High customer service	⇧ (open up)	⬆ (filled up)	⇧ (open up)
• Low transportation costs	⇧ (open up)	⇩ (open down)	⬇ (filled down)
• Low warehousing costs	⬇ (filled down)	⇩ (open down)	⬇ (filled down)
• Reduce inventories	⬇ (filled down)	⇩ (open down)	⬇ (filled down)
• Fast deliveries	⇧ (open up)	⬆ (filled up)	⇧ (open up)
• Reduced labour costs	⇧ (open up)	⇩ (open down)	⬇ (filled down)
• Desired results	⬇ (filled down)	⬆ (filled up)	⬇ (filled down)

Figure 8.7 Areas of conflict in the supply chain.

(4) The manufacturer monitored results with his field sales force to ensure understanding and adherence.

Within eighteen months, the overall availability of standard items was increased to the target level of 95% availability.

8.4 BARRIERS TO A SUPPLY CHAIN

The barriers to a supply-chain approach are tradition, organizational, legal and non-integrated management systems. Traditionally, supply chains of necessity have been managed and controlled functionally. For those portions of the supply chain that are captive to the manufacturer, there are usually strong organizational boundaries between activities, e.g., procurement and manufacturing, manufacturing and production control, manufacturing and distribution management, etc. The management objectives and measures for each of these functions are in fundamental conflict (see Fig. 8.7). Inventories, for example, are 'owned' and managed separately.

Independent businesses, vendors, and distributors add obvious barriers. The key here is establishing mutually advantageous relationships to make the chain work more smoothly and at lower costs. The tools available to work with are volume, price, commitment horizon, schedule stability, and exclusivity of franchise.

Finally, information and control systems are often barriers. These have usually been developed for each functional area on a piecemeal basis. Lack of integration across the supply chain often precludes the visibility and timeliness required for managing the chain as a single entity.

The analytical tools necessary to analyse and control complex and often multinational supply chains are now available. It is clear that the use of these tools can provide firms with the opportunity to use their inventory and distribution systems to gain competitive advantage in the market segments they serve.

CHAPTER NINE

Managing strategic lead times

Martin Christopher and Alan Braithwaite

Time is a business commodity which has an enormous opportunity cost. Yet normal business controls make no attempt to value or identify the scale or nature of this. This paper introduces the concept of strategic lead time management as a means of measuring and valuing the time efficiency of business.

Time concepts are embedded in every element of managerial activity. The idea of 'lead time' is generally accepted as a 'given' in most businesses. Yet most managers will accept that reductions in lead time and the more efficient use of time can confer benefits in terms of improved use of assets and enhanced competitive advantage in the form of better customer service, and lower costs.

In the current climate of high interest rates and extremely competitive markets, cost reduction and service improvement are worthwhile goals; yet few companies treat the management of time as a strategic issue, measure and report on their time efficiency, or review their methods of business control to identify systematic failure to manage corporate lead time.

In this paper we intend to show the value that is locked up in the strategic management of lead times, demonstrate the extent to which typical corporate operations waste time and describe a method by which corporate time efficiency can be assessed.

It must be the ultimate cliché that 'time is money'. We all recognize that we are dealing every day in concepts with time dimensions; bar charts and time tables are used to represent schedules for achievement;

Source: Christopher, M. and Braithwaite, A. (1989) *Logistics Information Management*, **2**(4), 192–7

budgets have a time dimension with revenue by period; 'just-in-time' is now a watchword in manufacturing. Time assumes a value in terms of how we manage our diaries and there is an opportunity cost attached to every personal scheduling decision we make.

Figure 9.1 shows the various terms applied to management's success and failure with time across the various functional areas. All of these relate to the speed with which results are achieved. Time is the common theme.

The importance of time across all the functional areas of management, as reflected in the words we use about it, supports the view that more could be done to take an integrated view of the time efficiency of business performance.

The shaded area in Fig. 9.1 contains the functions which are 'operations' oriented; these are the functions which are custodians of the firm's assets, consume the resources and deliver market-place performance. Within these functions lead time is already a critical concept; but it is an inconsistency of corporate process that allows companies to spend millions shaving a day off manufacturing inventories through the application of sophisticated computer systems while simultaneously maintaining inaccurate forecasting methods and lead times of two weeks to process an order! The requirement is to look across the functions at the lead times between the different elements of the organization and to measure the time that is consumed and the 'value' that is added by the system as a whole. The idea that the use of time can be 'value engineered' in an integrated way across the business functions has substantial economic potential. We have called this approach 'strategic lead time management'.

The concept of strategic lead-time is simple: How long does it take to convert an order into cash? Whilst management has long recognized the competitive impact of shorter order cycles, this is only part of the total process whereby working capital and resources are committed to an order.

From the moment when decisions are taken on the sourcing and procurement of materials and components through the manufacturing and assembly process to the final distribution and after-market support, there are a myriad of complex activities that must be managed if markets are to be gained and retained. This is the true scope of logistics lead-time management. Figure 9.2 illustrates the way in which cumulative lead-time builds up from procurement through to payment.

One of the basic functions of marketing is the provision of 'time and place utility' – more commonly expressed as 'the right product, at the right time, in the right place'. However, in practice, it is so often the

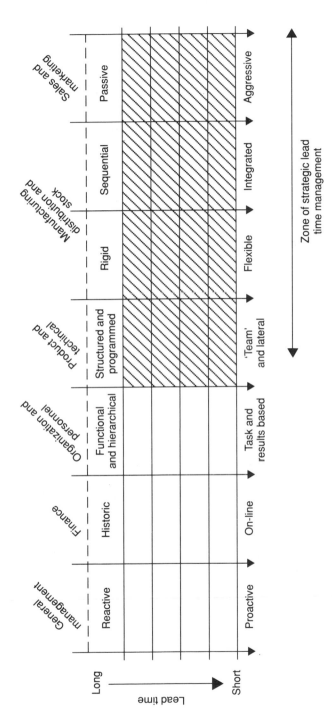

Figure 9.1 Time concepts in management.

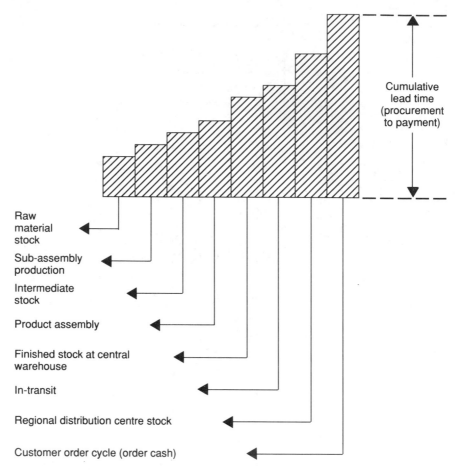

Figure 9.2 Strategic lead-time management.

case that the necessary integration of marketing and manufacturing planning to achieve this competitive requirement is lacking. Further problems are caused by limited co-ordination of supply decisions with the changing requirements of the market place and the restricted visibility that purchasing and manufacturing have of final demand; this is caused by extended supply and distribution 'pipelines'. To overcome these problems and to establish lasting competitive advantage by ensuring timely response to volatile demand, a new and fundamentally different approach to the management of lead times is required.

9.1 THE 'VALUE' IN LEAD TIME

A business with zero lead time is utopian; it has low inventory yet it can achieve 100% customer service. Most business people would dismiss such a notion out of hand on the basis that it would be both unachievable and impossibly costly in capacity and service costs. Such a dismissal fails to recognize the opportunity to challenge established lead times and measure their cost both in terms of inventory and customer service failure. The design and operation of corporate processes all embody the concept of lead time, yet because it is not an explicit factor, the consequences of the actual lead times are not understood. We have assembled three examples from our experience to illustrate this point.

9.1.1 Planning cycle/manufacturing lead time/pack size

A fashion retailer that also designs and arranges the manufacture of its garments is accustomed to working on two seasonal cycles per year. Indeed, this is the basis on which most fashion businesses operate with spring/summer and autumn/winter collections.

Its method of operation is to design and specify one season in advance. So, for example, it would be committed to its Autumn sales programme with its suppliers in February or March. This lead time is necessary in order to show the garments and gain their acceptance from the franchisee's, as well as 'book' the capacity with its suppliers. When the goods are ready for distribution to the outlets, the unit of dispatch tends to be either threes or sixes by size within a style. The selection of the size of the distribution quantity is made at clerical level without reference to the outlets' capability to sell the garments allocated or the probability of the requirement to distribute a second tranche later in the season. During the selling season, the company is generally unable to respond to styles which have sold especially well by securing more supplies since the workshops are already committed to next season's production. The company also proved incapable of moving garments between outlets to respond to variations in both style and size across the country. The consequence of this method of operation has been that average stock holding is in excess of four months and 60% of all products are sold at a discount in the 'end of season sales'. It is a tribute to the amazing gross margins of the high-fashion sector that the company remains profitable. Consider the lead-time components of the business;

(1) Design – nine months
(2) Manufacture – five months
(3) Remanufacture in season – infinite, i.e. not possible
(4) Redistribution between outlets – infinite, i.e. not possible.

The cost of inventory financing and lost profit due to mark-down represents nearly 30% of actual turnover and is almost equivalent to the entire annual manufacturing budget. Even a modest improvement in the company's lead-time efficiency would double profits. It is not sufficient to fall back on the excuse that the industry practice cannot be changed; Benetton have shortened their total cycle time to as little as four weeks by the use of integrated lead-time arrangements from the point of demand to the factory.

9.1.2 Forecasting and ordering of supplies

A computer company is sourcing its production on a worldwide basis to sell in individual national markets. Factories/suppliers require a six-month 'build plan' to enable components to be sourced and to plan factory loadings. National sales and marketing operations are required to forecast requirements in line with this lead time. Because of the rapidly changing market place, the individual countries regularly suffer from the twin difficulties of excessive slow-moving stock and an inability to service customers with the items they really want. Forecasting accuracy can be less than 50% at the marketing-company level and there are constant disputes with factories and suppliers over supply accuracy due to the frequency with which requirements are changed.

The consequence of the situation has been inventories 40% above those which are really necessary, together with an increased risk of technical obsolescence and inventory write-off. There is also a significant level of lost sales due to inability to supply. The opportunity cost for the current operation was as much as 5% on gross margin.

The lead time to make any substantial changes to the supply programme is four months or more, and with such low forecast accuracy the benefits of changes to requirements are somewhat doubtful. Furthermore, experience has taught management to hold higher levels of safety stock in terms of weeks of cover in order to meet customer service goals. Time is locked solidly into this operation and is attracting major costs, i.e.

(1) Lead time of supply – four months +
(2) Safety stock – one month +
(3) Forecast review – two months +

9.2 WAREHOUSE PICKING AND DISTRIBUTION

A company distributing parts to field service engineers established a 'hot order' channel to allow the engineers to request urgent shipments of parts for machines on repair. The service concept was simple: i.e. order and pick today, dispatch tonight, receive and fit tomorrow. Management was delighted that the concept received strong acceptance and the proportion of items dispatched by this method increased rapidly to 60%. Subsequent survey work showed that 70% of all parts dispatched by this method remained unfitted seven days after receipt. The company was effectively wasting premium dispatch costs in excess of £100 000 per year through its poor management in lead times, e.g.

(1) Lead time to complete repair – up to two weeks but assumed as 24 hours universally
(2) Lead time to deliver parts – 24 hours.

It was also found that non-urgent dispatches handled on a 24-hour basis occasionally affected customers who really required prompt service by putting parts temporarily out of stock.

These are just isolated examples of lead times which are embedded in company systems. In all cases, the opportunity for reducing cost and improving customer service through better management of lead-times is substantial.

9.3 THE EFFECT OF LEAD TIME

One of the most important areas of lead time management is in inventory replenishment. We have carried out extensive modelling on alternative inventory management techniques combined with different lead times of supply; all applied to the same basic customer demand scenario.

The example we have taken is based on the management of three inventory items at a local branch, selling at the rate of 1, 5 and 12 per day respectively. The distribution about the average daily rate of sale was assumed to be normal.

The aim was to predict average inventory levels for each rate of sale based on:

(1) Lead time of supply of 5 days and 10 days
(2) Methods of inventory management based on 'continuous review' or 'periodic review' of 5 days and 10 days.

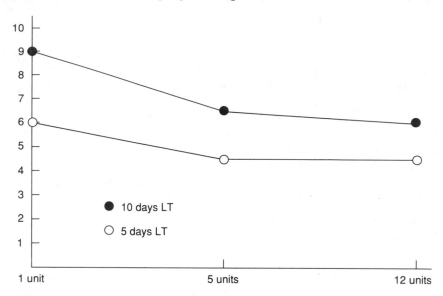

Figure 9.3 Average days stock vs average demand on reorder-level system with continuous review and reorder quantity of five.

The model was able to project the average inventory level and monitor the customer service achieved on each simulation. As far as possible, conditions were created to ensure that service levels of 98–100% were achieved. Figures 9.3 and 9.4 illustrate the main conclusions.

, Figure 9.3 shows that a reduction of lead time from 10 days to 5 days using a continuous review system and a re-order quantity of five can reduce average inventory by 30%.

Figure 9.4 shows that the combined result of both inventory control method and lead time combined can reduce inventory by as much as 50%. A detailed trade-off analysis is then required to ensure that, with the cost of possible increased shipping frequencies, the growth still provides an optimum total cost for the business. However, few companies can afford to ignore the opportunity to reduce inventory by even as little as 25%.

It can be surprising to see the extent to which the method of inventory management can add to the throughput efficiency of the system. This confirms the point that every lead-time component of a company's system must be challenged, both individually and for its effect on the total business, to ensure that the firm is securing the maximum value from its assets and the optimum customer-service performance.

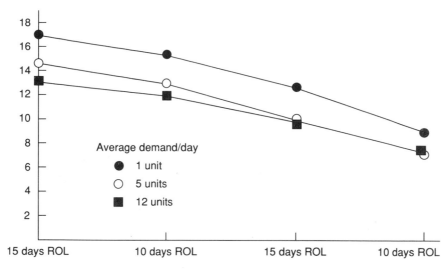

Figure 9.4 Effect of inventory control method and lead time on average stock.

To support this concept we have developed the example detailed in Fig. 9.5. It has been designed to illustrate how a large integrated corporation can add time and cost to the process of making its product and serving its customers without adding significant value. There are two parallel tracks which can be addressed:

(1) Throughput efficiency
(2) Process efficiency.

This notional corporation has a total throughput time of 37 weeks, from procurement to payment, yet it is operating sound methods in manufacturing and has a full range of computer systems in operation to support its processes. Its process chain is a little less at 26 weeks. It is scarcely surprising that captains of industry can be compared to the masters of super-tankers where the results of a change of direction can be such a long time in their realization. The reality is that the majority of time is absorbed adding cost rather than 'value'. An analysis of the time efficiency of the business will show that opportunities exist to simultaneously lower costs, raise quality, increase variety and market-place flexibility and, not least, raise standards of customer service.

The answer is to address all the lead-time components in the business as a total system and act to reduce total corporate cycle times in terms of both throughput and process.

All of what we have said seems obvious; so why have companies not picked up on this more quickly? The reasons seem to be fourfold:

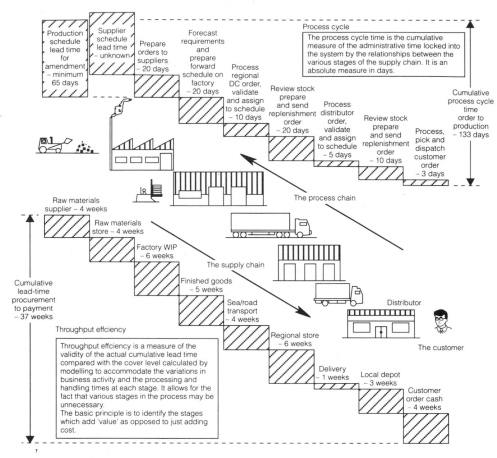

Figure 9.5 Throughput efficiency and the process control.

(1) Few directors retain a grasp of process at the 'coal face'; as a result, the way things get done can reflect convenience for the doers, a desire to protect functional boundaries, and a lack of understanding of the consequences both up and down stream of individual processes.

(2) Initiatives for change are largely functional and seldom reflect the total cost of the system. So, for example, manufacturing based on JIT can externalize inventory back on to the suppliers or into finished goods warehouses. On occasions this can actually increase total cost and reduce flexibility since the success of the operation is ultimately conditional on the accuracy of the forecast and the lead

time over which changes can be introduced. In this context 'flexible' manufacturing has extremely rigid constraints.

(3) Lead times are 'protected' by their custodians as a means of keeping people off their backs, and as a way of providing some hidden flexibility to respond. Individual functional lead times inevitably contain some slack, and where these become embodied in a company's processing system, then they are institutionalized.

(4) Systems hold lead times as parameters which are taken for granted. Few executives will dare to challenge the basic principles of the computer systems in the business, far less the accuracy with which they complete the task. As a result systems regularly operate on outdated or inappropriate lead-time constraints which have not been reviewed for years.

These factors together combine to create considerable inertia to achieving a strategic focus for the management of lead time.

The lack of any definitive systems architecture in which lead time is a consistent corporate wide dimension has meant that information technology cannot be used directly to provide information on the opportunities being missed. This does not imply that lead time is ignored by systems such as MRP2, DRP, forecasting and planning modules; simply that these systems are all functionally orientated and do not recognize the strategic dimension of lead time. Each of these systems is parameterized by lead-time factors; the point is that none of these systems is designed to reduce or manage lead times. They are also connected sequentially through the various business processes so that the additive effect of the lead time at each stage is not understood.

The nearest systems concept to managing lead time in the supply-chain area is 'virtual inventory' where information on regional, country, European or global inventory is substituted for the item itself; goods are shipped from where they are held to the point of demand. Such a system eliminates the lead time and cycle times for controlling inventory on a store-by-store basis. With the advent of 1992, more and more companies will need European wide virtual inventory and demand management systems, as well as methods to integrate customer service with the supply chain.

The benefits of such methods will only be clear when it is possible to:

(1) Measure the company-wide lead-time efficiency.
(2) Carry out trade-off analysis to assess the benefits of reducing these time constraints.

We have developed two measures which, when used together, provide an indication of corporate lead-time efficiency.

9.4 THROUGHPUT EFFICIENCY

Figure 9.5, which shows the total dwell time in the system, is dramatic but does provide an accurate measure of the extent to which long dwell times are really necessary. It is essential that any measure of throughput efficiency recognizes the real external and internal constraints and measures the degree to which the supply chain is adding 'value' as opposed to pure cost. By employing time-based simulation techniques, it is possible to establish the extent to which the 'buffer' is needed to cope with variations in demand, reasonable levels of forecast inaccuracy and economic production and purchasing cycles, at each stage in the supply chain.

The computer model calculates the throughput cover, expressed in time, across the whole business necessary to service the projected customer demand. It also enables the components which make up the total time efficiency of the business to be tested individually and their effect on the total cover to be evaluated. It is not unusual to find that complete segments of the supply chain are entirely unnecessary in the context of meeting customers' requirements. They are just adding an additional tier of cost and administrative complexity, as well the opportunity to let more customers down through failure to deliver with accuracy and on time.

The total actual throughput time for the business can be measured using sampling techniques based on conventional method study.

The measure of throughput efficiency using this approach is simple. It is calculated as a single percentage measure as follows:

throughput efficiency

$$= \frac{\text{actual chain cover (days)} - \text{modelled cover (days)}}{\text{Actual chain cover (days)}} \times 100$$

9.5 PROCESS EFFICIENCY

Unlike the measure of throughput cover, which reflects a limit to the opportunity to create a stockless environment with zero lead-time processing, the process efficiency of the business should be viewed as an absolute measure. As we have already shown, the requirement for 'visibility' all the way from customer demand to the start of the supply chain is crucial to achieving a strategic dimension for lead-time management. Since computers using electronic data interchange (EDI) are capable of providing nearly instantaneous visibility of all events to all players in the chain, the assumption can be made that perfect information can exist and any process cycle represents an inefficiency. The process cycle, expressed in days, with all the components of the cycle treated as additive, is therefore not a bad absolute measure of efficiency. So, for example, the company in Fig. 9.5 would have had to report a process cycle of 133 days. It is not difficult to measure the process cycle although careful interpretation is required to distinguish the process cycle and lead time inside and outside established production schedules. For some manufacturing companies it may be necessary to measure both.

9.6 CONCLUSION

Armed with these two measures, what is management to do? The preparation of the analysis will have helped to identify the pressure points and enabled them to be prioritized, both in terms of value and ease of change. Based on this understanding, a decision can be made on whether to go for piecemeal improvement or a radical redesign of the supply chain and the lead-time parameters.

In many cases the results of the measurement process will be quite alarming and the scale of the financial opportunity will demand action. The basis for change will be in information technology (IT), whatever the approach and timescale adopted. IT will provide the EDI and the real-time information on the status throughout the chain. However, the systems requirements to meet the goals of strategic lead-time management have barely been defined, let alone implemented. The possibility of being able to buy a single package to manage total lead time is still some way off.

Nevertheless there is much that can be done to realize some of the benefits through focusing on just parts of the supply and process chains. Indeed this is likely to be a desirable course of action, given the major risks attached to large IT projects. Once the strategic direction of a lead-time management programme has been set, it is likely to be more effective to opt for progressive implementation through a series of systems, connected by EDI, each delivering local functionality, and 'feeding' special decision support modules to provide both the strategic overview and interfunctional control.

In the context of the financial and market place benefits, the new perspective of strategic lead-time management will be a major tool for securing competitive advantage; the opportunity to introduce it progressively makes it especially attractive.

CHAPTER TEN

Fast-cycle capability for competitive power

Joseph L. Bower and Thomas M. Hout

All managers appreciate, at least intuitively, that time is money, and most will invest to save time – and the money it represents – if they see a clear opportunity. The travel agent computerizes to be able to confirm customers' reservations instantly. The apparel manufacturer develops a just-in-time production process to make what's wanted and avoid the inevitable discounts caused by overproduction.

But actions like these don't create much competitive advantage, because competitors will soon see the same opportunity and most will do the very same thing. Taking time out of a business gets interesting, however, when it represents a systematic change in the way a company accomplishes its work and serves its customers. Then saving time can provide sustainable competitive advantage.

Fast cycle time is not a new operating concept in business strategy. It has long been a key factor in the success of businesses ranging from Hong Kong's custom tailors to McDonald's. But today, executives in more and more large, complex businesses are achieving sustained competitive advantage by making radical changes in how they manage time within their companies. These companies make decisions faster, develop new products earlier, and convert customer orders into deliveries sooner than their competitors. As a result, they provide unique value in the markets they service, value that can translate into faster growth and higher profits.

In these top-performing companies, fast cycle time plays two important roles. First, it is an organizational capability, a level of performance that management shapes and builds into the company's operating systems and the attitudes of its employees. The basic idea is to design

Reprinted by permission of *Harvard Business Review*, 'Fast-cycle Capability for Competitive Power', Joseph L. Bower and Thomas M. Hout, November / December 1988

an organization that performs without the bottlenecks, delays, errors, and inventories most companies live with. The faster information, decisions, and materials can flow through a large organization, the faster it can respond to customer orders or adjust to changes in market demand and competitive conditions. Less time is spent fighting fires and coordinating. More time is available for planning, for initiating competitive activity.

Second, fast cycle time is a management paradigm, a way of thinking about how to organize and lead a company and how to gain real advantage over competitors. It is a powerful organizing message because its basic premise is so simple. It is also extremely effective since compressing time reinforces and supports what capable managers are already trying to do.

Analysis of competitive developments in a wide range of industries indicates that fast-cycle capability contributes to better performance across the board. Costs drop because production materials and information collect less overhead and do not accumulate as work-in-process inventory. Customer service improves because the lead time from receipt of order to shipment diminishes. Quality is higher because you cannot speed up the production cycle overall unless everything is done right the first time. Innovation becomes a characteristic behaviour pattern because rapid new-product development cycles keep the company in close touch with customers and their needs.

Developing fast-cycle capability is not easy nor can it be done overnight. It requires fundamental rethinking of how a company's goods or services are delivered to customers, and it means that various parts of the organization will have to work together in new and different ways. But these days, the penalty for standing still is far higher than the cost of change.

10.1 EVERY COMPANY IS A SYSTEM

People in fast-cycle companies think of themselves as part of an integrated system, a linked chain of operations and decision-making points that continuously delivers value to the company's customers. In such organizations, individuals understand how their own activities relate to the rest of the company. They know how work is supposed to flow, how time is supposed to be used.

In small companies, this way of thinking is usually second nature. People find it easy to stay focused on creating value because almost everyone works directly on the product or with a customer. Policies, procedures, practices, or people that interfere with getting the product out the door are easy to see and can be dealt with quickly.

As companies grow, however, the system-like nature of the organization often gets hidden. Distances increase as functions focus on their own needs, support activities multiply, specialists are hired, reports replace face-to-face conversations. Before long the clear visibility of the product and the essential elements of the delivery process are lost. Instead of operating as a smoothly linked system, the company becomes a tangle of conflicting constituencies whose own demands and disagreements frustrate the customer. 'I don't care what your job is', the overwhelmed customer finally complains. 'When can I get my order?'

Fast-cycle companies – especially the big ones – recognize this danger and work hard to avoid it by heightening everyones's awareness of how and where time is spent. They make the main flow of operations from start to finish visible and comprehensible to all employees, and they invest in this understanding with training. They highlight the main interfaces between functions and show how they affect the flow of work. They are aware of the way policies and procedures in one part of the company influence work in others. They compensate on the basis of group success. And, most important, they reinforce the systemic nature of the organization in their operations architecture.

To illustrate, let's look at Toyota, a classic fast-cycle company. Figure 10.1 presents a simplified diagram of the company's key operating activities. As the diagram shows, the heart of the auto business consists of four interrelated cycles: product development, ordering, plant scheduling, and production. Over the years, Toyota has designed its organization to speed information, decisions, and materials through each of these critical operating cycles, individually and as parts of the whole. The result is better organizational performance on the dimensions that matter to customers – cost, quality, responsiveness, innovation.

Self-organizing, multifunctional teams take charge of product development, focusing on a particular model series. In rapid response to demand patterns, they develop products and manufacturing processes simultaneously to collapse time and ensure better manufacturability. The teams are responsible for managing ongoing styling, performance, and cost decisions, and they control their own schedules and reviews. They also select and manage suppliers, who are brought into the design process early on. The result is an ever-faster development cycle – three years, on average, as compared with four or five years in Detroit – frequent new product introductions, and a constant flow of major and minor innovations on existing models.

The production cycle begins as soon as a customer orders a car from a dealer. Dealers in Japan are connected on-line to the factory scheduling system, so that an order, complete with specifications and the customer's option package, can be entered and slotted into the factory schedule right away. Toyota schedules its plants to minimize sharp fluctuations in daily volume and to turn out a full mix of models every day. Customers get on-the-spot confirmation of their expected delivery date. Suppliers are automatically notified of the new order and given a stable production schedule so that they won't deliver the wrong components on the day of final assembly.

Actual production is executed in small lots by flexible manufacturing cells that can accommodate a mixed flow of units with little changeover time. Plants are managed to maintain high up time (all the steps in the production sequence are functioning) and high yield (all the production processes are under control and turning out quality products). The result is a fast-paced production cycle, which squeezes out all the overhead except what's needed to get work done right the first time through, and a reliable, continuous manufacturing process.

Much of Toyota's competitive success is directly attributable to the fast-cycle capability it has built into its product development, ordering, scheduling, and production processes. By coming up with new products faster than competitors do, it puts other manufacturers on the marketing defensive. By translating a customer's order into a finished product delivered faster, it captures large numbers of time-sensitive buyers and puts cost and inventory pressure on other manufacturers. By continuously bringing out a variety of fresh products and observing what consumers buy or don't buy, it stays current with their changing needs and gives product development an edge market research cannot match. The faster Toyota can develop and deliver automobiles, the more it can control the competitive game.

In their ability to preempt new sources of value and force other companies to respond to their initiatives, Toyota and other fast-cycle companies resemble the World War II fighter pilots who consistently won dogfights, even when flying in technologically inferior planes. The US Air Force found that the winning pilots completed the so-called OODA loop – observation, orientation, decision, action – faster than their opponents. Winning pilots sized up the dynamics in each new encounter, read its opportunities, decided what to do, and acted before their opponents could. As a result, they could take control of the dogfight, preempt the opposition's moves, and throw the enemy plane into a confused reactive spiral.

Companies in many industries are operating in much the same way today. Responding to a challenge from Yamaha, Honda nearly doubled its range of motorcycle models in less than two years – destroying Yamaha's short-lived edge. Liz Claiborne has introduced two addition-

Toyota performs critical operations faster ...

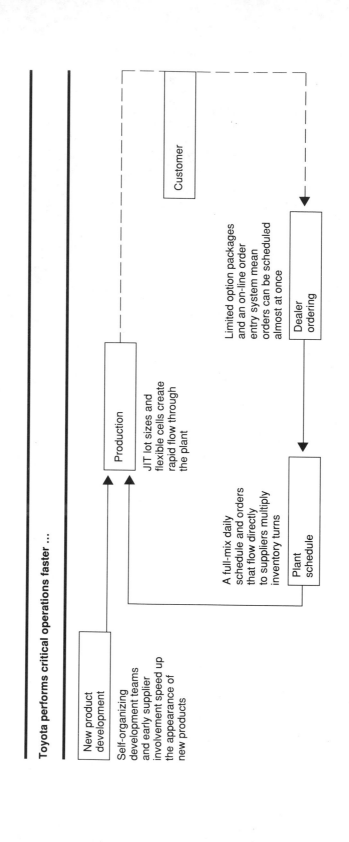

New product development

Self-organizing development teams and early supplier involvement speed up the appearance of new products

Production

JIT lot sizes and flexible cells create rapid flow through the plant

Customer

Dealer ordering

Limited option packages and an on-line order entry system mean orders can be scheduled almost at once

Plant schedule

A full-mix daily schedule and orders that flow directly to suppliers multiply inventory turns

... so it cuts time at every turn.

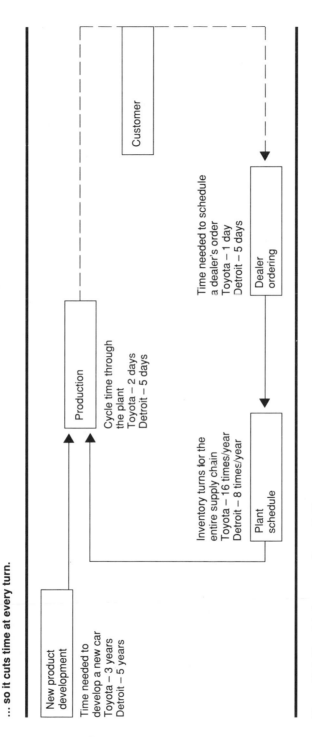

Figure 10.1 Toyota's key operating activities.

al apparel seasons to match consumer buying patterns more closely. Seiko has strengthened its hold on the watch market with a highly automated factory capable of producing new models each day. In semiconductors, the battle for global share is being fought largely on the basis of the speed with which new technology can be applied to larger chips.

Other manufacturing companies go beyond their own boundaries to include customers and suppliers in one integrated delivery system. Milliken, the large US textile manufacturer, collaborates with General Motors on auto interiors, with Sears on upholstery fabrics, and with Wal-Mart on apparel. Because they see one another as partners in delivering a product, not separate operations, Milliken and its customers have been able to share upstream order input and scheduling information, coordinate production cycles to minimize imbalances, and eliminate duplicate inspections and buffer inventories. The results are dramatic. Costs have fallen. Inventory turns have typically doubled. Sales have risen. Stock shortages and mark-downs occur less often. The time it takes the Milliken customer system to fill an order has been cut in half.

Finally, competing through fast-cycle capability is as powerful a strategy in services as it is in manufacturing. By automating its analysis and trading functions, Batterymarch, the Boston-based equity fund manager, collapsed the time it takes to decide on a portfolio change for a customer and put it through. The customer gets into rising stocks and out of falling ones faster than before. Batterymarch has lower costs and higher profits: revenues per employee triple the industry average.

10.2 WHAT MAKES FAST-CYCLE COMPANIES RUN

Fast-cycle companies differ from traditional organizations in how they structure work, how they measure performance, and how they view organizational learning. They favour teams over functions and departments. They use time as a critical performance measure. They insist that *everyone* learn about customers, competitors, and the company's own operations, not just top management.

Each of these characteristics is a logical outgrowth of the management mind-set Toyota examplifies, the mind-set that sees a company as an integrated system for delivering value to customers. Conversely, practices and policies that compartmentalize the company – a strong functional organization, for example, or buffer inventories, or measurement and control systems that focus exclusively on the numbers – have to be modified or done away with. In a fast-cycle company they're counterproductive, however useful they've been in the past and however reassuring they are to employees.

10.2.1 Organize work in multifunctional teams

To compress time and gain the benefits, a company has to work in and manage through relatively small, self-managing teams made up of people from different parts of the organization. The teams must be small because large groups create communication problems of their own and almost always include members whose areas of responsibility are peripheral to the team's task. The teams must be self-managing and empowered to act because referring decisions back up the line wastes time and often leads to poorer decisions. The teams must be multifunctional because that's the best – if not the only – way to keep the actual product and its essential delivery system clearly visible and foremost in everyone's mind.

AT&T and Ford have used teams staffed with members from different disciplines to develop new telephones and new cars. By bringing people from product engineering, manufacturing, marketing, and purchasing together throughout the development process and giving them the authority to make the real business decisions, these companies have cut enormous time and expense out of their new product efforts. In the telephone business, for example, it takes laggards three to four times as long to bring their products and services to market.

Fast-cycle companies use multifunctional teams for everyday work at all levels, not just for special projects. One bank we're familiar with successfully reorganized its personal lending practices and collapsed the time it takes for a customer to get a decision from several days to 30 minutes. Formerly loan applications were handled by a series of supervisors, with clerks as intermediaries to do the processing work. Now an application comes to a single group made up of a credit analyst, an experienced collateral appraiser, and a bank procedures expert who can draw on their collective knowledge and experience to respond to the customer almost at once.

As this example suggests, putting together a successful team often means broadening the scope of individual jobs, organizing the team around market-oriented purposes rather than departmentally defined tasks, and placing business responsibility as far down in the organization as possible.

In effect, it redefines what is commonly meant by multifunctional work. In our experience, many large companies like to think that they work multifunctionally because they form special task forces that cross organizational lines or encourage managers to wander around informally and share their observations. And devices like these can make employees more aware of a company's working mechanisms and opportunities to improve them incrementally, to be sure. But they cannot create well-designed, day-in and day-out, cross-functional relationships down in the organization, where the work gets done and the opportunities to learn are greatest.

Similarly, skunk works that bypass the organization's regular review mechanisms won't develop fast-cycle capability or help managers root out quality and time problems in their operation. Fast-cycle managers know that routine work determines a company's effectiveness, not special projects. So rather than circumvent a slow-moving core by creating outlying units that are smaller, quicker, and more responsive, these executives work to build those qualities into the company as a whole – even if that means taking themselves out of some critical decision loops.

Senior managers typically have lots of good ideas to contribute. But their interventions also carry great weight and often come at awkward times in a project's life. Moreover, their calendars are so crowded that the more they get involved in a project, the harder it becomes to schedule important meetings and keep decisions on track. Senior executives in fast-cycle companies understand this problem and appreciate the way the bottlenecks they create can demotivate junior people. They concentrate on improving the system, therefore, and delegate routine operating decisions to others.

Because of all these differences, the organization charts of fast-cycle companies bear little resemblance to the traditional pyramid of hierarchical boxes. Neither responsibility nor authority is so neatly decentralized and isolated. Instead, the organization chart is more likely to be a set of interlocked circles or a systems flow chart with arrows and feedback loops indicating the actual path of decisions and work. The organization chart for the Taurus-Sable product development effort at Ford, for example, was a circle with the core project management team in the centre and working groups branching out in all direction (Fig. 10.2).

10.2.2 Track cycle times throughout the organization

To assure that information and materials will move through the entire organization with little or no delay, fast-cycle companies manage both the cycle time of individual activities and the cycle time of the whole delivery system – the number of days it takes to ship a customer's order, for instance, or develop a new product. Managers in these

Pyramids Are the Buggy Whips of Organizations

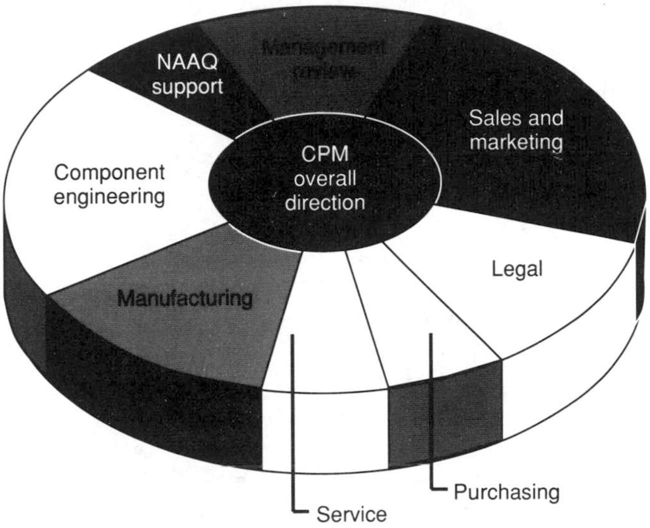

Ford put car programme management at the centre of the organization chart for Team Taurus

Figure 10.2 Organization chart.

companies track each stage's output to see that it is flowing easily into the next and meeting that user's specifications. They make continuing efforts to reduce each activity's characteristic cycle time and therefore the time of the entire sequence. And they are alert to opportunities to compress time by eliminating stages, for example, combining once-separate data-preparation and processing activities.

Most organizations manage the cycle time of the longest or most visible part of their operation, but neglect others that are less obvious like order processing or engineering tests. They also allow information in process and decisions to pile up between stages. In-company studies indicate that often less than 10% of the time between receipt of an order and shipment of the product is spent adding value. Material and information spend the rest of the time waiting to be acted on. In factories, for instance, processing in large batches slows down total plant throughput because each workstation has to wait for a large batch to accumulate before it can begin to work. And the same thing happens in white-collar work such as scheduling shipments and pricing orders. Often the only measures used to control these build-ups are limits on working capital and overhead expense. Those costs are merely a crude approximation of the lost value to customers.

In contrast, Toyota appears to manage all the cycle times in its operation chain. As we have seen, for example, its management recognized that applying just-in-time principles to production would not greatly change the time a customer had to wait for a new car if retail orders spent weeks moving through the company's regional sales and scheduling departments. So Toyota's order-entry and scheduling procedures are designed to couple without intermediate steps or queues. Toyota's near-term goal is to produce and deliver a new car within a few days of the customer's order.

Benetton, the well-known Italian sportswear producer and retailer, is another company that owes much of its explosive growth and success to across-the-board cycle time reduction. Time compression starts in new product development, where a CAD system automatically explodes the new design into a full range of sizes, then transmits these patterns to computer numerically controlled fabric-cutting machines to await orders for the new product. Fabric is inventoried in neutral greige and then cut and dyed to order. This allows the company to minimize rolled-goods inventory and still respond quickly to the full range of customer demand. Orders are sent to a chain of pull-scheduled, just-in-time factories that allow Benetton to replenish its US retail shelves in 15 days, a response time previously unimaginable in fashion retailing. That not only satisfies customers but lets the company avoid under- and over-production as well.

Finally, fast-cycle companies know just where in the system compressing time will add the most value for customers. Not surprisingly, those are the activities they attack first and upgrade regularly. For example, consider Freightliner, which has more than doubled its share of the US heavy-duty, on-highway truck market over the last decade. Unlike many companies in this customized business, Freightliner didn't invest heavily in speeding up its in-plant production process. Instead, its management invested in pre-engineering hundreds of possible truck combinations, so that customers can order the drive trains, cabs, and other optional features they need from a pretested menu. The company avoids the on-line errors that plague some competitors and make hasty redesign and rework necessary. And it can deliver a truck weeks ahead of most of the industry at a lower price.

A key factor in achieving end-to-end, fast-cycle time is a disciplined approach to schedules. Time-based competitors avoid the seemingly inevitable delays of organizational life by creating calendars for important events and insisting that everyone meet their commitments, so review and decision activities stay on track.

10.2.3 Build learning loops into the organization

Markets, products, and competitors move so quickly today that organizations with centralized intelligence functions simply cannot keep up. This is why fast-cycle managers want active sensors and interpreters of data at every level of the company, and why they emphasize on-line learning, which is the catalyst for continuous process innovation.

Designing rapid feedback loops into routine operations is a standard practice in fast-cycle companies. Benetton, for example, collects data daily at the retail level so it knows what is selling and what is not. Because what sells changes from month to month and from neighbourhood to neighbourhood, these data help the company decide what to produce currently, what new styles and colours to develop, and what merchandise to stock in particular outlets. Fast-cycle companies like Benetton don't waste time building inventory that won't be used immediately to satisfy customer needs.

Companies with fast-cycle capability also emphasize informal, *ad hoc* communication. Current information goes straight to where it can be most useful. It doesn't get lost in the chain of command. At Marks and Spencer, the great UK retailer, for example, managers at all levels are taught to bring important market information to senior management's attention at once. Thus the manager of a key store would be expected to call a vice chairman immediately if deliveries of basic products suggested the possibility of a system-wide shortage. From retail sales assistants, who are expected to reject defective merchandise and provide feedback on customer satisfaction, to a hands-on top management, everyone works to speed goods through the stores and information to the managers who can use it.

Companies with fast-cycle capability don't stay that way automatically. Their managers frequently renew and redesign the delivery system, continually gathering information about what makes it effective and what is getting in the way. They study competitors and superior performers in other industries for helpful ideas. They use new technologies like artificial intelligence to cut time out of routine activities. They encourage an unusual degree of mobility and initiative among their employees. At Du Pont, for example, production workers now visit customers just as salespeople and product engineers do to learn their needs firsthand.

10.3 GETTING THE CLOCK STARTED

Delivery dates, lead times, upcoming production dates – managers deal with time every day in an episodic manner. But they rarely stand back and consider time systematically or as a key to competitive position. Two facts of organizational life explain why time is so easily overlooked and undermanaged.

First, decision options are rarely presented to managers in terms of the effect they would have on time. A proposal for a new production process may highlight cost and labour savings but neglect to mention that the larger economic batch size will slow the whole organization down. Proponents of a new headquarters building will talk about more space and amenities but fail to point out that the floor plan separates marketing from engineering and thus will lengthen the new product development process. In short, it takes a special effort for executives to focus routinely on elapsed system time as something to be managed.

Second, and more problematic, most people in organizations like to have stability in their working procedures and social patterns. Serious efforts at cycle-time reduction disrupt both. Multifunctional teams break up existing departments and routines. Compressing cycle time sweeps away long-standing crutches such as quality inspection and redundant data entry that existed only because work wasn't designed or done right the first time through. Some valued specialists are exposed as the cause of bottlenecks, while others become completely unnecessary. You don't need sophisticated short-term market forecasts if you can respond immediately to any change in the level of demand.

Strong as these internal forces are, however, today's executives have an even stronger incentive to manage their company's cycle time – the competitive world outside. Fast, smooth, skilful operations and an ability to learn in real time are potent sources of competitive advantage. Based on our observations in successful companies, here are some suggestions that can help management get started.

10.3.1 Examine cycle times and raise standards

First, calibrate your performance against that of your toughest competitors, not only on response time but also on cost, quality, and rate of innovation because all these are causally related. Then use these performance benchmarks as minimum targets in your strategic plan: improvements of 5% per year won't challenge the status quo. When Toyota set out to achieve a one-minute die change on a 50-ton press to make a cheap custom car possible, that wasn't incremental; it was inconceivable! But it is a foundation of Toyota's new level of competitiveness.

Map and model your company's decision-making and operations flows so you can identify major interfaces, bottlenecks, and behaviour patterns. Find out exactly where and how time is wasted and where quality problems arise, and share this intelligence with all of your employees. The organization has to learn how it actually works before it can usefully talk about changes.

Describe and highlight past successes in making changes, even modest ones, in how the company works. Build a belief that the company's circuitry is not fixed, that people can design and implement better ways to operate. Keep raising performance standards.

10.3.2 Set up unusual organization mechanisms to focus on cycle time

Form temporary teams to study what's slowing down a few key cross-functional activities in the company. Staff these teams with energetic, well-respected middle managers who must make the eventual solutions work. Ask them to articulate and evaluate a few options, especially radical ones. Crudely remap how the company would work under each proposal, then test it and determine what changes in policies and behaviour would be needed to make it work. Keep discussing the best proposals until people begin to accept their feasibility.

Pursue conflict in meetings as a way to uncover and explore how the organization's working mechanisms slow down and where people's assumptions and beliefs diverge. After identifying the core of the conflict, develop a way to resolve it with data, not more opinion.

Treat bottlenecks, down-time problems, and other breakdowns as opportunities to learn. Don't just ascribe them to 'life in a large organization' and assume they have to be lived with.

Keep asking 'why' until you get to the root of a problem. Companies vary greatly in how they attack operating problems. Many fix today's problem: they adjust the machine that's turning out bad parts. Some go further and find the immediate cause of the problem: they adjust the machine and replace the worn tool that's throwing it off. Superior companies don't stop until they find the root cause – the poorly designed process or defective part that made the tool wear down in the first place.

10.3.3 Develop information systems to track value-adding activities

Distinguish the main operating sequence – the organization's central, value-adding activities – from time-consuming support and preparatory steps. Move the latter off-line. Give decision authority and responsibility for results to employees involved in the main sequence.

Organize working units around the flow of decisions, information, and material, not to accommodate departmental neuroses that have deformed the process over the years. Use training to give these groups the skills and support they need.

Connect stages in the operations chain as directly as possible. Design away gaps and queues. Develop target cycle times for specific stages, and schedule decisions and work flows so that people can meet them routinely.

10.3.4 Make time count in managing employees

Evaluate individuals on the basis of their contribution to the working team of which they are part. Be explicit about the group's cycle time and quality objectives and the individual's role in meeting them.

Avoid creating specialists unless they're absolutely essential. Specialists tend to be cut off from other perspectives and often have difficulty understanding new contexts. They also tend to push issues higher up in the organization where valuable management time gets taken up resolving them. Multifunctional teams can usually settle these issues at a working level.

Ask each individual to have at least an informal plan for the positive changes he or she intends to make. Get people accustomed to challenging and rethinking their activities continuously in the working-team context.

10.3.5 Position your people to accelerate their learning

Vary interactions among key managers, especially senior executives. Have them spend more time with peers on work substance and less time on policy problems. Imagine what would happen if you moved your senior managers' desks into a single room for three months, as Honda sometimes does, so that they could get to know the day-to-day business from their colleagues' point of view.

Devote meeting time to the effect of cycle time on the company's competitive position. Make sure everyone knows where the bottlenecks are, especially those they contribute to themselves.

Maximize key managers' exposure to operations downstream that depend on them. Sometimes an exchange of jobs between adjacent department heads is useful. With good people, a tour of duty that brings the vice-president of marketing and sales to manufacturing – and vice versa – can be positive all around.

Ask each senior manager to prepare a flow chart that maps out how key reports make decisions and relate to one another operationally.

Then compare the map with what the organization chart says. Explore the contrast and how it affects cycle time.

10.3.6 Implementation – a delicate balance

Managers who begin to move their organizations toward time compression face an inescapable dilemma: how to achieve faster cycles in the long term without being badly damaged by work interruptions in the short term. Most organizations cover their delays and errors with slack resources and loosely fitting interfaces. But when a company begins to compress its cycles, the delays and errors can rarely be fixed as quickly as the slack is taken away. Temporary breakdowns occur, and fast response to customers – the whole objective –is undermined.

Every management must find its own pace and mechanisms to walk this tightrope. A pilot project – walking before running – often helps. So does a simulation of new procedures before they are fully implemented. Temporary buffers of material or information may also help as long as they are deliberately reduced during the transition period. What's critical is that managers keep pushing the change process and don't suspend their efforts when the inevitable problems arise. As fast-cycle competitors everywhere remind us, operating crises are opportunities to learn and improve.

Many of these suggestions run counter to traditional ideas about good management. Efficiency was often thought to follow from fixed objectives, clear lines of organization, measures reduced to profit, and as few changes in basic arrangements as possible. But that was the logic of the mass-production machine. It has been superseded by the logic of innovation. And that logic, in turn, demands new organization and management practices.

CHAPTER ELEVEN

Manufacturing logistics systems for a competitive global strategy

Christopher Gopal

Corporate management in the increasingly competitive manufacturing world has begun to explore concepts of global manufacturing to secure its organization's position in the current market place. The key to successful implementation of such concepts is an effective integrated information system. This article explores aspects of that system and the logistics chain, from purchasing through distribution, necessitated by a global policy.

In an increasingly complex and competitive business environment, manufacturing executives are finding that to maintain the status quo is to lose ground and that traditional management techniques must be supplemented with planning that incorporates all market factors. This need has led to the growth of global manufacturing policies.

Both domestic and foreign companies are examining the concepts of global manufacturing more closely than ever. Unlike a multinational manufacturing policy, which emphasizes local production for each market, a global manufacturing policy requires a 'world-system' perspective. Products or parts can be produced at different locations and shipped wherever a market exists, responsibilities of a particular production location are determined by existing conditions, and centralized planning keeps company operations in line with overall goals. The

Source: Gopal, C. (1986) Information Strategy. *The Executives' Journal*, Fall (1988), 19–25
Published by Auerbach Publishers, New York

following complex, sometimes conflicting trends and factors are leading executives to adopt a global manufacturing strategy:

(1) national markets newly opened or reopened to foreign goods and competition;
(2) import restrictions and local content laws in many countries;
(3) policies in many developing countries that make licensing of foreign firms contingent on their ability to develop export markets;
(4) foreign domination of formerly strong domestic markets;
(5) foreign firms' use of multinational sourcing and manufacturing to gain cost and quality advantages;
(6) US firms entering foreign markets, often in competition with strong domestic and multinational firms;
(7) an increasingly globalized marketplace that supports common products, albeit with local difference and preferences.

The benefits of adopting a global manufacturing policy include improved efficiency through logical planning of manufacturing facilities and centralization of capacity management, improved communication and resource transfer between the domestic product division and international operations, and the development of a strategy that addresses global competition (W.H. Davidson and P. Haspeslagh, Shaping a global product organization, *Harvard Business Review* **60**, 125–32, July–August 1982.

Corporate management must proceed carefully when implementing a global manufacturing policy. The cornerstone of a global policy is centralized planning, purchasing, and distribution functions. Such centralization entails the development of a strong logistics network, which is often a difficult task. Logistics strategies are complex even in purely domestic environments, and problems can increase dramatically when strategies are transferred to international operations.

Quality standards must be maintained throughout the logistics network, making effective vendor evaluation and development programmes essential for local and international manufacturing operations. A careful assessment of local market requirements and manufacturing capabilities should guide decisions involving the location, configuration, and automation of production facilities. Also, an often-overlooked concern in implementing a global policy is that a manufacturing information system must be designed to support a global strategy.

11.1 MANUFACTURING SYSTEMS INTEGRATION

A manufacturing information system to support the centralized planning dictated by a global policy is vital. Figure 11.1 lists elements of a

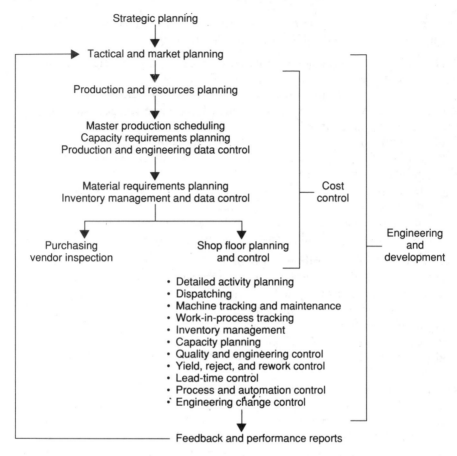

Figure 11.1 Elements of a traditional manufacturing information system.

comprehensive traditional manufacturing information system that can be adapted for global manufacturing.

Most packaged systems are designed for a single plant, and their bills of material (BOMs) typically list only component and lead-time requirements. Such BOMs do not provide the comprehensive details of manufacturing supplies, facilities, and materials that global manufacturing requires.

Most manufacturing resource planning (MRP) systems focus on plant functions, such as obtaining materials on time, manufacturing on time, and maintaining certain levels of raw material, component, work-in-process (WIP), and finished-goods inventories. Global manufacturing requires that such functions be made applicable to multiple suppliers and customers. Traditional systems support data entry to a single host computer through terminals located within the facility; global manufacturing requires rapid data transfer between hosts at separate facilities. Centralized planning demands that accurate and up-to-date inventories be available for all locations to facilitate purchasing and distribution.

The nature of global manufacturing implies the use of different technologies at different manufacturing plants. Therefore, an integrated system must aggregate and present data from different shop-floor control modules. Performance measurements and systems also differ from plant to plant, depending on the focus, technology, and goals of each plant. Hence, performance measurements should not be applied across the board but should change as requirements change. Effectiveness, rather than efficiency, must be the goal.

However, an integrated manufacturing information system does require some standardization across the logistics chain, such as standard part numbers for unique item identification, common documentation for engineering change control, and a common understanding of capacity and resource use parameters. Standardization in such areas is vital if planning for the logistics chain is to be centralized.

To properly support a global manufacturing policy, the integrated system must address the needs dictated by centralized planning. The following paragraphs explore the minimum requirements of an integrated information system for global manufacturing.

11.1.1 Multiplant product structure

A system must support multiple sources, plants, and planning parameters (e.g. lead times, yields, and rejection rates) for the same item produced at various locations.

The structure should allocate production responsibilities based on such factors as fixed percentages, capacity limitations, and mandatory practices (e.g. sourcing from a plant in India may require that a certain amount of Indian material be used, in conformance with local content laws). Production can be allocated to several plants if multiplant manufacturing is necessary for a certain component, assembly, or product.

11.1.2 Multitiered planning

Production planning and master scheduling should be multitiered to accommodate multiple plants. Traditionally, a product master schedule is based on a single plant's capacity. The system should be able to plan and assess multiple scenarios for products that can be sourced from more than one plant. Such 'what-if' analyses can help the company quickly reevaluate manufacturing plans if labour costs, material availability, local content laws, political conditions, or other factors change at a particular plant.

11.1.3 WIP tracking

The manufacturing system must maintain up-to-date WIP status from multiple sources to provide a complete picture of manufacturing operations. This includes tracking products and components, from raw material through the finished-goods stage. For example, if components from Mexico are needed to build subassemblies in the US, which are then assembled into the finished product in China, each component and subassembly must be separately tracked.

11.1.4 Vendor evaluation

Vendor evaluation must be part of the global purchasing system. Traditional evaluation criteria, such as delivery performance, price, and reliability, must be augmented by qualitative measures that can be converted to qualified ratings for evaluation purposes. Such measures include stability, technology, capacity, and ability to handle higher technologies and more complex designs. Lists of current and potential vendors should be maintained and updated within the system.

11.2 OTHER ISSUES IN GLOBAL SYSTEMS IMPLEMENTATION

Table 11.1 lists many external factors that affect the implementation of a system for global strategy. Corporate management must carefully assess the ramifications of each factor on the company's proposed system.

11.2.1 Technology policies and strategies

An effective global manufacturing system requires a rational plan for establishing appropriate levels of technology at different production facilities and assigning products, components, or subassemblies to be manufactured at each location. It may be necessary to perform final assembly in a certain country with subassemblies manufactured in another country. Figure 11.2 illustrates a case in which a lower level of technology is necessary for the assembly of the finished product than for the manufacture of the subassemblies. If the finished product is

Table 11.1 Non-manufacturing issues in system implementation

Issues	Factors
Technology policies and strategies	Level of technologies Location of plants Technology transfer Research and development information dissemination Market potential Supplier potential Regulations Standards
Centralization versus decentralization	Information flow Reporting Performance measurement Planning Logistics
Education	All aspects of manufacturing
Management commitment	Espoused Actual Perceived
Communication	Policies and procedures

an electronic measuring instrument, for example, integrated circuit manufacturing would require a higher level of technology than final assembly.

In some countries, laws require a certain percentage of local labour and material content, which may justify a lower level of technology. However, a country's potential market growth could outweigh this factor because local production may minimize transportation costs and increase response time to market demands. In such a case, the manufacturing technology may be established at a lower level but should be easily upgraded.

11.2.2 Centralized management

Corporate planning managers are often unaccustomed to planning a widespread logistics chain and assuming the responsibilities that a global system entails. Local managers in established plants, on the other hand, are accustomed to a higher degree of autonomy in plan-

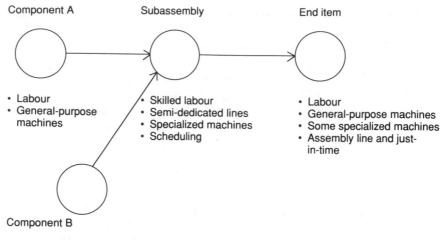

Figure 11.2 Possible technology requirements of different production stages.

ning, scheduling, and execution than a global system allows. Managers at all levels must be educated on quality awareness, planning and scheduling responsibilities, and job co-ordination and co-operation.

Since performance measurement techniques must be changed to accommodate each new situation, traditional cost-based measures, such as variance and contribution, are obsolete and may be dangerous. Performance measurements must assess the following factors, which constitute the rationale for adopting a global manufacturing policy:

(1) *Delivery performance* The speed and accuracy of delivery to geographically dispersed plants and customers must be carefully measured.

(2) *Quality assurance* The cycle of inspection, rejection, return, and replacement is very costly and time-consuming, and shortages of components attributable to faulty manufacturing can result in stoppages of subsequent processes if safety stock is not maintained. With the increased emphasis on foreign production, quality is a vital concern.

(3) *Cost* A major incentive for manufacturing abroad is lower production cost. Therefore, value-added tracking (i.e., comparing actual cost roll-ups with standards) should be an integral part of the assessment.

Determining and maintaining standards are vital steps in central-ized planning. Valid standards are essential for controlling non-manufacturing activities (e.g. corporate software development) and production activities. Their development should be based on reason-able assumptions and measurements or on well-reasoned hypotheses, if data is unavailable. Standards should be maintained by comparing actual performance with previous standards, and the standards should be updated as new technologies are introduced and efficiency improves.

11.2.3 Commitment, education, and communications

The most important non-information system factors that affect the implementation of a global manufacturing policy are human resource factors. Whether executives can obtain commitment to the change from employees, educate them in the new system, and communicate and synchronize organizational direction may be the ultimate test of their ability to oversee the project.

11.3 THE LOGISTICS CHAIN

The requirements for a global manufacturing system will be deter-mined by the configuration of the logistics network. Each logistics function should be analysed in two ways: as it is currently performed and as it must be adapted to fit the overall plan and direction. A system perspective, or top-down analysis, should be used to avoid the 'islands-of-information' syndrome and deter the tendency to directly transfer a local system to an international environment.

Based on the overall strategic plan and direction of an organization, a detailed analysis of all aspects of the logistics chain should be made. In this way, long-term and short-term objectives can be translated into policies and procedures for operating the system. Figure 11.3 illustrates the methodology for analysing and developing the system and the various issues and parameters that must be considered.

The following aspects of the logistics chain should be addressed by an integrated information system for global manufacturing:

(1) Multiple vendors for similar parts
(2) Warehouse planning
(3) Accurate lead-time analysis and determination of multiple sources
(4) Transportation and lead times
(5) Scheduling

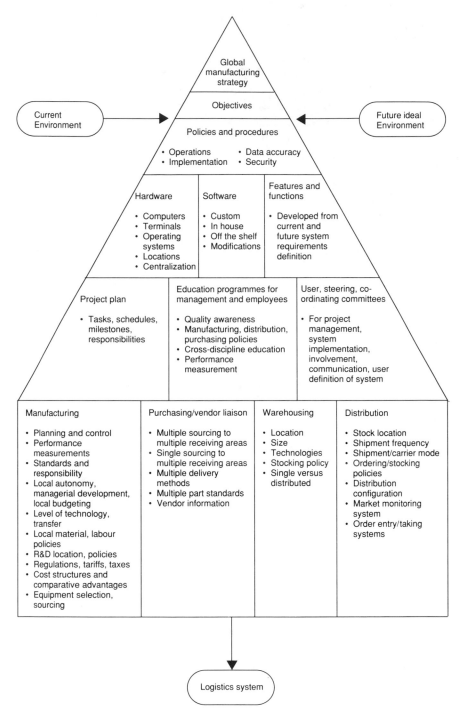

Figure 11.3 Manufacturing system analysis and development.

(6) Delivery performance
(7) Variable quality standards
(8) Varying scrap, yield, and rejection rates
(9) Safety stock requirements
(10) Total throughput time (from design through distribution)
(11) Varying cost structures.

11.4 CONCLUDING COMMENTS

Designing, obtaining, and implementing a manufacturing system to effectively support a global manufacturing policy is a major effort but one that can be eminently worthwhile. A global policy may not be necessary when a company uses foreign manufacturing facilities solely to reduce labour and material costs for domestic competition, but when worldwide market conditions dictate a global manufacturing policy rather than a multinational policy, implementing a global manufacturing system is essential to survival. Increasing world-wide competition, market regulation, and market sophistication are spurring the adoption of global manufacturing strategies by large, multinational manufacturing corporations.

Before a global policy is implemented, a fresh perspective on the capabilities of manufacturing systems and a re-examination of company policy are needed. Such issues as centralization and decentralization, local autonomy and managerial development, education and training, and standard setting and enforcement must be considered, and a company-wide investment of resources must be made. Benefits of a global system include better co-ordination of customer service in multiple markets, fast and accurate information transfer, less difficulty in complying with local laws and regulations, and conformance of both centralized and local planning to overall objectives. The ultimate pay-off is the ability to compete effectively in world markets.

CHAPTER TWELVE

International supply-chain management

John B. Houlihan

Competitive pressures and changes in the economic climate have forced management of international companies to evaluate afresh the operation and structure of international supply chains. Swings between 'local for local' and 'international supply centre' strategies for manufacturing and distribution have dramatic implications for organization, structure, control systems and costs to serve the customer.

New approaches to managing change in international chains have emerged and been proved in recent years. This article describes the concepts underlying these approaches, the barriers that need to be overcome and some of the lessons learned from experience of implementation.

12.1 THE CHANGING ROLE OF THE LOGISTICS MANAGER

In the world of the logistics manager ten years ago – another era altogether in terms of business economics – the mission, while perhaps not always readily achieved, was at least clear: balancing inventories between both production capacity and the demands of customer service. While the manager might have understood intellectually that assets should be employed to make the most of both factors, it was also accepted that hidden costs were bound to creep into even the best-managed system – and that these could be borne.

Now all that has changed. The job of the logistics manager has begun not only to overwhelm him or her, but also to have an increasing significance for overall corporate health. What were once simple

Source: Houlihan, J.B. (1988) *Manufacturing Issues*
© 1988 Booz, Allen and Hamilton, New York, USA

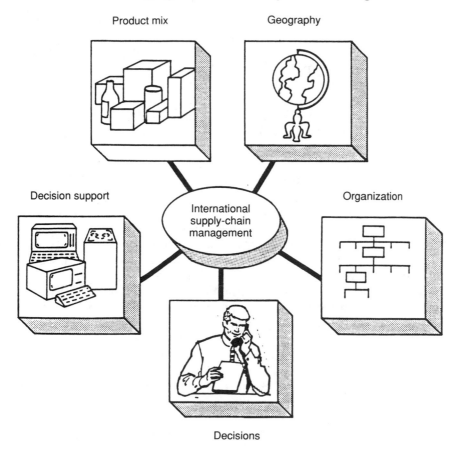

Figure 12.1 The role of the logistics manager.

trade-offs seem to result, with increasing frequency, in what is not merely a suboptimal utilization of assets, but, in the worst cases, a no-win materials management policy. Companies are faced with the prospect of incurring double or even triple costs in order to build up inventories to support marginal increases in customer service, but at the same time more intensive competition in slow-growth markets, combined with the rising costs of other production and supply factors, means that many firms can't afford not to supply a level of service that results in a competitive edge.

Over the last few years, our analyses of the particular problems of national and multinational companies in the context of today's more challenging economic environment resulted in a fundamental shift in our own perceptions about materials management. What were hitherto considered mere logistics problems have now emerged as much more significant issues of strategic management. Through our study of firms in a variety of industries in the USA, Japan and Western Europe, we found that the traditional approach of seeking trade-offs among the various conflicting objectives of key functions – purchasing, production, distribution and sales – along the supply chain no longer worked very well. We needed a new perspective and, following from it, a new approach: **supply-chain management**.

12.2 CHALLENGES OF THE MARKET PLACE

To appreciate the urgency in the move towards adoption of new approaches to logistics, executives need look no further than the current economic and competitive environment. Within the macroeconomic sphere, the cost of capital alone stands out as a major concern. Between 1977 and 1981, the prime rate tripled in the USA and the relevance of that to European financial health is seen not just in parallel high European rates but in the acrimonious international debates surrounding the issue. This factor, coupled with generally slower growth and uncertainty in demand, makes investment decisions all along the supply chain – whether in capacity, systems or inventories – riskier than ever before.

Economic uncertainty and, in particular, the swings in and out of recession are, by themselves, problematic from the viewpoint of materials planning. The natural inertia of the supply chain itself and of its decision-making mechanisms magnifies the impact of such changes, producing major inventory surpluses or shortages in sharp succession. So wrenching are these swings that even politicians have started to monitor national inventory trends. Add to this problem the tendency of management to overreact to these ups and downs in the hope of providing a safety net for the next swing, and the incurring of still further costs and risks is almost guaranteed.

Evidence of such behaviour can be found in various functions all along the supply chain. Marketing, for example, may boost its forecasts in order to secure large allocations from manufacturing so as not to be caught short in a potential upswing. In response, the manufacturing and distribution functions may develop their own independent forecasts or try to second-guess actual sales and inventories. Functions all along the supply chain tend to exhibit a certain possessiveness, and as a result inventories accumulate like snowdrifts at organizational fences. Finally, both short-term and long-term decisions on capacity, lagging as they do behind the market and inevitably reflecting the tendency to build in a safety net, as described above, very often make the firm even more vulnerable to subsequent changes in demand – if not actually influencing the market.

To a large extent, the driving force behind these conflicts and responses is another reality of the current business environment: increased competition in slower growth markets. Higher investment and operating costs cry out for increased market share as a means of assuring high (or at least adequate) return on investment. But as ever-stronger competitors vie for a larger part of the same (and, in some cases, shrinking) pie, the overall cost implications of increased performance in the distribution and marketing functions may be over-shadowed by the desire to enhance the firm's competitive position through greatly increased customer service.

The trouble is, certain competitors out there are doing a better job of not only providing a high level of customer service, but also simul-taneously keeping inventory costs down. Evidence of such perform-ance showed up in a Booz·Allen survey, completed in mid-1980, in which inventory turnover and facility utilization in some 1100 com-panies representing 18 industries were examined. The study showed that inventory turn over among Japanese firms had increased 31% over a 9-year period, compared with an increase of only 20% in the USA and a drop of 2% for European firms (see Fig. 12.2). And because the Japanese were starting from a higher base, they came out the undis-puted winner. This study showed, quite tangibly, why the 'Japanese challenge' should not be discounted merely because it has, by now, become a cliché.

It is not feasible, of course, to suggest that Western firms slavishly emulate the Japanese, either in terms of the particular features of their production operations (de-integration, smaller plants, narrowly fo-cused facilities, etc.) or in terms of their particular managerial style (consensus and 'bottom-up' decision making). Nor is it logical to sug-gest that the historical and environmental factors that have shaped Japanese industry – almost complete dependence on imported raw materials, a limited domestic market, and, as a consequence of the two, the need to build a strong presence internationally – have much rele-vance for the majority of Western firms today. However, the study does indicate certain characteristics that American and European firms successful in supply-chain management have in common with Japanese firms; these can, and probably should, be emulated. The strategic balance of supply and demand based on firm-wide objectives, and, more particularly, its support by a systems approach that places a premium on the fast transfer and accessibility of information across functional barriers are all highly relevant. While 'natural' conflicts be-

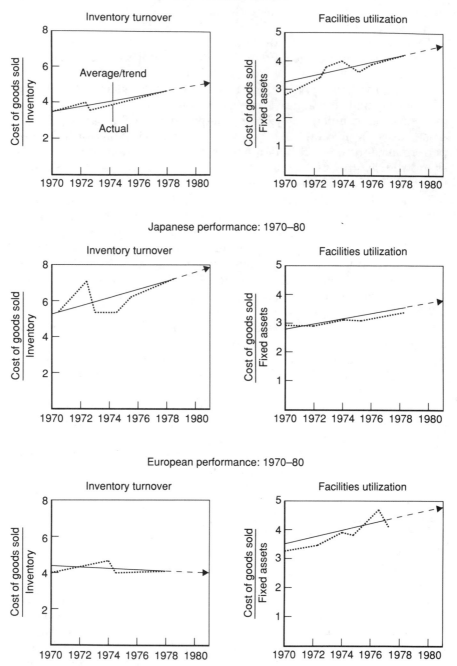

Figure 12.2 Inventory turnover and facilities utilization in the United States, Japan and Europe.

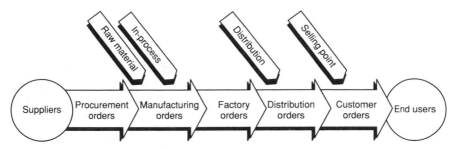

Figure 12.3 The scope of supply-chain management. Supply-chain management covers the flow of goods from supplier through manufacturing and distribution chains to the end user.

tween functions may be inevitable, common and shared data encourage the development of a broader perspective on supply-chain management and foster decision making that is more likely to be keyed to the overall objectives of a business than to the local or parochial functional objectives that have tended to dominate in the past.

12.3 FUNDAMENTALS OF SUPPLY-CHAIN MANAGEMENT

Supply-chain management differs significantly from classical materials and manufacturing control in four respects. First, it views the supply chain as a single entity rather than relegating fragmented responsibility for various segments in the supply chain to functional areas such as purchasing, manufacturing, distribution and sales (see Fig. 12.3). The second distinctive feature of supply-chain management flows directly from the first: it calls for – and, in the end, depends on – strategic decision making. 'Supply' is a shared objective of practically every function on the chain and is of particular strategic significance because of its impact on overall costs and market share. Third, supply-chain management provides a different perspective on inventories, which are used as a balancing mechanism of last, not first, resort. Finally, supply chain management requires a new approach to systems: integration, not simply interface, is the key.

12.4 THE INTERNATIONAL CASE

Classical approaches to logistics have left companies vulnerable to change; in the international company this vulnerability is magnified

International supply-chain management

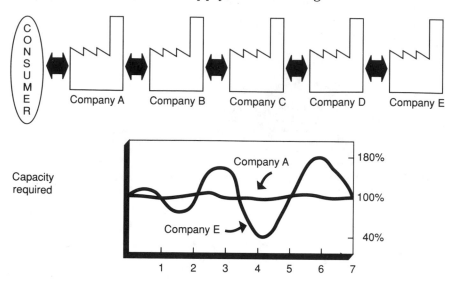

Figure 12.4 Industrial dynamics and the supply chain.

even more than in the simplest case of local for local production and distribution. Vulnerability to poor management of change can be demonstrated in models applying the techniques of systems dynamics to the industrial environment. The effects described by Roberts and Forrester[1,2] have shed much light on the distortion of information and data as they flow through decision processes in partitioned systems and organizations.

Periodic economic swings are inevitable and increasingly dangerous in many business sectors. However, companies themselves generally increase their vulnerability by inducing unreal business cycles and even further amplify them by localized protective policies.

A company's vulnerability can be considered in a dual context – the context of its external placement in a global supply chain and the context of its internal supply system. In the first case, the further a company is from the end user of its products the greater are the swings in demand it experiences (see Fig. 12.4).

The effects experienced by Company E are the culmination of time delays, planning distortions and inventory movements in preceding links of the chain. International supply chains even within one corporate entity tend to demonstrate the same characteristics. Frequently they consist of many autonomous organizational units in the same chain. The total planning cycle, when measured in time and taking inventory levels into account, frequently exceeds a year. Often the

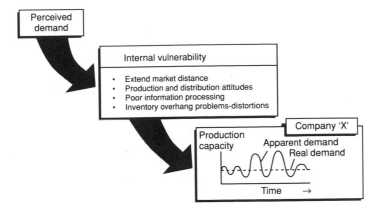

Figure 12.5 Vulnerabilities in the organization.

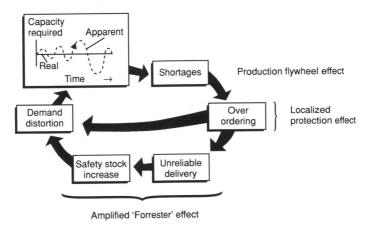

Figure 12.6 The 'Forrester' effect and the supply chain.

informational and procedural relationships make their dialogues seem more like those normal in arms' length negotiations with third parties or licensees.

The effects of change in the external context are amplified in the company's internal system. Figures 12.5–7 show some of the contributants to, and results of, what one could call a company's internal vulnerability.

Figure 12.5 depicts the amplification effect and the major contributing factors. Figure 12.6 shows the additional amplification that stems from the weaknesses inherent in many of today's logistics systems.

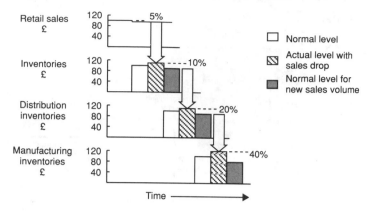

Figure 12.7 The effect on manufacturing inventories of a fall in retail demand.

(1) An upswing in demand produces shortage somewhere on the chain – not necessarily a customer shortage but at least inventories below target.
(2) The normal reaction to any threat of shortage is local protection – a 'place in the queue', the most frequent symptom of which is over-ordering.
(3) Since most internal forecasting mechanisms are order-book driven, this surge in ordering will most likely have an impact on the new forecast and serve to distort the internal perceptions of the upswing – 'the growth psychosis effect'.
(4) Additionally, current inventory control logic dictates that unreliable delivery should be compensated for by additional inventory investment. This is yet another source of demand and further distorts the profile of the upswing.

These characteristics are discernible even when single organizational units are handling cross-functional dialogues among marketing, distribution and management. They are all the more apparent in the international chain because of the greater complexity of integrating systems, data flows, functional objectives and attitudes and, not least, national approaches. Often 'local for local' subverts the corporate policy of 'international supply centre' by pulling inventory to the market place.

Figure 12.7 shows the effects of decoupled inventory planning cycles on the manufacturing and distribution chain; a 5% downturn in sales is later interpreted as a 40% downturn in manufacturing requirement.

Aggregating and accumulating changes along the chain create the illusion of massive swings; it is not unusual on international supply chains for a 10% market movement to cause management to view the apparent capacity–demand mismatch as though it were a serious structural imbalance.

External and internal vulnerability are, therefore, serious threats to international operations today. At their worst they are the principal contributants to the lack of performance in the chain that management wants to correct – inadequate customer service, high working capital investment and excessive supply costs.

Successful approaches to such challenging problems for the international company rely on meeting three principal needs of the chain.

(1) Objectives and policies for functions on the supply chain are naturally in conflict both within and across operational units. Effecting a strategic balance reduces the need for system complexity and excess capital investment in inventory and capacity.
(2) Service, capacity and inventory are the currency of the balance. The drivers for the balance are functional objectives and policies. Managing the drivers is more profitable than administering the currency.
(3) Systems and procedural controls play an important role in managing the international chain as a unified process. Any compromise on the integration of the process will create further demands on capital, inventory and service costs.

12.5 BALANCING FUNCTIONAL OBJECTIVES

The conflicting objectives of marketing, sales, manufacturing and distribution are a fact of business life. The imbalances resulting from these conflicts have become almost structural in nature and traditionally have been bridged by inventory and excess capacity. It is not necessary to challenge the direction of the individual strategies of each of those functions. What is needed, rather, is a critical evaluation of the opportunities for trade-offs between the key elements of these strategies, and examination of the implications, such as:

(1) How the supply policy – embodied in the marketing strategy – is affected by the characteristics of the demand, the lead time and reliability of service and the quality of the information available to the customer;
(2) How the economics of manufacturing determine lead time, reliability, flexibility and run size;

(3) How the complexity of the range, variety and options in the product portfolio affect the supply policy.

Some companies tend to resist the notion that a better balance can indeed be achieved, claiming to be victims of their own structures, culture, and environment. Many companies also find it difficult to articulate their objectives at this level, particularly in manufacturing, where traditionally reactive positioning precludes 'objectives' and where management tends to talk in terms of 'constraints', in sharp contrast to the Japanese view of manufacturing as a 'competitive weapon'. Customer service objectives are frequently taken for granted and the use of certain supply points and lead times is considered fixed. Thus, the traditional approach to managing these imbalances is by inventory and sophisticated control systems.

Supply-chain management suggests a quite different approach: addressing the imbalances directly and evaluating opportunities for minimizing them. In our diagnostic studies for international companies, we found – sometimes to management's genuine surprise – that key functional strategies affecting logistics are, indeed, negotiable. It may be possible, for example, that delivery reliability to customers can, in some instances, be traded against lead times: a 99% reliability on a four-week lead time is frequently more acceptable to customers than 85–90% reliability on a two-week lead time. Moreover, such supply policies are usually negotiable by individual item based on relative volume or price.

In addition, the tendency of manufacturing executives to use the longest procurement time for materials as the basis for quoting standard lead times can be challenged – as can many attempts to protect manufacturing costs via batch sizes, particularly in times of low demand. We can see that decisions at these levels do have a fundamental and significant impact on inventory requirements. And as a consequence, the failure to achieve a balance of objectives at the strategic level will tend to put the burden on inventories alone, inevitably resulting in greater working capital requirements and increased costs.

12.6 CONFLICTING OBJECTIVES –
THE INTERNATIONAL DIMENSION

In an international context the conflicting objectives of high service, low inventory investment and least unit cost have another dimension – the transfer price or fiscal policy. Divisional or geographic unit autonomy is accompanied by local objectives which may conflict with that

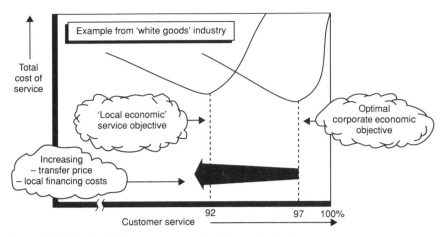

Figure 12.8 Trade-offs in the international supply chain.

which is optimal in the corporate view. Figure 12.8 shows, for example, two points of view on economic service level – balancing stock-holding cost with cost of lost sales. The local optimum would allow significant reduction of inventory at the expense of contribution to fixed cost in the transfer price. Fiscal policy needs to be consistent with supply policy in order to target an economic inventory investment.

12.7 SERVICE, CAPACITY AND INVENTORY ARE THE CURRENCY OF THE BALANCE

Analysing functional strategies and attempting to reduce structural imbalance to a minimum leads to a whole new role for inventory and supply policies. They become the mechanisms by which the inevitable residual imbalances are bridged, rather than the primary tool for managing the supply chain. The deployment of inventory as an asset, however, remains a strategic rather than an operational issue. At this level it should not focus on planning and batching rules or on systems tools, but on sourcing and supply policies, customer service and delivery performance objectives, and demand and supply decisions. This is the only way in which structural reductions in inventory requirements are likely to be achieved. The superior performance of Japanese industry – five and even ten times that of Western firms – highlights the opportunities for reducing the dependence on high inventory levels in the logistics systems of most European and US companies. This performance does not emanate from knowing how much is where but

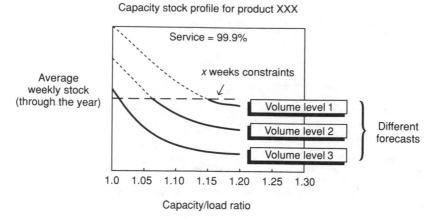

Figure 12.9 Capacity/stock profile – a conceptual view.

from why it is there? How many so-called inventory control systems in Europe and the USA today advance beyond mere 'status' into the areas of simulation and goal setting?

Figure 12.9 shows the conceptual relationships between stock and capacity for given service and volume levels. The premise is that any given service level can be achieved either with stock or capacity within certain constraints. In this instance the constraint is a management-imposed maximum of x weeks stock to protect shelf life. Equally, a minimum stock can be specified to cater for the minimum physical movement times of the chain.

Seeing service as being met by either capacity flexibility or inventory puts a different dimension on 'safety' investment. A safety requirement for a given supply chain and service objective can first be calculated. Whether that is best met by inventory or capacity depends on such diverse elements as the following:

(1) current inventory holding costs;
(2) current loading;
(3) costs of incremental capacity.

Clearly, the optimal solutions tend to vary with volume levels, finance costs, etc. Balancing, therefore, must be undertaken periodically and routinely if a supply chain is to remain optimally 'tuned' to the needs of the market place.

Balancing assets and service on international supply chains is clearly a difficult challenge since it requires not a change in control philosophies and techniques but also a change in management perspective to span the traditional organizational boundaries.

12.8 CONTROL SYSTEMS STRATEGY

Once the strategic framework has been established, then management and control mechanisms can be developed. It is only at this point that the issues of organization, tools, techniques and support systems should be addressed. The basic architecture of most systems today follows the traditional functional and organizational divisions of the supply chain – purchasing systems, production control systems, distribution systems, and sales order processing systems. This structure may do a fine job of supporting the hierarchical upward flow of data within any single function, but it is not very effective in the context of cross-functional or total supply-chain communication. The same holds true for 'interfaces' (frequently a synonym for time-consuming meetings), which by now have become a commonly accepted means of providing the necessary cross-functional communications.

The systems interface approach has several shortcomings, not the least of which is its hidden cost in terms of indirect manpower, and the related delay and distortion in the transfer of information. In addition, this approach frequently results in strategic and directional decision-making at too low a level. Furthermore, systems groups either directly or indirectly 'sell' their services separately to functional heads. Typically, there is no one 'client' for cross-functional communications, although the information processing technology needed to support supply-chain management has been available for some time. The end result is that systems modules have tended to reflect organizational segmentation with little or no emphasis on integration across the total chain.

Systems costs and system complexity are almost commutable. Nevertheless, it is striking how little recognition there is of the fact that systems complexity, the balance of functional objectives and logistical costs are all interrelated. Figure 12.10 depicts some powerful messages for management in that context.

(1) Asset and service costs can be squeezed by a balance of functional objectives and by application of appropriate control systems.
(2) Delegating the balance of objectives to control systems to an excessive degree increases the complexity of the system. Examples of

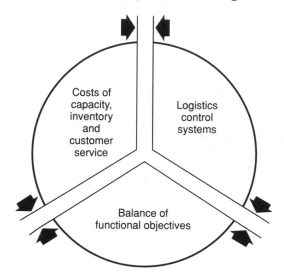

Figure 12.10 The inter-relationship of logistics decisions.

this persist today in misapplication of material requirements planning (MRP) and distribution requirements planning (DRP) systems because service degree, product range and manufacturing and distribution focus have not been rationalized by management. Compare the simplicity of the control system in a focused facility (see [3] and other publications by Wheelwright and Skinner in the *Harvard Business Review*) with the hugely complex capacity scheduling and sequencing systems that have been installed in mixed factories where management looks only to facilities utilization as a measure of success.

International supply chains place great obstacles in the path of information transfer; local autonomy, local systems standards and incompatible operating procedures make integration of international systems difficult. Frequently even the product nomenclatures differ so that translation is needed before orders are legible to any central polling system. The effects are manifested in great delays and distortions of the information flow. Figures 12.11 and 12.12 describe the filters that act on data and the effects on the operating functions.

Market movements are batched and filtered, giving the effect of peristaltic transmission. Despite real-time capture of customer orders at the order desk in each of the countries the replenishment cycle waits four weeks between signals to the distribution planner. Real market movements are now distorted by local inventory adjustments

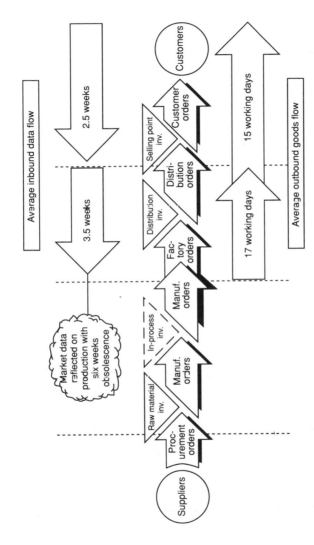

Figure 12.11 Time lags in the supply chain.

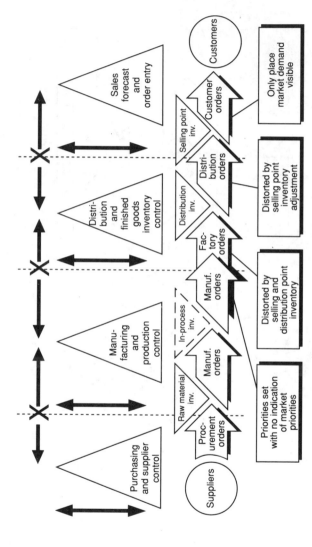

Figure 12.12 Distortions in the supply chain.

and about 2.5 weeks have on average been lost. The same effect is seen at the distribution point as it generates the monthly replenishment plan on manufacturing, adding another inventory adjustment and a further 3.5 weeks delay to the market movement.

The barriers to integration of such systems are not only in the systems architecture but also in the control philosophies that underpin the system and in the organizational relationships among the units. However, integration is no longer a luxury for many companies since changes in manufacturing and distribution strategy increasingly force a transition from 'local' to 'international' supply centres. Experience shows that some of the greatest barriers are in attitude and perception with the result that systems cannot be relied upon to fulfil the role of integrator. For example, some of the most serious problems encountered in the transition from local to international supply centres have been the following:

(1) The increased need for formal rather than information procedures; informality based on market proximity rapidly breaks down once the source of supply is moved away from the customer base; formal procedures need not be rigid but must be clearly understood; often such formalization is resisted only because some of the drivers of the business such as customer service objectives are not understood and are neither measured nor managed.
(2) Planning and allocating capacities across country boundaries become more complex; the role and responsibility of the logistics planner suddenly moves from inventory and distribution controller to 'capital broker' – allocating available capacity and inventory to best corporate advantage. In practice, what transpires short-term is often a degeneration of working relationships and substantial increases in capacity disruption and working capital, while the system is blamed for inadequacy.
(3) Shared information is associated with centralization and bureaucracy; central planning functions call for higher-quality information systems as well as better planners; excess centralization of planning functions is often the result of badly engineered systems which block visibility of supply and only serve to increase the feeling of uncertainty among the distribution channels.

12.9 INTEGRATION OF ORGANIZATION AND SYSTEMS FUNCTIONS ON INTERNATIONAL CHAINS

The systems and information flows already discussed need a degree of horizontal integration on an international chain. This requires:

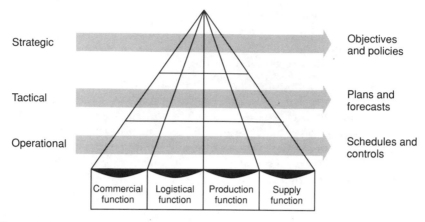

Figure 12.13 Integration of organization and systems functions.

(1) Management of data capture and flow across the functional bound-
    aries without delay and distortion;
(2) Linking systems for purchasing, production and inventory control,
    distribution, customer order entry and service;
(3) Shared ownership of information and a high degree of visibility
    across all functions of plans, allocations, inventories and customer
    – as well as replenishment orders.

Equally important to supporting effective international supply,
however, is the notion of vertical integration. Three discrete levels of
management control – strategic, tactical and operational – are often
employed in the successful model for the international chain. The
overall structure is shown schematically in Fig. 12.13. This dimension
to integration is the key to effective organization development; it
precludes the need to talk of centralized or decentralized logistics
functions as exclusive structures and permits the vital flexibility of
centralizing the strategic, decentralizing the operational, where practical,
and tuning the tactical decision making to the organizational preferences of the particular company.

12.10 THE CHALLENGE AND THE OPPORTUNITY

There can be no doubt that adopting such a holistic approach to the
management of international supply chains places additional burdens
on top management: it requires the incorporation of a logistics focus
into the strategic decisions of the business; it demands the rejection

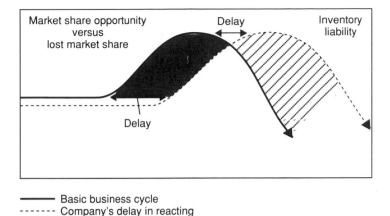

Basic business cycle
------ Company's delay in reacting

Figure 12.14 The costs of slow response.

of inventory as the easy 'buy-out' option to many of the troublesome balancing and trade-off decisions; it implies an approach to control systems which supersedes the traditional functional divisions and which is likely to have significant organizational implications in the longer term.

For many companies today the need to react faster to market changes is paramount. New product introductions threaten long-standing inventory investments; new levels of service emerge from smaller predatory competitors; old traditions in manufacturing and distribution delay the response. The real cost of the slower response is not only lost market share but also the liability of immovable working capital investments – see Fig. 12.14.

None of these are easy challenges, but the competitive environment of the 1980s for Europe and for the USA puts a high premium on meeting them.

CHAPTER THIRTEEN

Analytic tools for strategic planning

William Copacino and Donald B. Rosenfield

In this article the focus is upon analytic tools for strategic logistics planning. We discuss a broad set of tools roughly divided into two areas. One area is that of traditional tools such as functional cost analysis and the various modelling approaches and these are briefly reviewed. Principally, however, the discussion centres on newer tools which have not been as widely used and which can be highly effective for strategic planning and especially for strategic logistics planning. In addition, we will present a framework which outlines the various aspects or approaches for strategic logistics planning and identifies the analytic tools that are available and appropriate for each particular aspect of planning.

Our presentation is divided into four areas. First, so that we have a framework for looking at what analytic approaches might be appropriate, we will briefly review what is involved in strategic logistics planning. Then we will review why logistics planning is both important and difficult. We will spend the majority of time describing the various analytic methods and how they can assist in strategic planning. Finally, we will provide some summarizing comments and conclusions.

13.1 WHAT IS STRATEGIC LOGISTICS PLANNING?

In order to provide a framework for analysis, we first want to define what is involved in strategic logistics planning. We only want to touch upon some of the highlights or key points. Our goal is not to describe the process for strategic planning; rather we will describe tools or

Source: Copacino, W. and Rosenfield, D.B. (1984) *IJPD & MM*, **15**(3), 47–61
© 1984 Council of Logistics Management, USA
First presented to *National Council for Physical Distribution Management Conference* (1984), Dallas, USA

analytic approaches or types of analysis that can be used to aid the strategic planning process.

We want first to review some of the major steps of the corporate strategic planning process. Companies begin by going through a variety of steps in order to identify the means by which the corporation is going to compete. These generally include an assessment of the external environment, which includes a look at economic factors, regulatory factors, technology and technological changes, and competitive factors. Companies then examine their internal capabilities; this includes an assessment of their strengths and weaknesses, an identification of threats and opportunities facing the firm, and finally leads to a determination of objectives for the firm in terms of growth, market share, profitability, social responsibility and so forth.

A company then determines the specific means through which it will achieve the objectives. These are often described in terms of markets, products, basis of competition, sources of supply, the marketing channels, the service requirements in each market, product quality requirements, and so forth. Finally, the last step of the strategic planning process involves obtaining support for these plans with the cooperation of the major players, including logistics, operations, finance, marketing and so forth. Each of these functional areas develops detailed functional plans which support the overall corporate plan.

Figure 13.1 describes this process. We want to emphasize several points related to Fig. 13.1. First of all, it will be noted that the basis of the functional plans is the corporate plan. This is the starting point for all planning. Second, there is an important feedback loop from the functional plans to the corporate plans. That is, planning is done in a somewhat interactive manner where the functional plans have an input to, and a say in, forming the corporate plan. And lastly, marketing is generally the launching point for strategic planning; however, all functions should be given equal weight in the strategic planning process. That is, although marketing is the starting point for strategic planning, all functions must be given equal emphasis and priority in the process.

From our perspective, strategic logistics planning includes both manufacturing and physical distribution. Manufacturing involves a set of decisions that includes such things as the degree of vertical integration, the number, size and location of the manufacturing facilities, the process technology to be used, the type of production plan that will be followed (that is the choice of a level production plan or a plan that more closely follows or chases the demand pattern), which products are going to be produced and which are going to be purchased, and what products are going to be produced at what facilities for what markets.

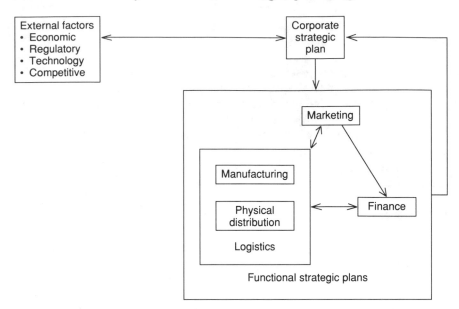

Figure 13.1 Strategic planning overview.

Physical distribution planning involves a different set of decisions looking at the number and location of warehouses, the deployment of inventories as well as the level of inventories to maintain, transportation mode selection and carrier selection and strategy, planning and control issues, organizational issues and so forth. We focus here primarily on the methods for strategic physical distribution planning, but we want to emphasize that a full logistics strategy involves both of these components.

Figure 13.2 then outlines the framework for strategic logistics planning. As can be noted, it begins with identification of the business goals and strategies (a key element of which are the customer service requirements) and proceeds with integrated logistics planning which looks at the quality of each link of the logistics system. The quality of each link or component of the logistics system is examined not only individually but also as they function as part of an integrated whole.

13.2 THREE MAJOR ASPECTS OF STRATEGIC LOGISTICS PLANNING

In the literature as well as in practice, strategic logistics planning means different things to different people. That is, individuals and

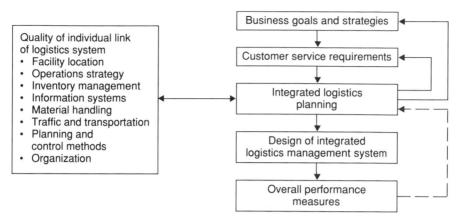

Figure 13.2 Aspects of strategic logistics planning.

companies have different things in mind when they use the term strategic logistics planning. We do not believe that it is important to establish a unified definition of strategic logistics planning: in fact, it may even be counter-productive to do so. However, we do believe it is important to identify, articulate and understand the various aspects of strategic logistics planning. We have grouped the different meanings that are often implied by the term strategic logistics planning into three major areas or aspects. We believe that it is important for managers to think along these lines and make these distinctions when they are involved in planning. The three areas are: leveraging logistics, evaluating the impacts of proposed corporate strategic plans, and supporting the corporate strategic plan. We want to talk briefly about each area.

In performing strategic logistics planning, companies often look for ways to leverage logistics. By that we mean that companies address the basic question of how logistics can be used to differentiate their company in the market place. That is, how can logistics be used to provide a distinctive, competitive advantage? Rather than focusing on ways to make the existing system more efficient (that is, faster, cheaper or more accurate, or in some way improve it along any of these dimensions) a company which is leveraging logistics is addressing the question of how it can meaningfully distinguish itself through its physical distribution capability.

The best way to provide a clear definition of this concept is through example and we want to discuss briefly two case histories. Consider the office-machine company that obtains a competitive advantage through superior customer service. Traditionally, when an office machine at a customer location broke down, the company would send a repairman from a service centre to repair that machine. There was often a delay in assigning the serviceman to the repair job, and there also was time required for a serviceman to travel to the customer location to fix the machine. Therefore, much time was lost in both allocating a serviceman to a repair job and in the travel of the service-man to the customer's office (resulting in considerable down-time for the customer). This method of operation also was rather costly since the highly trained and rather well-paid serviceman spent a fair amount of time travelling back and forth from repair jobs – rather than repairing machines. In trying to improve the performance of the system, many companies tried to find better ways to allocate and use the service-man's time; they sought better scheduling methods, improved ways to deploy and allocate salesmen, and so forth.

Another company took a radically different approach. They fully redesigned their logistics system and positioned inventories of loan or replacement office machines around the country. When a customer's machine broke down, they quickly shipped that customer a loan machine and sent the customer's machine to a service centre for repair. Not only did this reduce the machine down-time for the customer but it also reduced service costs because more of the expensive service-men's time was spent in repairing machines rather than travelling to and from jobs.

A second example is the American Hospital Supply Corporation's ASAP order entry system. American Hospital Supply developed an efficient system for its customers to purchase medical supplies by putting terminals in their customers' offices. This system simplified and facilitated the ordering process for the customers, and guaranteed a higher proportion of orders for American Hospital Supply.

In both of these cases logistics was a key element or reason why the company was able to distinguish or differentiate itself in the market-place and therefore obtain competitive advantage through its physical distribution capabilities; and that is what we mean by the term leverag-ing logistics.

The second aspect of strategic logistics planning is evaluating the impacts of proposed corporate plans. This involves participation in the corporate strategic planning process by physical distribution executives. Physical distribution managers should assist in developing, as well as in evaluating, corporate strategic plans. As part of the strategic planning process, the distribution executive should pose such questions as whether the marketing advantage gained by producing a full product line is worth the full cost (in terms of production, transportation, warehousing and inventory costs) of making and carrying this full product line. Or, is the competitive advantage of superior customer service (say a one-day delivery time to all customers) worth the cost of doing that? Alternatively, as part of the strategic planning process, the distribution executive may provide answers to such questions as what the full cost of serving a new market is, or what the costs of adding a new product line are.

The final aspect of strategic logistics planning involves supporting the strategic plan. That is, once a corporate plan is articulated and agreed upon, this aspect of strategic logistics planning involves developing a plan for the logistics area that supports this corporate plan and allows the functional area to perform in the most efficient manner possible.

13.3 IMPORTANCE AND DIFFICULTIES OF LOGISTICS PLANNING

There are five major areas of importance and difficulties that we want to address briefly. These are: the importance of customer service, the substantial impacts of logistics costs, external pressures influencing logistics, the complex trade-offs involved in logistics, and organizational conflicts that influence logistics. One of the main forces influencing logistics is the demand for improved customer service. In many industries and for many companies product quality is increasing in competitive importance. That is, product quality is becoming a more important basis of competition in many companies. An important element of product quality is quality customer service. In fact, many customers are demanding better customer service: they are measuring many different dimensions of customer service, and they are measuring customer service in more sophisticated ways. In the future customer service will become more important. As automation continues to enter our factories and plants, manufacturing costs will become both a less important cost element and a more equal cost element among various companies. Therefore, just like the process industries in the 1950s and 1960s, customer service will become a more important competitive factor.

At the same time, there has been a proliferation of new products in many companies, shorter product life cycles, and more complex delivery patterns (that is, delivery to more stores or customer locations). These influences make customer service a more difficult as well as a more important activity – but a key activity if a company is going to be a successful competitor in the future.

In addition to customer service, physical distribution is important because it represents a significant cost element for most companies. Physical distribution costs on the aggregate are just under 10% of the sales dollar for all companies. They can be up to 25–35% of the sales dollar in many companies or above 50% of the delivered cost of a product. In addition, as the diagram in Fig. 13.3 illustrates, physical distribution costs impact both sales and profitability, as well as the asset base of a company. Therefore, physical distribution can have a large impact on a company's return on investment and overall performance.

We have stressed the impact of logistics in terms of customer service and cost. What makes strategic logistics planning so difficult is that one is often shooting at a moving target. That is, there are many factors acting upon and influencing the logistics system. Figure 13.4 shows many of these. Starting at the lower left-hand corner of the figure, technology as a whole is strongly influencing the logistics system and creating pressures to which the logistics system must respond. This is particularly true in terms of advances in improved communications systems and information technology. It also applies to advance in materials-handling technologies, technological advances in the transport area, and so forth. These technologies are providing new opportunities which companies cannot afford to ignore.

Regulatory changes, particularly over the last four years and generally over the last decade, are creating pressures to which the logistics systems must respond. We have already discussed some of the influence of new customer service requirements and competitive pressures. Changes in cost structures are another force influencing logistics. The relationship among transportation, warehousing and inventory costs is changing and companies must adapt their logistics system accordingly. Other factors influencing logistics include the need to reduce inventory costs and overall costs; the need to improve financial performance; the aforementioned proliferation of products, shorter product life cycles, more complex logistics networks and delivery systems; and a change in the strength and the role of players in the distribution channels. For example, in the consumer goods area, retail stores are becoming stronger and more dominant players. In the industrial area, the role of just-in-time inventory policies and the pressures by many companies to alter the delivery patterns of their suppliers are creating pressures on the logistics systems of both suppliers and their customers.

Responding to these pressures for changes is not an easy task because of the complex interaction of parts of the logistics system. Logistics variables and costs interact in a complex and indirect way. A cost decrease in one area can influence a variety of other logistics costs. This entire set of complex interactions must, therefore, be examined together in a systematic way.

Finally, there are organizational conflicts that make logistics planning

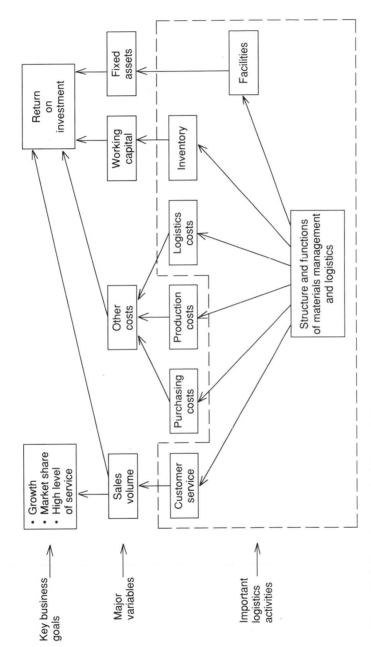

Figure 13.3 Importance of logistics activities.

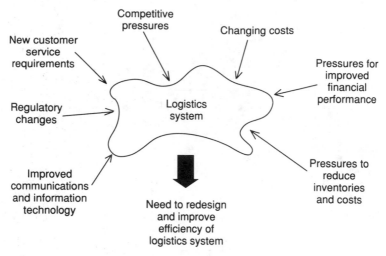

Figure 13.4 Pressures influencing logistics systems.

difficult. First of all, even today the responsibility for many logistics activities is spread throughout the organization. There often is no clear single authority that spans all of the logistics activities. Second, as shown in Fig. 13.5, different organizational functions have different interests and these create conflicting objectives and requirements for a logistics system. Fortunately, there are numerous analytic tools to help sort out these complexities and difficulties.

13.4 WHAT ANALYTIC METHODS CAN HELP?

We want to emphasize that there is no single analytic method for strategic logistics planning. Because of the complexities, there are several methods available – each appropriate for a different aspect of the strategic logistics planning process. So in answering the question of what analytic methods can help, we need to identify a range of methods – each appropriate for a specific aspect of the overall process. This creates a framework or mapping of methods or tools to applications or aspects of planning. To understand this framework, we again review the three aspects of strategic logistics planning. **Leveraging logistics** involves how most effectively we can distinguish a company in the market place. This aspect requires a knowledge of the offerings of the market place and the offerings of the company, and hence the methods that we select must address both of these. **Evaluating the**

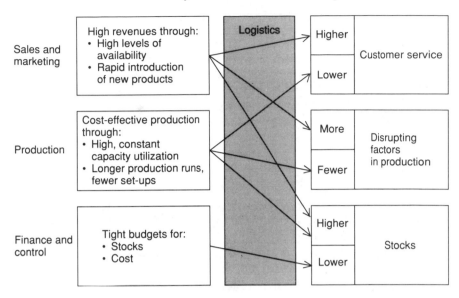

Figure 13.5 Classical conflicts of interest.

impacts of proposed corporate strategic plans implies measuring the effect of alternative logistics configurations. Traditional types of models can be used effectively for this purpose. Finally, supporting the corporate strategic plan implies the need to determine the most efficient ways to meet the corporate and logistics objectives. Again, traditional methods can be used quite effectively.

There is actually a wide range of methods or tools that can be used for each aspect of logistics planning. These include logistics cost analysis, decision-support models, traditional manufacturing strategy tools, the Shapiro grid framework, and cost–service trade-off curves. **Logistics cost analysis** or functional cost analysis is an analysis of the logistics costs by functional area or by other dimensions. **Decision-support models**, mostly computer models, are common today in many companies and can be used to address the issues of the network configuration, number of facilities, inventories versus cost, and so forth. While we will not focus at length on traditional manufacturing strategy tools, we will discuss them because they are useful for assessing manufacturing strategies and they are good examples of the concept of leveraging. The **Shapiro grid framework**, developed by Roy Shapiro of the Harvard Business School, aids in examining how companies place themselves in the universe of logistics offerings. Finally, the **cost–service trade-off curve** is an explicit means of quantifying

Table 13.1 Analytic tool and application

Analytic tool	Leverage logistics	Evaluate impacts	Support plans
Logistics cost analysis			×
Decision-support models		×	×
Traditional manufacturing strategy tools	×	×	
Grid framework	×		
Cost–service trade-off curve	×		

cost and service and for computing these costs and service offerings with other companies in the marketplace. Figure 13.6 illustrates how the various tools can be matched with the various aspects of the strategic planning process. We want now to discuss each of the five analytic tools listed in Table 13.1.

Logistics cost analysis, also known as functional cost analysis, can be used to analyse logistics costs by:

(1) channel of distribution
(2) product
(3) type of customer
(4) geographic market or
(5) logistics function.

One can also combine any two of these dimensions, say analyse costs by channel of distribution and product family. Traditional accounting systems do not summarize costs by the dimensions noted above. Accounting and operating data must be analysed together, and costs must be recast along dimensions that are meaningful to management so that logistics operation can be fully understood. As an extension of functional cost analysis, revenues can also be assigned along these dimensions, allowing a company to understand the breakdown of marginal contribution or profits along any of these lines. By understanding these costs, the most efficient method of operation can be determined. This analysis is also useful as an input to broader analyses, such as decision-support models, which is the next analytic tool we want to discuss.

Decision-support models are becoming commonplace in more and more companies. They are useful for measuring the impact of proposal plans, as well as for determining the most efficient way to support the corporate plan. They can address strategic concerns such as the number and location of plants, the number and location of warehouses, the determination of supply patterns – specifically what products should be made at what plants for what markets, freight consolidation methods, and inventory deployment strategies. These models also can be used for determining the network and facility requirements necessary to obtain a given level of service. They can be used to determine what configuration is necessary for a proposed new product line. They can be used to determine the most efficient configuration and product assignments to obtain a stated level of service. They also can be used to determine the best way of improving service through new warehouses or faster delivery.

There are two basic approaches to decision-support models – 'what-if' simulation and optimization. What-if simulation is the direct calculation of all logistics costs, often for a limited number of alternatives. Direct calculation of costs normally involves the calculation of inventory costs (both pipeline and facility inventories), transportation costs and handling costs. As an example of the notion of direct calculation of costs, freight rates are tabulated based on actual freight rates and weight breaks, and inventory costs are based on actual safety stock requirements and shipping frequencies.

Optimization is a determination of optimal flow and/or facility locations for a logistics network subject to all the constraints and requirements of the network. In each case, transportation, inventory and handling costs are modelled, for example, as linear functions or generally in a less precise manner than the direct calculation methods used in what-if simulation. Optimization is necessary when there are a significant number of constraints or a very large network with complex interactions.

The choice of a modelling approach for a particular problem is often a matter of art and depends on several factors, principally the nature of the constraints and the importance of inventory costs. What-if modelling is generally preferred when there are fewer facilities and fewer choices or when precise cost estimates are required. In a transportation-dominated network with large numbers of products, large numbers of facilities and many constraints, optimization is generally preferred. For example, optimization is often the method of choice for a complex freight consolidation problem. To determine the actual location of one or two new facilities that are unconstrained in size, what-if simulation can often be used effectively. Finally, if an inventory deployment strategy needs to be chosen (that is, deciding to stock inventory at a master location or at field locations for a small number of facilities), what-if simulation is also the method of choice.

Both approaches can be very effective in supporting the strategic plans of the company and in determining the most efficient means of supporting the corporate plan. Sometimes the two methods can be used together. In a recent case study, we determined the optimal location and size for two new warehouse facilities for a rapidly expanding consumer goods company. They had an existing warehouse that was constrained in size. We developed a what-if simulation model in which the current facility was constrained and we used an embedded optimization routine to determine the optimal product flows subject to that constrained existing facility.

Decision-support models offer several advantages for strategic logistics planning. They can be used to evaluate quickly a large number of alternatives that must be analysed in many strategic planning problems, and they can incorporate all the complex trade-offs that we discussed earlier.

We now want to discuss briefly some traditional manufacturing strategy tools. These methods are useful because they assist in the leveraging of logistics. There are three that we want to mention. The first is the learning curve, which is an empirically derived method of analysing how costs vary as cumulative production volume increases. They can be to analyse one's own and one's competitors' manufacturing cost structures. A useful example is the strategy of Texas Instruments in the semiconductor market in the early 1970s. By understanding how its costs were going down as volume was increasing, Texas Instruments was able to develop a pricing strategy to maintain its cost advantage and maintain its position as a market leader.

The second manufacturing strategy method that we want to mention is life-cycle costing, which deals with how the market for a product will grow and mature. In the early stages of a product life cycle, demand for a product will grow rather rapidly; but then it will reach a saturation point and level off. By understanding how fast a market will grow and where the saturation will occur, a company can determine its appropriate manufacturing strategy and capacity plan.

A third method, which is more of a framework than a method, is the product–process matrix which helps to determine how manufacturing should be matched with a given product. For example, mature industries are generally more cost competitive, and companies need a manufacturing process with a continuous flow or at least some type of repetitive flow-through. High-volume products generally should be produced in a more flow-oriented manufacturing facility. The product–process matrix permits a graphic display of the process and product match. A related approach to the product–process matrix is the Skinner notion of the focused factory, which states that given factories should be defined to meet a fairly narrow mission.

Table 13.2 Shapiro grid framework

Breadth of
product line

		Narrow	Broad
Location of inventory	Decentralized		A
	Centralized	B	

The manufacturing strategy tools presented above are important for two reasons: first of all, manufacturing is part of logistics so we should deal with how strategic questions should be addressed. Second, as leveraging methods, these tools address both what a firm is offering as well as what the market and competitive environment is like.

This leads to the last two methods which are both methods for leveraging logistics. We believe that any method of strategic logistics planning in the area of leveraging needs to address three factors: cost, service and the nature of the market.

The first method is the Shapiro grid framework, developed by Roy Shapiro. This method is based on the notion that service consists of many dimensions, and the framework presents a way of examining two of the most important dimensions and of identifying where a company stands relative to its competition in respect to these dimensions. The two dimensions that we are talking about are the breadth of the product line and the location of the inventories (specifically, whether inventories are centralized at a few master locations or decentralized in many field locations). These dimensions are incorporated in the framework in Table 13.2. When a company offers a broad line of products and a decentralized distribution system (point A in Table 13.2), it has quite different logistics implications as compared with when a company offers a narrow product line and a centralized distribution system (point B). The framework is a simple concept which provides a company with the basis to see where it stands as compared with other companies and in which direction it prefers to move.

The final method is the cost–service trade-off curve. It is a concept which examines in detail the trade-offs between logistics costs and logistics service. The notion here is that it is necessary to examine

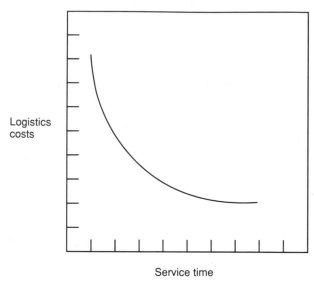

Figure 13.6 Cost–service trade-off curve.

simultaneously both costs and service. Service is a multidimensional concept. In the examples presented here, we will focus on one dimension of service, namely delivery time. However, the method can be applied to other dimensions of service as well.

Any company has a characteristic cost and service trade-off relationship, as illustrated in Fig. 13.6. This is not to say that cost and service cannot both simultaneously be improved, but states that all other things being equal, costs will go up as service improves. The point here is that a single curve can represent the range of choices available to a company. Each point in the curve represents a choice available to a company, and it can choose to locate anywhere along the curve. The curve also can allow a company to compare its cost–service offerings to those of other companies, as well as look at the effect that faster transportation, more warehouses, a new order-entry system, etc, would have on its location on the curve. The curve can be defined by the cost of different distribution strategies ranging from local finished goods stocking to customer manufacture at a single location, as shown in Fig. 13.7. In between are options such as regional finished goods inventory, central finished goods inventory, central work-in-process inventory, and so forth. In examining the curve, it is useful first to determine the shape of the curve and, second, determine how the shape affects the structure of the logistics system of a company, as well as the structure of the industry. Certain types of curves imply different

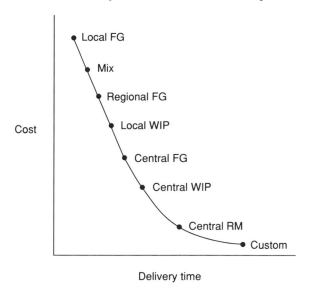

Figure 13.7 A hypothetical efficient frontier.

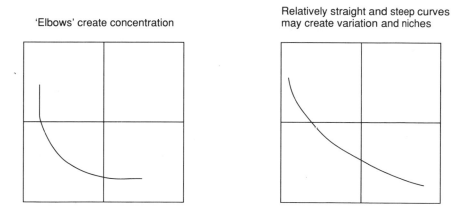

Figure 13.8 Differences in the cost–service curve.

types of industry structures. A curve with an elbow or a sharp bend as shown in Fig. 13.8, has predictable implications. When you move away from the elbow or bend, there are large increases in delivery times with only moderate decreases in cost. In going in the other direction, you have large increases in cost for only modest improvements in delivery time. In this case, most companies should locate near the elbow. In the other case shown in Fig. 13.8, a relatively straight or steep curve creates variation and more niches for different players. In this case, companies can obtain improvements in either costs or service with only modest changes in the other parameters. Understanding the curve can help a company understand the options available as well as its competitive position.

We have examined the bases of many curves, and we believe that there are three key factors that determine the shape of the curve. These factors are: the **structure of the demand and product variety** – which is basically the degree of stability in forecasting product demand; **transportation economics** – specifically what transportation costs for the product are relative to its unit value (coal, for example, has a high transportation cost per unit value and diamonds and pharmaceuticals have a relatively low cost per unit value); and the **structure of the value-added stream** in the logistics system – how much value (at each stage of production and distribution) is added to the product. It is useful to examine and understand the effects of the different key variables. The demand and variety parameters represent a measure of product stability. Products with higher demand, lower variations, higher regional correlation (that is, with demand that tends to move in the same direction in different parts of the country), and lower product variety tend to have a more stable demand pattern – which can be forecasted with greater accuracy and which requires lower inventory requirements. As these factors increase, product stability in turn increases and the curve tends to move downward as it is less costly to provide better service. It may change the curve in a number of different ways as shown in Fig. 13.9. As product demand becomes more stable (that is, as you move to the dashed curve), you obtain little benefit in costs if you are located at point A of either curve because companies have not invested that much cost in the logistics system. On the other hand, as you move further to the left there can be significant increases in cost for a given level of service.

Let us examine the effects of a second variable – transportation costs. A change in transportation costs per unit value for alternative modes can also reduce the curve. As this cost goes down it becomes more economically viable to use faster transportation modes and to consolidate inventory at fewer locations, as shown in Fig. 13.10. The curve is certainly useful for understanding trade-offs, as well as for examining offerings involved in competitive environment.

We should also point out that there is another aspect to this analysis which is what we call the willingness-to-pay curve. Different customers have different cost–service trade-offs, as shown in Fig. 13.11. In developing a cost and service strategy, it is necessary to understand how customers will react in the market place. All things being equal, one

Demand and variety parameter
An increase in this measure
- higher demand
- lower variation
- higher regional correlation, and
- lower product variety

Tends to lower the cost of decentralized inventory policies

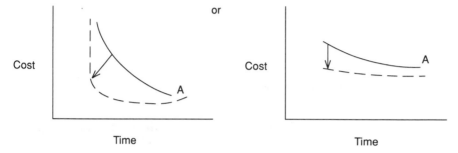

or

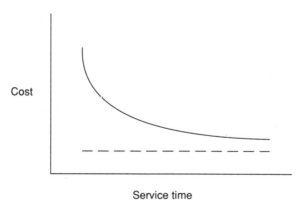

Figure 13.9 General effects of key variables.

Transportation cost
- Changes in transportation cost per unit value for alternative modes

Figure 13.10 General effects of key variables.

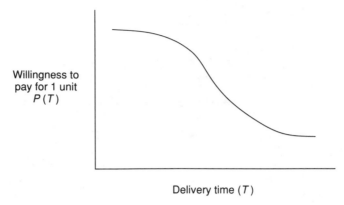

Figure 13.11 Different customers have different cost–service trade-offs.

would like to maximize the distance between the willingness-to-play curve and the cost–service trade-off curve (i.e. choose a cost–service offering that maximizes the difference between curves in Figs. 13.11 and 13.10). This concept introduces additional complications with multiple players that we do not address here. Suffice it to say that broader analysis can be useful in selecting a logistics strategy. In summary, the cost–service trade-off curve is a useful way to help a firm understand how various logistics costs relate, how its cost and service compare with those of its competitors, and how changes can affect a company's competitive position in the market place.

CHAPTER FOURTEEN

Customer service logistics

Warren Blanding

14.1 IS THE WORLD CHANGING – OR IS MANAGEMENT CHANGING?

The world is changing, but that's not news. For middle managers, the truly significant news comes when top management changes. And that's what's happening now.

We've heard repeatedly about the trend towards a service economy in the USA, but how true is this? A look at the record of the last several decades provides persuasive evidence that the USA has been and is a manufacturing-based distributive economy and shows little change.

For the great productive strides of those years are essentially a reflection of the ability to market and distribute an incredible variety and volume of goods. Technological advances including automation and process control have cut manufacturing employment as such, and much manufacturing has moved overseas for economic reasons. But how and where the manufacturing is done doesn't change the basic character of the distributive economy.

14.1.1 The emerging distribution company

Question: Does a company have to own manufacturing facilities to be called a manufacturing company?

Answer: No. historically, most manufacturing companies have contracted out portions of the manufacturing process. Today there is a clear trend among some types of companies to contract out the entire manufacturing process. Unlike so-called 'private label' products, these are fully proprietary items 'invented', designed and engineered

Source: Blanding, W. (1986) *Proc. Council of Logistics Management*, 361–76
First presented at the 1986 Annual Conference of the Council of Logistics Management, Anaheim, USA

by a company and manufactured to its specifications by a contract manufacturer.

We call these 'distribution companies', and they're a natural progression from companies in the automobile and dozens of other industries which have contracted out some models or product lines to overseas manufacturers. The principal difference is that the typical distribution company has evolved to the point where it has no manufacturing plants at all. In fact, its sole physical presence is likely to be an Eastern distribution centre, a Western distribution centre, and a corporate headquarters in a major market area.

14.1.2 Pressures of the distributive economy

This company faces some unusual challenges. Its 'plants' are located thousands of miles away – and, for many products, as many hours away in delivery times. The complexities of export-import aren't just a now-and-then event, but a full-time concern. Production planning – a tough job under the best of conditions – is compounded by barriers of time and language. How do you lean on a plant manager all those thousands of miles away when he doesn't speak your language, nor you his, and it's already tomorrow (or was it yesterday?) where he is?

This is another way of saying that in the distributive economy we can expect to see tremendous pressure for increased accuracy in forecasting and highly enhanced production planning. We can also expect comparable pressure for considerably increased production flexibility to accommodate a changing market place, requiring a far superior level of planning than most companies have today.

14.1.3 Where does the distribution manager stand?

How much of this responsibility will attach itself to the logistics or distribution manager? The question might better be phrased: how much of this responsibility is the logistics or distribution manager prepared to take on? Does this manager understand that logistics extends well beyond the traditional physical distribution role?

To answer these questions, we have to start with our original premise that to the middle manager what really counts is the way top management perceives the world, which is not necessarily the way it really is. Although what we've described here is a reasonably accurate description of the world as it exists today, chances are few managements would be impelled to initiate new strategies as a result of reading it.

Which may explain why relatively few top managements look to distribution (or logistics) as offering any significant contribution to their companies' future success (or survival).

14.1.4 The Coopers and Lybrand report

Survival? You'd better believe it! When you read the Coopers and Lybrand report you will get the distinct feeling that a lot of top managements in a lot of top companies are scared as hell.

The report is called 'Business planning in the eighties: the new marketing shape of American corporations'. At the time of this writing, copies were available without charge from the Business Planning Division of Coopers and Lybrand, 1251 Avenue of the Americas, New York, NY 10020, 212/536-3306.

The 24-page report is well worth reading – better yet, careful study – even total immersion. It's a summary of the findings of a survey of top managements of Fortune 500 companies in four categories: mature industries, high-tech firms, consumer goods manufacturers, and service industries. Perhaps the most significant single finding is that the CEOs themselves of these billion-dollar firms have determined that 'strategic marketing' will be their area of primary concern for the rest of this decade.

14.1.5 The Golden Rule

It's said that the Golden Rule can be defined simply as 'He who has the gold, writes the rule'. Top management's espousal of strategic marketing sends a clear message to middle managers: 'Like it or not, this is the way it's going to be.'

This means, according to the report, that

(1) Sales and Finance will have diminished influence on company operations. This has great significance for logistics and distribution managers who have traditionally been squeezed between the two. It can also be interpreted as a warning to quickly rethink the cost-reduction philosophy that has hitherto characterized many distribution departments.
(2) There will be a significant increase in direct involvement with customers. The report describes this as 'strengthening customer ties'. It reflects increasing management concern with the total customer-service process.
(3) The tradition of allocating budget in proportion to sales will be abandoned. This is another extremely important point for logistics and distribution managers! Under the new strategic marketing

orientation, says the report, marketing funds will be allocated on the basis of 'need and opportunity'. This recognizes distribution and customer-service activities as an investment rather than as cost incurred in 'after sales service'.

14.1.6 What the report doesn't say

On the other hand, distribution and logistics manager should be aware that the top managers quoted in the Coopers and Lybrand report appear to have little or no interest in distribution or logistics. As nearly as we could determine, the word 'distribution' appears only three or four times in the entire report (and then usually in another context), and the word 'logistics' not at all.

By contrast, references to customer service abound. A typical comment with particular relevance for cost-conscious logisticians/distributionists is this observation by a top manager interviewed for the report:

'We're moving from a 'tunnel vision' focus on controlling costs to a 'market' focus on customer service and competition.'

There are continued references to 'customer needs and wants', and an especially revealing comment by another manager about the new role of Finance:

'Financial management will be much more integrated with marketing than in the past. It will also be driven more by marketing goals than by cost control goals'.

The message should be quite clear. Management's concern – what top managers call 'strategic marketing' – sounds suspiciously like something we know as customer service. Right along here, middle managers who understand the significance of 'management style' to their CEOs may be thinking that it wouldn't be a bad idea to fall in line and start thinking strategic marketing themselves.

14.2 LOYALTY AND LOGISTICS

Each business discipline leaves its mark on its practitioners. Financial people think one way, sales people another and MIS people still another. Customer service is on its way to recognition as a full-fledged discipline in most companies, and has similarly developed an orientation of its own. That orientation is very much on target with the way management is currently thinking – and will most likely continue thinking for some time to come.

Although distribution people have long laid claim to customer service, in practice there are relatively few companies – less than 10% – where customer service actually reports to the distribution function. For the remaining 90%, the distribution philosophy or outlook and the customer service outlook are fundamentally different.

It's an important difference, given top management's current concern with customer service. Here's how the two philosophies spell out, in very general terms:

(1) Customer service recognizes the inevitability of customer service failures, has considerable scepticism about systems, sees 'customer keeping' as a major corporate goal.
(2) Distributionists and logisticians are more optimistic and have greater faith in systems: one of their central concerns is best described as 'optimizing the system'.
(3) Customer-service people are likely to be reactive, in the sense of being driven by events. Unplanned expenditures to overcome unexpected emergencies are a way of life.
(4) Distribution people tend to initiate change, to determine in advance what service levels should be, and then plan the least-cost configuration that will meet that level.
(5) Customer-service professionals see the creation of customer loyalty – the basis of future sales – as a primary goal of their departments. As a result, they tend to think of quality on a case-by-case basis.
(6) Distribution professionals tend to be operations-oriented rather than sales- or marketing-oriented. They have high concern for quality as a systems concept.
(7) Customer-service people have little direct control over costs, and thus see profits as a marketing goal but not their immediate responsibility.
(8) Distribution people feel a direct profit responsibility: identifying costs as a basis for strategic pricing, and containing and/or reducing costs as a direct means of maintaining and increasing profits.

A final point of distinction is a fairly common view that, while physical distribution or logistics can be precisely measured and stated as a percentage of sales, customer service 'can't be quantified'. But is this really so?

14.2.1 Customer service CAN be quantified!

'Customer services is important, but it can't be quantified.' This comment by the top financial executive of a major apparel manufacturer typifies the lack of understanding of how customer service contributes

Table 14.1 How customer loyalty goes to the bottom line

Year	70% Retention rate	80% Retention rate	90% Retention rate
1	$1000	$1000	$1000
2	770	880	990
3	593	774	980
4	456	681	970
5	352	600	961
6	270	528	951
7	208	464	941
8	160	409	932
9	124	360	923
10	95	316	914
TOTALS	**$4028**	**$6012**	**$9562**

(Based on 10% account growth annually)

Account retention and account growth are both measures of customer loyalty which can be readily quantified, as shown above. A firm with a customer retention rate of 70% or better is most likely offering superior customer service, based on American Management Associations data, and as customer service improves, revenues also improve quite dramatically. For example, in the table above, an increase in customer retention rates of only 10 percentage points – from 80% to 90% – would bring about a 59% increase in actual revenues from the same customer base.

to the bottom line, what it contributes to the bottom line and how readily the contribution can be measured.

(1) *Customer loyalty can get quantified* The American Management Associations says that at least 65% of a firm's business comes from its present customers. Existing accounts who receive good service tend to increase their purchases from year to year. The accompanying chart (Table 14.1) indicates the total revenue, over a 10-year period, at different levels of repeat business at a constant account growth rate of 10%.

(2) *ROI on improvements in customer service can be measured against return on advertising or other marketing investment* General Electric found that investment in stepped-up service after the time of the sale was much more productive of customer loyalty and repeat business than a much larger investment in advertising aimed at recapturing the same customers.

(3) *In industrial markets, a 5% decrease in service levels will result in a*

Table 14.2 Quantifying the customer-service contribution

Action	Results	Value ($)
Customer service relieves sales of administrative tasks like returns and credits, exchanges, qualifying leads, etc.	Each field salesperson can now make one more call/week, 50 calls/year. With 50-person sales force, this is 2500 calls/year, with each call worth $200-plus	500 000
Field sales has a 'hit rate' of one sale for every 10 calls, or 250 additional sales/year	Each completed sale has an average dollar value $40 000	10 000 000

Projection calculated for a major chemical company and based on its own numbers shows how support by customer service can add $10 million to actual sales revenues with no increase in selling cost, plus an increase in sales productivity valued at $500 000. If customer service performs lead qualification, an improvement in the 'hit rate' would undoubtedly increase sales revenues by at least another 10%.

24% drop in purchases by the existing customer base This was determined in a study conducted on behalf of the Council of Logistics Management.

(4) *Customer service can reduce selling costs and increase selling productivity in measurable amounts* Table 14.2 is a projection made for a major chemical company showing how transfer of certain administrative duties (e.g. returns and credits) from sales to customer service would represent a $500 000 improvement in sales productivity plus $10 million increase in sales at virtually zero cost. This is only one of many possible trade-offs between customer service and sales.

(5) *It costs five times as much to acquire a new customer as it does to service an existing one* This is a finding of the American Management Associations. As an example of how this works, a large publisher found that it was spending $8 to acquire a new subscriber, but only $1 to service a subscriber complaint. Since its advertising rates were pegged to its paid circulation, every subscriber lost through poor service at a $1 level had to be replaced by a much more expensive new subscriber at the $8 level. By a modest increase in the expenditure for customers service – complaint handling, in this case – the company was able to maintain a higher renewal rate and thus reduce the need for high-cost 'replacement subscribers'. This situation is not confined to the publishing business; it's valid in every situation where repeat business is an important consideration.

(6) *Customer service can help avoid cancellations and recover lost sales.*   This is another readily quantifiable contribution by customer service. It generally comes into play when a customer cancels, or indicates he/she will cancel because of stock shortages, unsuitable units of sale or unacceptable delivery dates. The customer service representative handling the transaction avoids or reverses the cancellation through one or more of the following strategies:

(a) Negotiation of a mutually acceptable delivery date.

(b) Offering substitutions by product or by pack or packaging, e.g. 50 packs of 24 instead of 100 of 12.

(c) Offering alternative logistics: truck instead of rail, bag instead of bulk etc.

(d) Negotiating a 'loan' of product from another customer with less urgent requirements.

(7) *Customer service can mitigate expense of mis-shipments and similar errors* This is also readily quantifiable: for example, when a truckload shipment is sent to a distant customer by error when only a pallet load has been ordered, the customer-service representative on the account can find another buyer in the area for the product and thus save the return freight costs as well as restocking and other handling expenses.

(8) *Customer service can upgrade orders and add significantly to revenues* This can be computer-assisted or done on the basis of decision rules, e.g. if a customer orders a certain amount of product the customer-service representative is instructed to recommend ordering additional product to take advantage of a price break. Or the suggestion may be to order related products, etc. Sales results can be readily quantified in all such cases.

14.3 DOES LOGISTICS HAVE A PLACE IN CUSTOMER SERVICE?

Logisticians have long laid claim to customer service by virtue of their involvement in it in some fairly conventional ways. However, there's little evidence that they have attracted much management attention in doing so. This is not to belittle their accomplishments, which include:

(1) *Consolidation programmes by region, day of week, etc.*   Primarily seen as cost-reduction techniques for the company, they often have benefits for customers as well in the form of lower freight charges. Some of these have been quite creative, and have enabled workload levelling in the warehouse and customer service activity in addition to significant cash savings.

(2) *Unit load programmes* These have been used successfully in the grocery industry for some years, and have generated numerous benefits for both manufacturers and their customers. In fact, the grocery products industry appears to have the highest proportion of distribution managers with direct responsibility for the customer-service department.

(3) *Warehouse locations and programmes* Although the logistics of warehouse location are usually viewed in the light of trade-offs with transportation cost, they are predicated on meeting specified customer service levels that in many instances have been determined to be acceptable and/or necessary for competitive reasons, in addition to locational aspects. Logistics is often involved in special warehouse services like drop shipments, storage in transit, labelling, price-marketing and similar arrangements.

(4) *Centralized parts support* This practice, now employed in many high-tech companies, was first introduced in the late 1950s and early 1960s by logisticians in the airline industry and in manufacturing organizations. It was adopted by foreign car manufacturers to get a foothold in the US market, and in addition to high tech uses is also used widely by heavy equipment manufacturers with customers worldwide.

(5) *On-line systems* Distributionists and logisticians can take well-deserved credit for pioneering the advanced on-line systems which enable fast response and high levels of customer service at minimum cost. The work of the TDCC (Transportation Data Coordinating Committee) in developing protocols for electronic data transfer and electronic funds transfer is probably the most important logistics advance in the last thirty years.

But there are less conventional logistics involved in customer service that remain relatively untapped by distributionists and logisticians. For example:

(1) *Inventory levelling* Employing customer service's capability for upgrading orders and/or retaining business by suggesting substitutions, some firms use these same techniques 'in reverse', i.e. to slow down sales of items that are selling ahead of forecast, and to speed up sales of goods that are moving significantly behind forecast. While this may appear at first glance to be a marketing procedure, in actual fact it is very sound logistics. Yet how many logisticians have explored it?

(2) *Total cost approach to claims and adjustments* Some companies have costed out the claims-adjustments process to the point where they can realistically evaluate the trade-off between investigating claims

before paying and simply allowing an automatic adjustment up to a certain dollar limit. This is a basic exercise in logistics – the total-cost approach – which relatively few logisticians appear to have practised.

(3) *Investment vs. 'avoidable cost'* Logisticians have traditionally concerned themselves with costs, so much so that the term 'avoidable costs' is sometimes applied to those that are generally termed variable costs (as opposed to fixed costs). In practice, the term 'avoidable costs' has attached itself to emergency shipments or the use of premium transportation in situations that presumably could have been avoided through better planning. By contrast, it's fundamental customer service that when it's necessary to spend extra money to solve a customer problem, this is a dollars-and-cents marketing investment in the on-going business relationship with that customer – and some companies are in fact able to precisely measure the return on that investment. Not surprisingly, the same principles are found in very similar form in the distributionist–logistician's work-outs showing the cost justification for an automated warehousing system, private fleet operation or whatever.

(4) *Recovering departmental costs* Increasingly, customer-service departments are becoming self-sufficient by recovering their operating costs through a combination of increased productivity plus add-on sales telemarketing and similar strategies. They have paid great attention to their internal logistics as well as their underlying marketing role. Gradually, they are changing the perception of their function from 'after sales' to 'sales stimulating'. In some instance, they, not the marketers nor the logisticians, are seen as the driving force behind kanban or just-in-time arrangements.

(5) *Communications logistics* The customer service department has been described as the 'nerve centre' of the company. This is an apt description because the main business of customer service is communications. Customer-service executives themselves are only beginning to recognize that effective communication is essentially a matter of sound logistical planning. Given the ever-increasing cost of field selling, this involvement of customer service managers in communications logistics couldn't have come a moment too soon. *Question:* Are they preempting what the logisticians–distributionists should have been doing a long time ago?

14.3.1 Where does logistics stop?

It doesn't. Logistics pervades the entire business organization. But logistics and distribution managers should realize that logistics is not another name for physical distribution, and that their companies can't be driven by the distribution philosophies that came into popularity about 20 years ago. Top management has indicated its concern with customer service and, for the present anyway, that concern doesn't appear to include much interest in logistics or distribution *per se*.

Which leaves the question: can distribution managers use their logistical know-how to capitalize on this new management outlook, or will they insist that their own logistics is the only logistics that counts?

14.4 THE TROUBLE WITH BETTER MOUSETRAPS

If quality is so important, why are quality-driven companies in trouble? For example, this 60-year-old Midwestern metal fabricator is indisputably the best in its field in the quality of its products. Unfortunately, it's also on the verge of extinction: it probably won't even enjoy the dignity of a takeover, because there's almost nothing left to take over.

For 50 of those 60 years, this firm operated on the better mousetrap theory, i.e. that as long as it made better-quality products, customers would come to it. This philosophy also took it for granted that customers would tolerate poor service and a certain disdain for customers as the price of obtaining such quality.

Because this company had a broad product line and had done little to encourage customer loyalty, it was an obvious candidate for skimming. And that's what the competition started doing; zeroing in on a few high-volume items. It offered acceptable quality (if not quite as good), competitive pricing and – because it was unhampered by an unwieldy product line – superior customer service. This process continued over a 10-year period, until today the Midwestern company gets the orders nobody else wants – those that require a high level of quality but are generally uneconomic because they are relatively small and infrequent.

14.4.1 When customer service is de-prioritized

This company is one of a number in a similar downward spiral. Their problem is not their focus on quality but rather their almost total de-prioritization of customer service. These are companies that for the most part are run by engineers or driven by an engineering philosophy.

Would they be in better shape if they were driven by a logistics philosophy?

To the extent that logisticians recognize production planning as both a logistics function and a customer service function, the answer is yes, these companies would do far better in a logistics mode than in an engineering mode.

This doesn't in any way depreciate either the engineering function *per se* or the importance of product quality. Rather it recognizes one of the most overlooked and little understood principles of business success in today's marketplace:

> The perception of quality in a firm's products often arises directly from the quality of the firm's service rather than from the products themselves.

This principle is exemplified in a familiar situation where an excellent piece of machinery stands idle for an extended period because a critical part is not available. Ultimately, the machine is seen as being of poor quality when in fact the problem is poor logistical support entirely unrelated to product quality.

But logisticians should realize that service embraces a good deal more than logistical support. For example, a fast-responding liberal exchange or replacement policy doesn't give customers time to dwell on product quality and in fact promotes the image of a quality company. Or, a firm that is equipped to give customers advance notification of possible delays or service failures in the future is quite likely to be perceived as having superior service when others may in fact be providing better overall service.

14.5 WHAT IS THIS SO-CALLED CORPORATE CUSTOMER-SERVICE CULTURE?

It isn't very complicated. Basically, the corporate customer service culture is what's reflected in the Coopers and Lyband report: a fundamental switch in management preoccupation, from preoccupation with production and finance to preoccupation with marketing and customer service. But it goes far beyond the superficial 'We love customers' themes and promotional hypes that are pursued from time to time – and which generally neither fool nor convince anybody. The signs that distinguish a genuine corporate customer service culture are:

(1) A specific statement of the strategic marketing role of customer service, supported by appropriate policies and decision rules.
(2) Equal status of the customer-service department with other major functions and career pathing within the department.
(3) Rewriting the rule of accountability within the company to require

each department to meet specific internal standards of performance required to meet strategic customer service goals.

(4) As an extension of No. 3, an active and on-going internal campaign to create and maintain awareness of the 'internal customer' concept, where departments are in effect one another's customers in producing the quality of customer service inherent in the firm's marketing strategy.

(5) Management encouragement of innovation and experimentation by the customer-service manager.

14.6 WHAT ARE CUSTOMER-SERVICE MANAGERS DOING NOW THAT LOGISTICS MANAGERS SHOULD KNOW ABOUT?

Besides the examples already cited, these marketing innovations in particular reflect the growing stature of customer service and customer-service managers:

(1) *Identifying candidates for kanban arrangements*   This is a logical and legitimate byproduct of the customer service manager's overview of total account activity as well as individual account profiles. Much if not all of the same data is available to distribution and logistics managers.

(2) *Mining the gold in the customer database*   Nobody is more completely in the mainstream of account activity than the customer-service department. The department's forecasts are generally more reliable – because they are more factually based – than forecasts by the sale department. Some managers have developed the data accumulated in order entry and account service into extremely sophisticated marketing tools to support corporate marketing, field sales and inside selling alike.

(3) *Cost sharing with customers*   While this is commonly exemplified by self-service in retail activities – getting customers to do more of the work – there are also numerous industrial applications. These include computer-to-computer order entry, 'educating' customers in inventory and reorder points, persuading customers to accept discontinuance of order acknowledgments and confirmations (one firm saved $100 000 in this respect), upgrading orders, negotiated deliveries and similar arrangements.

(4) *Shared forecasting*   Closely related to kanban philosophies, this is one of the most exciting concepts to emerge so far in corporate customer service culture. As its name implies, shared forecasting occurs when a customer firm literally shares its own production

forecasts with selected vendors so that they in turn may fine-tune their own forecasts.

(5) *Production planning* Involvement of customer service managers in shared forecasting has opened the door to direct involvement in production planning. Here again, customer service's familiarity with customer profiles has been a real asset, particularly in capital-intensive businesses where combined runs and advance planning can generate substantial economies for the company as well as its customers.

(6) *Proactivism* In the past, customer-service departments have mainly reacted to customer demands. Today, there is an increasing tendency to ask customers 'Why?' – a realization that what customers perceive as the solution to a particular problem is not necessarily the best solution for either customer or company. This often leads to proposal – and acceptance – of alternatives that are better for both parties. In similar vein and departing from the tradition of arm's-length dealings, many departments recognize the value as marketing strategy of detecting and preventing customer errors in specification and ordering (including routeing and other logistics) that in the past would have been considered the customer's sole responsibility. This is an area where distributionists and logisticians have considerable experience in contrast to smaller customers who may be inexperienced in physical distribution matters. It is worth pursuing to greater lengths in regard to overall customer service.

14.7 LOGISTICS IS MORE THAN PHYSICAL DISTRIBUTION

Much of the significant progress in customer service management in the last decade is based on principles well known to – and often first introduced by – distributionists and logisticians. But not all such individuals recognize that logistics is indeed much more than physical distribution – and that a truly golden opportunity awaits those who can bridge the gap and become truly involved in **customer-service logistics** in areas like these:

(1) Telephone and other communications systems which offer multiple opportunities for cost reduction and profit improvement through the numerous potential trade-offs plus system optimization.
(2) Applications of queueing theory – a fundamental principle in logistics which is pervasive in customer service and offers many opportunities to support the new management concern with strategic marketing.

(3) Workload levelling in the customer service department, a direct transfer of methods used in warehouse and distribution centre management.
(4) Workload levelling between warehouse, shipping and customer service – an extension of accountability that relatively few companies have exploited thus far.
(5) New concepts in branch sales office design and location, an area which some companies are now treating as a matter of logistics rather than a sales or marketing decision.
(6) On-line systems, which still offer many opportunities for improvement and refinement.
(7) Enhancement of parts support and distribution, including integration of service in such innovative applications as carrier delivery personnel with sufficient 'low-tech' training to install new parts and return exchange parts on a single trip.
(8) Recognition that, for the immediate future, customer service is indeed the 'business of the business' – and offers great opportunities for distributionists and logisticians to broaden and expand their roles in corporate management.

This leaves only one question to be asked: are you ready – and able – to capitalize on these opportunities?

It is hoped that the answer will be a resounding 'Yes!'

CHAPTER FIFTEEN

Audit your customer service quality

Martin Christopher and Richard Yallop

INTRODUCTION

In recent years there has been a major transformation in attitudes towards services and quality. Customers have become more demanding, more knowledgeable, more sophisticated – and more likely to vote with their feet. Throughout all sectors of industry the search for service excellence has become the over-riding concern. Managers now recognize that substantial competitive advantage can be gained through superior customer service and, equally important, customer service becomes a powerful means of differentiating the company from the competition.

Many markets are now more 'service sensitive' than they are 'price-sensitive'. What this means is not that price has become unimportant – far from it. Rather it suggests that service has assumed a new significance to today's time-sensitive customer. For example, to the just-in-time manufacturer, reliable delivery is just as important as product quality and price. Similarly the retailer seeking to maximize selling space productivity looks for an equivalent level of delivery reliability.

A further powerful aspect of customer service is its ability to provide distinctive differentiation of the basic core product. It is no longer sufficient, in any market, to compete solely on the basis of product features or technology. The search for competitive differentiation has become a key priority in most market-orientated businesses. As Fig. 15.1 suggest, the ability to expand the 'product surround' through the

Source: Christopher, M. and Yallop, R. (1990) *Focus*, **9**(5), 1–6

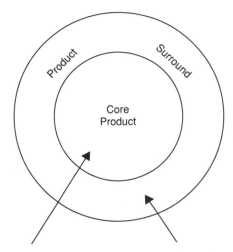

Tangible elements
- Quality
- Product features
- Technology
- Durability
  etc.

Intangible elements
- Delivery service frequency
- Delivery reliability and consistency
- Single point of contact
- Ease of doing business
- After-sales support
  etc.

Figure 15.1 Using service to augment the core product.

addition of service-related intangibles makes the core product vastly
more saleable.

More recently many companies have begun to widen their definition
of quality away from a narrow product feature basis towards the wider
concept of the total product offer. In other words, total quality equates
to the core product and the product surround combined. Thus to
become a quality supplier in the eyes of the customer, the organization
must meet customer requirements and expectations on all aspects of
the offer – both the core and its surround.

Clearly, therefore, because of the potential that the product surround
provides, both for differentiating the product and for enhancing the
customer's perception of total quality, the management of service
assumes the highest importance.

In the marketing environment of the 1990s the need to develop a
detailed understanding of the relative service performance vis-a-vis
competition will be even more vital than it is today. However, managing service implies an ability to measure it and, hence, to control it.
This is the role of 'competitive benchmarking'.

15.1 COMPETITIVE BENCHMARKING

Competitive benchmarking was pioneered by Rank Xerox. In an attempt to identify those areas where competition had gained advantage over themselves, Rank Xerox set out, department by department, to compare their performance against their competitors. This comparative analysis extended from a comparison of technical features of equipment and cost data, through to a detailed examination of customers' perceptions of quality and service.

Working on this baseline information, Rank Xerox began a programme of quality and service improvement which has led to their regaining market share which had previously been lost.

In the specific context of customer service, how does the benchmarking process work?

The first point to emphasize is that customer service is perceptual. Whatever our own 'hard' internal measures of service might say our service performance is, perceptions are the reality. The company might use measures which, whilst providing useful measures of productivity, do not actually reflect the things the customer values. For example, whilst 'stock availability' is a widespread internal measure of performance, a more appropriate external measure from the customer's viewpoint could be 'on-time delivery'. Hence it is critical that we develop a set of service criteria that are meaningful to customers.

The approach to service benchmarking that we favour follows a four-stage process:

Step 1   Identify the key components of customer service as seen by customers themselves.

Step 2   Establish the relative importance of those service components to customers.

Step 3   Identify company position on the key service components relative to competition.

Step 4   Analyse the data to see if service performance matches customers' service needs.

Table 15.1 summarizes the four-step customer service audit process.

5.1.1 Step 1: Identifying the key components of customer service.

It is a common fault in marketing to fail to realize that customers do not always attach the same importance to product attributes as the vendor. The same principle applies to customer service. Which aspects of service are rated most highly by the customer? If a supplier places its

Table 15.1 The customer-service audit

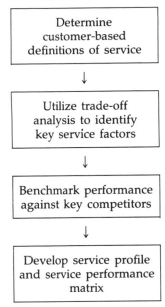

emphasis upon stock availability, but the customer regards delivery reliability more highly, it may not be allocating its resources in a way likely to maximize sales. Alternatively a company that realizes that its customers place a higher value on completeness of orders than they do on, say, regular scheduled deliveries, could develop this knowledge to its advantage.

Therefore it is important to understand the factors that influence buyer behaviour and, in the context of customer service, which particular elements are seen by the customer to be the most important.

The first step in research of this type is to identify the relative source of influence upon the purchase decision. If for example, we are selling components to a manufacturer, who will make the decision on the source of supply? This is not always an easy question to answer as in many cases there will be several people involved. The purchasing manager of the company to which we are selling may only be acting as an agent for others within the firm. In other cases his influence will be much greater. Alternatively if we are manufacturing products for sale through retail outlets, is the decision to stock made centrally by a retail chain or by individual store managers? The answers can often be supplied by the sales force. The sales representative should know from experience who are the decision makers.

Given that a clear indication of the source of decision-making power can be gained, the customer service researcher at least knows who to research. The question remains as to which elements of the vendor's total marketing offering have what effect upon the purchase decision.

Ideally once the decision-making unit in a market has been identified an initial, small-scale research programme should be initiated based upon personal interviews with a representative sample of buyers. The purpose of these interviews is to elicit, in the language of the customers, firstly the importance they attach to customer service vis-a-vis the other marketing mix elements such as price, product quality, promotion etc., and secondly, the specific importance they attach to the individual components of customer service.

The authors were involved in a customer service study to determine the elements of customer service in the market for a packaged grocery product and an initial series of personal interviews were conducted with senior buyers responsible for the purchaser of that product in major retail outlets. As a result, a number of customer service elements were generated as follows:

(1) Frequency of delivery
(2) Time from order to delivery
(3) Reliability of delivery
(4) Emergency deliveries when required
(5) Stock availability and continuity of supply
(6) Orders filled completely
(7) Advice on non-availability
(8) Convenience of placing order
(9) Acknowledgement of order
(10) Accuracy of invoices
(11) Quality of sales representation
(12) In-store merchandising support
(13) Regular calls by sales representatives
(14) Manufacturer monitoring of retail stock levels
(15) Credit terms offered.

The importance of this initial step in measuring customer service is that relevant and meaningful measures of customer service are generated by customers themselves. Once these dimensions are defined we can identify the relative importance of each one and the extent to which the customer is prepared to trade off one aspect of service for another.

15.1.2 Step 2: Establishing the relative importance of customer service components

One of the simplest ways of discovering the importance a customer attaches to each element of customer service is to take the components generated by means of the process described in Step 1 and to ask a representative sample of customers to rank order them from the 'most important' to the 'least important'. In practice this is difficult, particularly with a large number of components, and would not give any insight into the relative importance of each element. Alternatively a form of rating scale could by used. For example, the respondents could be asked to place a weight from 1 to 10 against each component according to how much importance they attach to each element. The problem here is that respondents will tend to rate most of the components as highly important, especially since those components were generated on the grounds of importance to customers anyway. A partial solution is to ask the respondent to allocate a total of 100 points amongst all the elements listed, according to perceived importance. However, this is a fairly daunting task for the respondent and can often result in an arbitrary allocation.

Fortunately a relatively recent innovation in consumer research technology now enables us to evaluate very simply the implicit importance that a customer attaches to the separate elements of customer service. The technique is based around the concept of 'trade-off' and can best be illustrated by an example from everyday life. In considering, say, the purchase of a new car we might desire specific attributes, e.g. performance in terms of speed and acceleration, economy in terms of petrol consumption, size in terms of passenger and luggage capacity and, of course, low price. However, it is unlikely that any one car will meet all of these requirements so we are forced to trade off one or more of these attributes against the others.

The same is true of the customer faced with alternative options of distribution service. The buyer might be prepared to sacrifice a day or two on lead time in order to gain delivery reliability, or to trade off order completeness against improvements in order entry etc. Essentially the trade-off technique works by presenting the respondent with feasible combinations of customer service elements and asking for a rank order of preference for those combinations.

Let us take a simple example where a respondent is asked to choose between different levels of stock availability, order cycle time and delivery reliability. For the sake of example the following options are presented:

Table 15.2

		Order cycle time		
		2 days	3 days	4 days
	75%			9
Stock	85%			
availability	95%	1		

		Order cycle time		
		2 days	3 days	4 days
Delivery	±1 day	1		
reliability	±3 days			6

		Stock availability		
		75%	85%	95%
Delivery	±1 day			1
reliability	±3 days	6		

Stock availability (%)	75
	85
	95
Order cycle time (days)	2
	3
	4
Delivery reliability (days):	±1
	±3

The various trade-offs can be placed before the respondent as a series of matrices (Table 15.2).

The idea is that the respondent should complete each matrix to illustrate his/her preference for service alternatives. Thus, with the first trade-off matrix between order cycle time and stock availability, it is presumed that the most preferred combination would be an order cycle time of two days with a stock availability of 95% and the least

Table 15.3

		Order cycle time		
		2 days	3 days	4 days
	75%	6	8	9
Stock	85%	3	5	7
availability	95%	1	2	4

		Order cycle time		
		2 days	3 days	4 days
Delivery	±1 day	1	3	5
reliability	±3 days	2	4	6

		Stock availability		
		75%	85%	95%
Delivery	±1 day	4	2	1
reliability	±3 days	6	5	3

preferred combination an order cycle time of five days with a stock availability of 75%. But what about the other combinations? Here the respondent is asked to complete the matrix to show his/her own preferences. An example of a typical response is given in Table 15.3.

Using computer analysis the implicit 'importance weights' that underlie the initial preference rankings can be generated. For the data in the above example the weights given in Table 15.4 emerge.

Thus, for this respondent, stock availability would appear to be marginally more important than delivery time and both were in the region of twice as important as delivery reliability. Information such as this can be most useful. It can tell us, for example, that in this hypothetical case, a stock availability of 85% with 2 days' delivery and a reliability of ± 1 day is seen as being equally acceptable as a 95% availability with 2 days' delivery and ± 3 days' reliability (a combined weight of 0.695 compared with 0.697), thus suggesting that a tighten-

Table 15.4

Service Element		Importance weight
(1) Stock availability (%)	75	−0.480
	85	0
	95	+0.480
(2) Delivery time (days)	2	+0.456
	3	0
	4	−0.456
(3) Delivery reliability (days)	±1	+0.239
	±3	−0.239

ing up on reliability might reduce stockholding and still provide an acceptable level of customer service.

A further benefit of this type of information is that it enables us to distinguish the responses between types of customers – a most important consideration when examining the possibilities for differentiating the service offering by market segment.

15.1.3 Step 3: Identifying company position on key components of service relative to competition

Now we know from the previous two steps the key components of customer service and their relative importance, the next question is: 'How do my customers rate me on these components compared to the competition?'

The first two steps were accomplished using relatively small samples and in effect they served as a 'pilot' study to provide the basis for a larger-scale survey of the company's customers. This wider survey can often be achieved by means of a postal questionnaire, the sample for which should be chosen to reflect the different types of customer. The main purpose of the questionnaire is to present the components of service as elicited in Step 1 and to ask the respondents to rate the company and its competitors on each of these elements in terms of their perceived performance. Table 15.5 reproduces part of a typical questionnaire for use in service benchmarking. For each competing company in that market the respondent is asked to rate its performance on each of the relevant dimensions of service identified in Step 1. When the responses are aggregated by trade sector or market segment patterns may well emerge. On each customer service element it is possible to see how each competing supplier compares in terms of each other.

Table 15.5 Customer-service benchmark questionnaire

How would you rate ABC on the following: (Score from 1 to 5; 1 = very poor, 5 = excellent)

Please circle

Order cycle time	1	2	3	4	5
Stock availability	1	2	3	4	5
Order size constraints	1	2	3	4	5
Ordering convenience	1	2	3	4	5
Frequency of delivery	1	2	3	4	5
Delivery reliability	1	2	3	4	5
Quality of documentation	1	2	3	4	5
Claims procedure	1	2	3	4	5
Order completeness	1	2	3	4	5
Technical support	1	2	3	4	5
Order status information	1	2	3	4	5

Other analysis can include regional breakdowns and analyses by size and type of customer. The usual statistical tests can be applied to identify if different scores on any dimensions have significance. To ensure an unbiased response to the questionnaire it is preferable if the survey can be carried out anonymously or via a third party such as a market research agency. Also, as in Steps 1 and 2, it is important to make sure that the people to whom the questionnaire is sent represent the decision-making structure within their concerns.

Management now has customer-service database upon which it can make a number of crucial decisions regarding the design of more cost-effective customer-service policies.

Analysis of the data will then enable service profiles of each company to be constructed and again this data can be presented alongside the importance ranking identified from the earlier trade-off analysis (Figure 15.2).

Further profiles can be produced by disaggregating the data by customer type, market segment, region, etc. Competitive service profiles can provide additional insights if non-users or lapsed customers are also included in the survey. Companies who have conducted these types of competitive analyses find that they provide a clear guide for action. Often competitive profiles point to weaknesses that had not previously been recognized. Additional benefit can be derived from repeating these studies on a regular basis to monitor changes and trends.

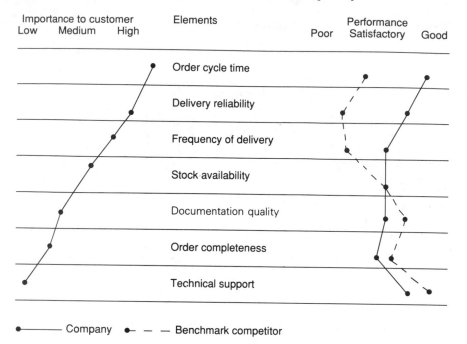

Figure 15.2 Customer-service profile.

15.1.4 Step 4: Comparing service performances with customers' service priorities

Using the data generated from the customer-service audit we are in a position to contrast two key findings: firstly what are the important dimensions of service and secondly how well is the company perceived to perform on those key dimensions?

A simple way of displaying this data is to represent the findings in the form of a service performance matrix. On one axis we measure the importance rating (usually on a scale of 1 to 5) and on the second axis is shown the actual perceived performance rating (also on a 1 to 5 scale). Table 15.6 shows such a matrix.

In this hypothetical example we have shown the scores on five dimensions jointly for importance and perceived performance. The five dimensions might be taken to be:

(1) Order cycle time
(2) Order completeness
(3) Documentation quality

Table 15.6 The service-performance matrix

Importance to customer
(1 = unimportant; 5 = highly important)

		1	2	3	4	5
	1					
Perceived	2				(i)	
Performance						
(1 = poor	3		(ii)			(iv)
5 = excellent)	4			(iii)		
	5	(v)				

(4) Delivery reliability
(5) Technical support

The interpretation of this matrix is simple. It is clearly crucial that the company be seen to be performing well in those service dimensions that the customer deems to be important. Conversely it can be argued that if the service dimension is seen to be less important to the customer, then high performance on that dimension amounts to 'service overkill' or a misuse of resources.

Thus in this case we are underperforming on dimensions (1) and (4) – order cycle time and delivery reliability – and possibly overperforming on (5) – technical support.

Figure 15.3 generalizes this point.

Similar charts can be produced for individual market segments, sales areas, distribution channels or whatever by further analysis of the data emerging from the customer service audit.

Management is now able to identify the priorities for customer-service improvement and possibly to consider a reallocation of resources so that every £1 invested in customer service can generate the maximum return.

15.2 CONCLUSION

The service-quality revolution is now well under way. However, the success or failure of any quality-improvement programme will be determined in large part by the ability of the organization to identify the

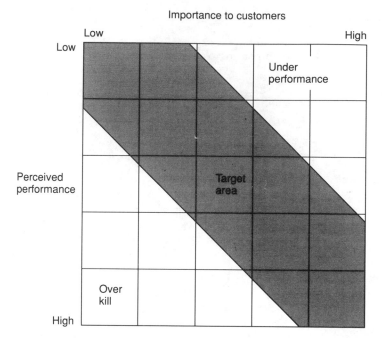

Figure 15.3 Customer-service management indicators.

key customer service factors and to monitor competitive performance on those factors.

In today's competitive market place there is a clear advantage to be gained by a recognition of the factors that influence customer demand. Competitive benchmarking, combined with trade-off analysis, is a highly practical way to identify the 'order winning criteria' that under-lie the customer's choice of supplier.

The methodology that we have described here has been used successfully in markets varying from industrial chemicals to cosmetics and toiletries. The companies that use competitive service profiling and benchmarking tend also to be the leaders in the service quality arena.

As in all things, the motto seems to be: 'If you can't measure it, you can't manage it.'

CHAPTER SIXTEEN

Reducing logistics costs at General Motors

Dennis E. Blumenfeld, Lawrence D. Burns, Carlos F. Daganzo, Michael C. Frick, and Randolph W. Hall

Automobile and truck production at General Motors involves shipping a broad variety of materials, parts, and components from 20 000 supplier plants to over 160 GM plants. To help reduce logistics costs at GM, the decision tool TRANSPART was developed. In its initial application for GM's Delco Electronics Division, TRANSPART identified a 26% logistics cost savings opportunity ($2.9 million per year). Today, TRANSPART II – a commercial version of the tool – is being used in more than 40 GM plants.

General Motors Corporation – popularly known as GM – traces its roots to 1897 when the Olds Motors Vehicle Company produced its first automobile. Nineteen years later, GM was incorporated and encompassed four automobile manufacturing operations, a truck marketing firm, and an export company. Today, GM is one of the largest corporations in the world. In 1984, it marketed over forty different vehicle models, sold 8.3 million cars and trucks worldwide and netted $80.5 billion in vehicle sales.

Roughly 13 000 different parts, varying widely in size and value, must be fabricated and assembled to produce a typical vehicle. A massive production and distribution network is required to accomplish this. In 1984, this network consisted of 20 000 supplier plants, 133 GM parts plants, 31 GM assembly plants, and 11 000 dealers in the USA and Canada. GM's 1984 freight transportation cost was $4.1 billion,

Source: Blumenfeld, D.E., Burns, L.D., Daganzo, C.F., Frick, M.C. and Hall, R.W. (1987) *Interfaces*, **17**(1), 26–47

with about 60% for material shipments and the remainder for finished vehicle shipments. In addition, GM's 1984 inventory was valued at $7.4 billion (about 70% for work-in-process and the remainder for finished vehicles), with much of this inventory being attributable to material and vehicle shipments. The 164 GM facilities are organized into 32 divisions or profit centres.

Because of the size, scope, complexity, and cost of GM's production network, it is imperative that effective decisions be made regarding the shipment of GM materials and vehicles. In the middle to late 1970s, several factors increased the importance of these decisions:

(1) The deregulation of the freight transportation industry was impending;
(2) Interest rates and energy costs were increasing rapidly;
(3) A recession was imminent;
(4) Overseas competitive pressures in the auto industry were escalating; and
(5) Just-in-time manufacturing and shipping were emerging as potentially attractive strategies for US industry.

In 1978, to help prepare GM for the materials management challenges ahead, the GM Research Laboratories formed a new research group. The mission of this group is to perform fundamental logistics research that provides an improved scientific basis for GM's logistics decisions (that is, decisions affecting the flow of materials over GM's extensive production network). The authors of this paper were either members of this group or consultants to it.

In 1981, GM's Delco Electronics Division (currently, Delco Electronics Corporation) confronted a problem in shipping its products which was the catalyst for the management science accomplishments reported here. Delco designs and manufactures a variety of vehicle components. Its products in 1981 included

(1) Electronic control modules produced in Milwaukee, Wisconsin;
(2) Radios produced in Matamoros, Mexico; and
(3) Radios, speakers, heater controls, and a variety of small plastic products and electronic sensors produced in Kokomo, Indiana.

The small size and high value of these electronic products play an important role in how they are shipped.

Figure 16.1 depicts Delco's product shipping network as it was in 1981. Products from Milwaukee and Matamoros were shipped by truck to a Delco warehouse in Kokomo, where they wee consolidated with products made in Kokomo. The consolidated production was then shipped by truck directly to about 30 GM vehicle assembly plants in

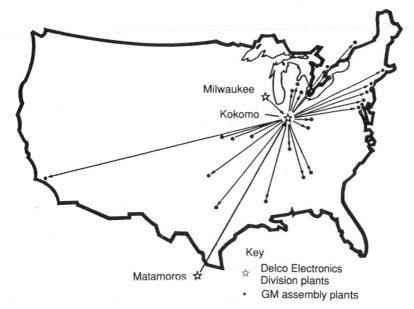

Figure 16.1 The Delco Electronics product distribution network in 1981 with its three plants (☆) shipping to about 30 GM assembly plants (●) via the Kokomo warehouse.

· North America. The warehouse served to combine shipments and store production.

In 1981, the logistics costs associated with Delco's product shipping network were shared by several GM organizations. Specifically, Delco incurred

(1) Inventory cost at its three plants and its warehouse due to load make-up;
(2) Freight transportation and in-transit inventory costs on the links to the warehouse; and
(3) Inventory costs at the warehouse due to material-handling time.

In addition, the GM assembly plants incurred

(1) Inventory costs due to load consumption; and
(2) Freight transportation and in-transit inventory costs on links from warehouse.

Delco, like all GM divisions, was focusing on ways to enhance product quality and reduce product cost. As part of this effort, Delco's manager of material control, Jim Schneider, was responsible for reducing finished product inventory. He recognized that inventory played an important role in allowing Delco to take advantage of the transportation costs efficiencies inherent in large shipments. This is especially important to Delco because its products are small and valuable.

Jim Schneider realized he might be able to reduce inventory by shipping directly from each Delco plant to each GM assembly plant; however, this would increase freight transportation costs substantially, and also affect the share of costs incurred by different GM organizations. While his charge was to reduce inventory, he concluded that he first needed to fully understand the trade-offs in inventory and transportation costs on a network-wide basis.

On 30 June 1981, when Jim visited GM Research, his objective had evolved to one of minimizing the combined corporate cost of inventory and transportation for all Delco products shipped to GM assembly plants. He wanted an analytical tool that would allow convenient and quick evaluation of alternative strategies for shipping Delco's products.

We suspected that several other GM component divisions faced similar challenges and that Delco's situation was a special case of a new and important generic research area for GM. In retrospect, these initial perceptions were correct.

Delco had a complex network that could not be analysed properly with standard mathematical programming techniques. Given Jim's desire to fully understand cost trade-offs and the advantage of using simple, transparent analysis techniques in practical settings, we concluded that there was a need to understand fundamentals and an opportunity to make fresh and original research contributions. We focused on reducing total corporate costs associated with shipping Delco's products and examining the impact different strategies would have on different GM organizations.

16.1 RESEARCH

Transportation costs result from freight charges incurred in shipping products. Inventory costs result from products waiting to be shipped from Delco plants, products in transit to GM assembly plants (including products in the warehouse), and products waiting to be used at assembly plants. Material-handling costs at the warehouse were factored into the cost of carrying inventory there. Modelling the trade-off between transportation and inventory costs over the entire network used to ship Delco products became the key to reducing cost.

16.2 DECISION VARIABLES

Shipping strategies are represented by two types of decision variables:

(1) Shipment sizes (or frequencies) on the network links; and
(2) Routes over the network.

Shipment sizes affect trade-offs between transportation and inventory costs. Shipping large loads infrequently on a specific link reduces the transportation cost per item because the fixed cost of a shipment can be spread over more items. However, large loads increase the inventory cost per item because of the added time incurred to make-up and use loads of more items. Alternatively, shipping smaller loads more frequently results in a higher transportation cost per item, but reduces the inventory cost per item because the loads can be made-up and used more quickly. Thus, transportation and inventory costs are interrelated, and a trade-off exists between them that depends on shipment size (or frequency).

The route selected for each shipment also affects transportation and inventory costs because it determines the amount of material shipped on each link. Routeing options for shipments from each Delco plant to each GM assembly plant include

(1) Making all direct shipments;
(2) Making all shipments via the warehouse;
(3) Making direct shipments between some Delco-assembly-plant pairs, shipping via the warehouse for others, and using a mixture of these two options for yet others; and
(4) Peddling (that is, delivering items from a Delco plant or the warehouse to several assembly plants in one truck load).

These options result in different allocations of transportation and inventory costs to different GM organizations. While we focused on reducing total corporate costs, we also had to consider the organizational implications of different routeing options.

16.3 RESEARCH OBJECTIVE AND APPROACH

Our research objective was to develop a method that would help Delco determine the best shipment sizes and routes (from a total corporate perspective) for its products. To achieve this objective, we had to develop an improved understanding of

(1) The way transportation and inventory costs depend on shipment sizes and routes;
(2) Trade-offs between transportation and inventory costs on complex networks; and
(3) The sensitivity of costs to system conditions.

In our research, we tried to keep the models and analyses as simple as possible. We accomplished this by first studying the simplest type of network and then gradually considering more complex networks.

16.4 SINGLE-LINK 'BUILDING BLOCK'

The first step was to develop a model to analyse the trade-off between transportation and inventory costs on a single link and to examine how total link cost depends on shipment size. We developed equations for transportation and inventory costs that reflect the structure of freight charges, the mixture of items that constitute loads, truck capacities in both weight and volume, and total inventory in the system.

Freight charges could have been inferred from freight rate tables that depend on specific plant locations, commodity type, and shipment size (in pounds). However, we found that the freight charges could be approximated exceptionally well by a parameter that depends only on distance. Incorporating this approximation into the equations allowed the optimal shipment size (that is, the shipment size that minimizes total cost) to be determined as a solution to a standard economic order quantity (EOQ) problem (Arrow *et al*. 1958; Magee and Boodman 1967).

Sensitivity analyses were performed to see how total cost varied around the optimum as a function of material flow (that is, demand) on the link. The equations assumed constant demand, and sensitivity analyses allowed the cost impact of demand fluctuations to be studied.

16.5 NETWORKS

The single link results served as a building block for studying networks with several links. They showed that the optimal shipment size on a link increases with the square root of flow. They also showed that the minimum total cost on the link per unit time increases with flow at a decreasing rate until there is sufficient flow to justify full truck loads, at which point cost increases linearly (Fig. 16.2).

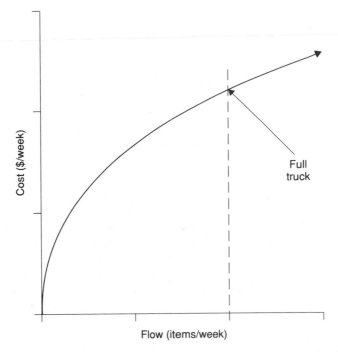

Figure 16.2 The concave relationship between cost and flow on a link, showing how the minimum cost per week increases with a flow at a decreasing rate, up to a full truck load, and linearly afterwards.

The concave relationship between link cost per unit time and flow means that the cost per item shipped on a link decreases with flow. As a result of this scale economy, routeing and shipment size decisions for all Delco–assembly-plant pairs are interrelated. This means that minimizing total network cost requires simultaneously determining optimal routes and shipment sizes.

Because total cost on a link is not a convex function of flow, routeing decisions cannot be evaluated with standard mathematical programming techniques. This problem is very complex. Fortunately, because of concavity, we were able to show that only two routeing options had to be considered for each Delco–assembly-plant pair: ship all products direct, or ship all products via the warehouse. Routeing options that involved shipping some products direct and some via the warehouse for the same plant pair are always more costly. This powerful 'all-or-nothing' principle is discussed in Newell (1980).

All-or-nothing routeing simplified the problem substantially. However, an enormous number of routeing options still remained because the decision to ship direct for one Delco–assembly-plant pair affects total flow through the warehouse and therefore affects costs and routeing decisions for other pairs. For the Delco network, there were 90 such plant pairs (three Delco plants and 30 assembly plants). Without accounting for peddling possibilities, there were $2^{90} \simeq 10^{27}$ different routeing options.

Attempting to solve Delco's combinatorial problem directly would have involved large-scale computing, with no guarantee of finding a solution. Because we wanted to keep the analyses simple and transparent and provide results in a timely manner, we were motivated to find a simpler solution technique. We observed that if shipment sizes were fixed (instead of optimal) on each inbound link to the warehouse (that is, from Milwaukee and Matamoros to the warehouse), total cost per unit time on these links would be linear with flow. As a result, we could prove that, for fixed shipment sizes on the inbound links, the total Delco network could be decomposed into independent subnetworks, each involving just one assembly plant (Fig. 16.3) (see the appendix for the proof given in Blumenfeld *et al.* 1985). Each subnetwork could then be easily solved by enumerating just four routeing options and using the previously described EOQ methods to determine optimal shipment sizes on the links to the assembly plant. The four routeing options on each Delco subnetwork are

(1) All direct;
(2) All via warehouse;
(3) Milwaukee and Kokomo via warehouse; and
(4) Matamoros and Kokomo via warehouse.

These are the only practical options because the warehouse is located adjacent to the Kokomo plant.

The optimal shipping strategy for the entire Delco network was identified by

(1) Generating a variety of fixed shipment-size combinations on the inbound links,
(2) Determining the optimal shipping strategy on each subnetwork for each shipment-size combination,
(3) Summing the resulting minimum costs on all subnetworks for each shipment-size combination, and
(4) Selecting the combination (and corresponding optimal strategy on each subnetwork) that results in the overall minimum cost.

Since there were only two inbound links, the number of shipment-size combinations to consider was relatively small.

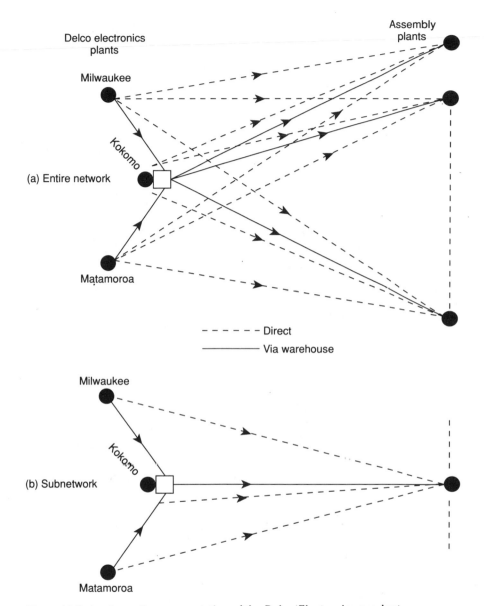

Figure 16.3 A schematic representation of the Delco Electronics product distribution network for the entire network and for a subnetwork isolating one GM assembly plant.

This decomposition method provided a new contribution to network optimization theory. It allowed the optimal shipping strategy (shipment sizes and routes) to be determined quickly and easily for routeing options involving a combination of direct and warehouse shipping. This is accomplished using only basic calculus and arithmetic.

In addition to direct and warehouse shipping, our solution technique also applied to peddling (that is, shipping material to several assembly plants in the same load). This was achieved by visually grouping together assembly plants in close proximity to form peddling regions. Each peddling region was treated as a single assembly plant with a total material flow equal to the combined flow to assembly plants in the region. The transportation cost was approximated by the cost to the nearest assembly plant in the region plus the cost of travelling between plants in the region. This additional cost was estimated from the distance travelled on the peddling route and the number of plants in the region. Shipments consisted of a mixture of items (according to demand) destined for each assembly plant.

Having discovered a simple solution technique, a fast FORTRAN-based decision tool was easily developed for Delco's network. This tool was named TRANSPART.

16.6 DECISION TOOL

The decision tool TRANSPART was developed to allow Delco to conveniently examine the impact on total corporate cost of different shipping strategies for its products. It contains the model for analysing transportation and inventory cost trade-offs and the solution technique for determining the minimum cost for the entire network.

TRANSPART requires the following input data:

(1) Value, weight, and density of each product;
(2) Demand for each product by assembly plant;
(3) Freight charge on each link;
(4) Transit time on each link;
(5) Warehouse material handling time; and
(6) Inventory carrying charge.

Product values are the prices Delco charges assembly plants and are needed in the calculation of inventory costs. Product weights and densities (weight per unit volume) are inferred from packaging data, account for container characteristics, and are needed to ensure their shipment sizes do not exceed truck capacity (maximum weight or volume).

Demands are the number of each product required per week by each assembly plant and are obtained from records of assembly-plant production volumes.

Delco produces about 300 different product types grouped into about 40 families of similar products. Each shipment from a Delco plant to a GM assembly plant typically contains a variety of products. To properly reflect this mix, the notion of a **composite product** was developed. A composite product is a proportional mixture of all of the product types shipped together on a link. The value of the composite product is the demand-weighted average of the values of the different products shipped on that link. Composite product weight and density are determined similarly.

The freight charge on each link is the cost of a truck shipment on this link. This charge was modelled as a fixed amount per load, independent of the size or weight of the load. This representation is supported by actual freight rate data and the fact that a carrier's operating expenses are nearly the same whether the transportation equipment travels empty or full. The freight charge was taken to be the full-truckload rate, available from freight rate data. This means, for example, that shipping trucks half full (to reduce inventory costs) results in a transportation cost per item that is double that of full-truck shipments.

Transit times (days per shipment) were obtained from historical data on truck shipments. An estimate of the average warehouse material handling time was provided by Delco. As a first approximation, this time was assumed to be independent of the total flow of material through the warehouse.

The inventory-carrying charge reflects the cost of holding products in inventory. It is expressed as a percentage of product-value-per-unit time. An estimate of this percentage was provided by Delco for its product inventory. This estimate reflects the opportunity cost of money and the cost of insurance, material handling, storage space, and obsolescence.

The FORTRAN program written for TRANSPART uses the network decomposition solution technique described above to evaluate the costs of alternative shipping strategies. This program provides as output the routes and shipment sizes that minimize total corporate costs for Delco's network. It also provides a breakdown of cost by link. This allows the cost of shipping products from each Delco plant to be accounted for separately and identifies which costs are paid by Delco and which by other GM divisions. This organizational impact is important when implementing results. Finally, for each link, the tool analyses the sensitivity of total cost to changes in shipment size around the optimum.

This is important in identifying links for which shipment size has a big influence on cost.

16.7 THE RESULTS FOR DELCO ELECTRONICS

The research results, network model, computer program, and data allowed Delco to answer questions regarding

(1) Trade-offs between transportation and inventory costs;
(2) Costs associated with alternative shipment frequencies and routes;
(3) Cost differences between the optimal (that is, minimum cost) routeing strategy and routeing strategies that are simpler and easier to manage (for example, all-direct shipments or all-warehouse shipments),
(4) The sensitivity of results to changes in key parameters such as warehouse material-handling time, inventory-carrying charge, and freight rates, and
(5) The impact of different routeing strategies on the shipping costs of Delco products incurred by different GM organizations (for example, individual Delco plants, the warehouse, and GM assembly plants).

We feel that providing Delco with the knowledge to answer such questions properly was more important than the immediate dollar savings. Delco no longer had to speculate about the merits of alternative strategies. It could evaluate them objectively instead. Delco was also in a position to adjust its shipping strategy as conditions changed (for example, as inventory-carrying costs changed with changes in interest rates). In fact, we believe that Delco had the opportunity to reduce product shipping costs in 1981 primarily because conditions had changed substantially since the company decided to build its warehouse in the late 1970s. Between 1979 and 1981, the freight industry was deregulated, and interest rates increased significantly.

16.8 SINGLE-LINK RESULTS

Because we focused on trade-offs and provided graphical answers, the usefulness of our work and the merits of various strategies could be illustrated easily. Figure 6.4, for example, was used to demonstrate the effect of shipment size on direct shipments between the Delco plant in Milwaukee, Wisconsin and the GM Assembly Plant in Baltimore, Maryland. While this figure presents a standard economic order quality

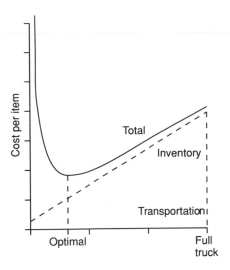

Figure 16.4 The economic order quantity (EOQ) relationship between cost and shipment size on a link, showing the trade-off between transportation and inventory costs for shipments from Delco Electronics Milwaukee plant to GM's Baltimore assembly plant.

(EOQ) relationship, showing it graphically is enlightening. At a glance, one can see that transportation and inventory costs need to be managed together and that myopically pursuing one objective (for example, minimizing transportation costs) can result in radically higher total costs. One can also tell that a wide range of shipment sizes result in costs close to the minimum. Finally, the penalty incurred by shipping direct in very small quantities to meet just-in-time delivery objectives can be inferred. Such graphical representations of the trade-offs would later prove to be very important in attaining corporate-wide use of our research results.

16.9 NETWORK RESULTS

Presenting trade-offs graphically was also effective in evaluating Delco's entire product shipping network (Fig. 16.5) Results are presented for shipping full loads, routeing all shipments direct, and routeing all shipments through the warehouse, because these strategies are relatively easy to control and manage. Results are also presented for shipping optimal load sizes, using a combination of

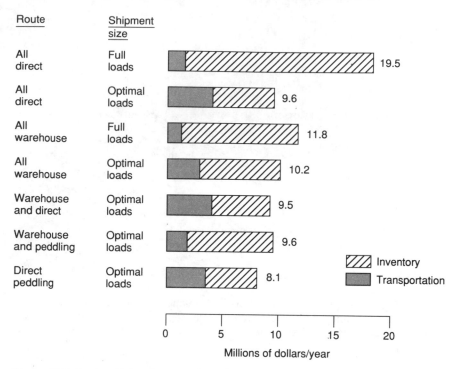

Figure 16.5 Trade-offs between total transportation and inventory cost estimates for various shipping strategies over Delco Electronics' entire North American product distribution network.

direct and warehouse routeing, and peddling, because Delco had no means of evaluating these more complex strategies prior to our research.

Figure 16.5 reveals that

(1) Delco's decisions regarding shipment sizes and routes were highly interrelated. As an example, the attractiveness of the all-direct and all-warehouse strategies depends on the extent to which optimal load sizes are used. Using optimal shipment sizes is not as important for the all-warehouse strategy because consolidating flows on links reduces the sensitivity of link costs to shipment size.
(2) The best mixture of direct and warehouse routeing (without peddling) was only 1% less costly than the simpler all-direct strategy. This best mixture had 56% direct routeings.
(3) Peddling direct was significantly less costly than the other routeing strategies considered. (This strategy defined nine peddling regions

based on the geographical proximity of GM assembly plants. These regions varied in size from one to five plants.)

16.10 SENSITIVITY ANALYSES

In 1981, Delco was routeing all shipments through the warehouse. GM's cost-accounting methods made it difficult to isolate actual transportation and inventory costs for Delco's products for a given set of conditions. We therefore had to estimate a range of potential savings. We knew Delco shipped full loads on some (but not all) warehouse links. Thus, an upper bound on their 1981 cost was $11.8 million per year (all full loads) and a lower bound was $10.2 million per year (all optimal loads). This suggested a potential savings of 21–31% ($2.1–3.7 million per year) by peddling direct from each Delco plant. Our best estimate of the overall savings is the middle of this range, 26% or $2.9 million per year. This estimate is the total corporate savings, accounting for the cost impact on both Delco and GM assembly plants.

We were delighted by the results. Peddling direct, which only recently had become attractive because of trucking industry deregulation, offered significant freight consolidation advantages without a high inventory cost and without the additional transportation cost of routeing via the warehouse. However, before concluding that Delco should begin peddling direct from all of their plants, we wanted to better understand the sensitivity of our results to changes in key parameters. Two parameters were especially important: inventory-carrying costs and warehouse material-handling time.

Inventory-carrying cost is difficult to estimate precisely. In addition to the opportunity cost of capital, carrying cost depends on insurance, handling, storage, and obsolescence costs of holding inventory. Furthermore, because interest rates had been increasing rapidly, we were convinced that carrying cost would continue to fluctuate.

As shown in Fig. 16.6, the savings potential associated with direct peddling (relative to the previously discussed base case) varies from 21% to 28% as the carrying charge doubles from 15% to 30% per year. Thus, a significant savings opportunity existed for a broad range of carrying charges. This sensitivity analysis was far simpler than precisely measuring the carrying charge for Delco's products, and it increased our confidence in the merits of direct peddling.

Warehouse material-handling time directly affected the attractiveness of the warehouse-routeing strategies. Embarking on an effort to reduce handling time may have been the most cost-effective way to reduce Delco product shipping costs.

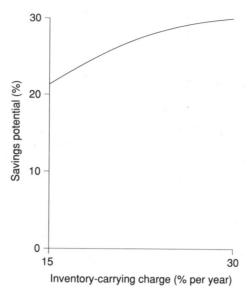

Figure 16.6 The cost-savings potential from the direct peddling strategy, showing a significant savings opportunity for a broad range of inventory-carrying charges.

Figure 16.7 illustrates the sensitivity of results to warehouse material-handling time. Delco's best estimate of this time in 1981 was two days. Figure 16.7a pertains to non-peddling strategies and Fig. 16.7b pertains to peddling strategies.

We learned from Fig. 16.7a that without peddling, the base case all-warehouse strategy is less costly than the all-direct strategy with optimal loads when handling time is less than a half day. Furthermore, as would be expected, the warehouse/direct strategy is always better than either all-direct or the base case. The cost difference here is about $1 million per year for handling times ranging from zero to two days. Finally, we learned that reducing material-handling time from two days to a half day would reduce base case costs by about $1 million per year. Certainly, making an effort to do this was one viable strategy for Delco.

We learned from Fig. 16.7b that peddling direct and peddling from the warehouse are less costly than the base case for all-warehouse material-handling times. Also, warehouse peddling becomes less costly than direct peddling when warehouse-handling time is below a half day. Again, attempting to reduce material-handling time appeared to be a key option for Delco. More importantly though, peddling (while somewhat more complex than the direct or warehouse strategies)

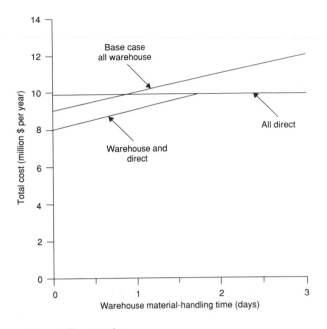

(a) Non-peddling strategies

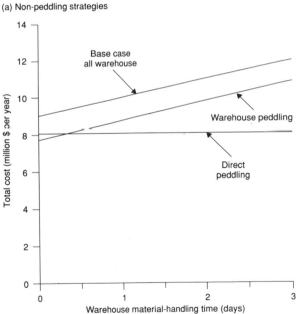

(b) Peddling strategies

Figure 16.7 The effect of warehouse material-handling time on total network cost estimates for different shipping strategies.

appeared to offer a promising opportunity for a broad variety of conditions.

Given that peddling looked promising, we decided to examine its impact on products shipped from each Delco plant. It turned out that 66% of the total savings accrued to products shipped from the Milwaukee plant. These products accounted for only 16% of the total products shipped by Delco. This suggested that a major savings might be realized by changing only the routes for products shipped from Milwaukee.

The preceding results made it clear that Delco could use a variety of strategies to reduce their product distribution costs. They could attempt to change shipping routes, ship optimal load sizes, reduce warehouse material-handling time, or renegotiate freight rates. By adjusting shipment sizes and routes alone, costs could be reduced by $2.9 million per year (26%). More important though, Delco was now in a position to evaluate a wide spectrum of strategies under a wide variety of conditions objectively. For example, because routeing and shipment size decisions are short term in nature, the model can be applied to quickly respond to fluctuations in demand, which are characteristic of the car industry.

16.11 THE IMPACT ON DELCO ELECTRONICS

In April 1982, Delco began applying the model on their own and pursuing strategies to reduce costs. Initially, they decided to continue their all-warehouse strategy (but use optimal shipment sizes) and to try to reduce warehouse material-handling time. These options offered immediate savings without having to adjust routes. However, because of congestion in the warehouse, Delco concluded that material-handling time could not be reduced significantly without reducing the amount of material flowing through the warehouse. This gave them an added incentive to use routeing strategies other than the all-warehouse strategy.

Delco's next step was to begin shipping direct from Milwaukee since this was the plant that offered the largest savings from changing routes. This also reduced warehouse congestion for the remaining products routed through the warehouse. Delco used a combination of direct shipping and peddling from Milwaukee, depending on the relative proximity of assembly plants. They continue to do this today.

Since 1982, Delco has applied the model to address several changes and to explore new strategies. Examples of how it continues to use the model include determining

(1) The best shipping strategy for a new Delco product manufactured in Hillsdale, Michigan – the Delco/Bose sound system;
(2) The best use of foreign trade zones for products shipped from Mexico;
(3) When electronic control modules should be shipped to distant assembly plants by air;
(4) Whether to use sea or air transportation for products from Singapore;
(5) The merits of combining Delco's Milwaukee products with other GM freight from Milwaukee in 'collecting' routes to assembly plants; and
(6) The best route for speaker components purchased from a Japanese supplier.

16.12 CORPORATE-WIDE IMPLEMENTATION

The success at Delco motivated us to implement our research throughout the corporation. We suspected that our results might apply in some form to almost every material shipment made to GM's component and assembly plants. This included opportunities to shift modes (truck, rail, sea, air), adjust shipment sizes, or change routes. It was an exciting and timely endeavour because of the rising popularity of just-in-time delivery strategies and because of new shipping strategies growing out of freight deregulation.

How could we effectively, efficiently, and quickly get our results disseminated and used throughout GM? We sent reports that documented the research, data and computer program, and results underlying our experience at Delco to all of the transportation (traffic) and materials management executives in GM. We also hosted a one-day workshop with representatives from each GM division. This sparked interest, but did not lead to rapid, corporate-wide implementation. Several impediments existed: (1) data were not readily available for most divisions, (2) the FORTRAN computer program written for Delco was tailored to its operation and was not user-friendly, and (3) our reports and workshop used equations which several potential users found difficult to apply.

We needed to overcome these impediments. One option was to work toward a new corporate information system that provided computer access to required data and a general computer program that applied to all divisions. We were concerned that this would be costly and require a long lead-time. While we were seeking an alternative to this top-down, centralized approach, an idea surfaced from a potential user, Jerry Spencer, Assistant Traffic Manager at the Chevrolet Flint Engine Plant. He had read one of our reports and was looking for a way to apply our findings without having to manually stick numbers in formulae. He began experimenting with using our research results on his personal computer to solve problems confronted by his engine plant.

Personal computers were just becoming available in GM. When Jerry shared his idea with us, a light went on! We did not fully recognize it at the time but, in retrospect, Jerry's idea was the key that opened a door to an exciting new approach to decision-support-system development and implementation in GM. We proceeded to develop a prototype of a user-friendly personal computer decision tool on an IBM-XT, which captured key features of the Delco model and presented solutions graphically. Our prototype, which focused on transportation/inventory cost trade-offs for direct routeing, took about three days to develop.

We then developed a more user-friendly prototype that took advantage of colour graphics and incorporated several additional analysis options. This second prototype was programmed by one systems analyst in about three months.

Next, pilot tests were performed at five GM plants. At that time, GM had created a new management science activity that is currently called the Decision Technologies Division (DTD) of Electronic Data Systems (EDS). Its objective was to gain widespread use of decision analysis tools throughout GM.

Decision Technologies viewed our decision tool as one of several around which they could begin building their organization. Greg Herrin of Decision Technologies, and Tom Matwiejczyk, then of GM Logistics Operations and now of the GM Truck and Bus Group, took the lead in pilot testing our prototype to refine it and to ascertain its value under a variety of settings.

The pilot tests were encouraging and useful. GM plants provided suggestions that made the tool easier to use and more general. Decision Technologies finalized the software and now had evidence that TRANSPART would be a valuable product to market widely. The pilot tests also identified several savings opportunities for the plants involved. Greg Herrin and Bob Lawson of Decision Technologies marketed the final product throughout GM and provided support for its use.

Decision Technologies' product, called TRANSPART II, is used today in over 40 GM plants and is being considered for sale outside GM. The following quotes describe the kinds of effects it has had:

With the aid of the TRANSPART system, GM of Canada saved approximately \$157 000 on carrier selections in four months. Currently we're very active in developing an inventory control system that lends itself to the 'just-in-time' concept. Our traffic department uses TRANSPART in all transportation-inventory analyses. The system has helped us complete our transportation-inventory studies in a more efficient and timely manner.

> *Jeff Abbott, Supervisor of GEEM and Expedited Services, Oshawa Traffic Department, GM of Canada*

We've known all the variables in inventory costs for a long time. But before TRANSPART we never had a way to consider all the variables in time to make decisions about inventory levels. I used TRANSPART over a period of four weeks to analyse the total costs involved in setting our maximum in-plant inventory level. I discussed my proposed changes with Production Control to make sure they made sense. The adjustments we agreed upon are saving us over \$35 000 per year.

> *Wayne Starr, General Supervisor of Inventory Management, Pontiac Motor Division (now with Chevrolet–Pontiac Canada Group)*

TRANSPART was very effective in helping us make rail vs. truck carrier comparisons for our [Astro/Safari] Van project in Baltimore. In Logistics, we're always dealing with transportation costs and shipping frequency. Trying to come up with an optimum strategy considering those factors individually – plus inventory costs – is almost hopeless without a computer. TRANSPART takes this complex situation and handles it for you. It ties into 'just-in-time', the name of the game today. Once you've seen how TRANSPART can help you, it's obvious you should use it. Eventually we want to integrate TRANSPART into our whole materials scheduling system. Now that's a big project. TRANSPART is a bandwagon we're going to jump on right now!

> *Larry Lamon, Senior Administrator, Central Office Logistics, GM Truck and Bus Operations*

A key ingredient in the successful and rapid evolution of TRANSPART II was the decentralized approach to system development and implementation offered by personal computers. This approach provides many independent users with the autonomy (from the standpoint of both system support and budget) to apply tools on their own and in the privacy of their own offices. As a result, they can take full responsibility and credit for their use of a tool. They do not need to seek approval or wait for priority. And, they are not dependent on the results and schedules of others.

16.13 MORE COMPLEX NETWORKS

We also had an opportunity to extend our research to solve problems for more complex networks. This included networks with many supplier plants, several consolidation terminals (including warehouses), and many destination plants. It also included collecting and peddling (that is, making pick-ups from more than one supplier per load and deliveries to more than one destination per load) on networks with hundreds and even thousands of suppliers and destinations.

Our research in dealing with more complex networks followed two paths. The first extended the solution technique developed for Delco. This extension identifies optimal routes for networks with over 1000 suppliers and on the order of 30 destinations (or vice versa); and one or more consolidation terminals. The routeing decision on such networks is a minimum-cost, multi-commodity flow problem with concave cost functions (Zangwill 1968). this important class of problems has received much less attention than network flow problems with linear or convex cost functions. The solution method developed here finds optimal routes graphically and is sufficiently efficient to be programmed on a hand calculator or personal computer.

This extended tool has been applied successfully by the GM Warehousing and Distribution Division to identify a significant savings opportunity. This division has a network of about 1000 suppliers, seven consolidation centres, and about 40 distribution centres. The application involved evaluating routeing strategies for shipping sheet metal parts from one of its main suppliers to the distribution centres. The network decomposition technique described previously allowed the evaluation to be performed properly without the need for information on other suppliers. The division selected this technique over several others it considered because it was the only one that correctly accounted for freight scale economies and because it required minimal data.

The second path used methods from geometric probability to develop formulae that help identify optimal collecting and peddling strategies when hundreds or even thousands of suppliers or destinations exist. These methods have been published in Daganzo (1984a, 1984b, 1985), Burns *et al.* (1985) and Hall (1985). They focus on the spatial densities of suppliers and destinations, and the distributions of production volumes and demands, rather than precise data on each individual location. This simplifies the analysis of logistics problems by eliminating the need to specify a detailed network and corresponding flows. It also results in formulae that allow cost trade-offs to be understood clearly, rather than in mathematical programming techniques that, in their pursuit of optimization, tend to obscure trade-offs.

The formulae for collecting and peddling costs are useful for practical applications and require only estimates of a few easily measurable parameters. For example, in 1983 the collecting formulae were used to evaluate shipments from a large number of suppliers to a GM warehouse in Westland, Michigan. This application identified an opportunity to save 44% of transportation and inventory costs for these shipments. The formulae have also been applied in planning material shipments to GM's Buick City Plant in Flint, Michigan. Finally, the collecting formulae are incorporated in TRANSPART II.

16.14 SUMMARY OF THE EFFECTS ON GENERAL MOTORS

The research, decision-tool development, and implementation described here have had a number of major effects on GM:

(1) GM has a new proven approach to decision-support-systems development and implementation. It is decentralized, expedites implementation benefits, and avoids large-scale system development costs. It involves
   (a) Focusing on simple, transparent decision models that require minimal data, highlight trade-offs, and present results graphically;
   (b) Rapid prototyping, using personal computers and involving potential users (to create a sense of user ownership);
   (c) Pilot testing in real settings to obtain quick prototype refinement and documented savings; and
   (d) Providing widespread corporate exposure by disseminating descriptive brochures, users' manuals (with real examples from pilot test), and diskettes.
(2) GM has new and simple techniques for analysing and solving large, complex network problems. They are based on decomposing a network into much simpler subnetworks and using analytical formulae to evaluate shipping strategies. The techniques are original research contributions to network theory and have been published in refereed journals. They are used in GM to reduce logistics costs and plan logistics operations, and they allow GM to solve network problems that it could not solve before.
   GM can now also resolve the conflicting objectives that result in logistics networks due to organizational boundaries. These occur

because shipping materials typically results in ownership changes, and traffic and material control departments sometimes function independently. The techniques focus on trade-offs and therefore help bridge organizational boundaries.

(3) GM has an improved understanding of the implications of just-in-time manufacturing on freight transportation costs. GM Divisions can now evaluate freight consolidation strategies, such as collecting and peddling, as means of attaining just-in-time delivery objectives (that is, frequent, small loads) without changing supplier locations or increasing freight transportation costs significantly.

(4) Delco Electronics has a new computerized decision tool for evaluating its product shipping strategies. It is used on a regular basis and allows Delco Electronics to properly adjust strategies to changes in conditions and thus avoid cost increases that could result from these changes.

(5) Delco Electronics has implemented strategies that have an estimated product shipping cost reduction of 26% ($2.9 million per year). They are based on extensive sensitivity analyses Delco Electronics performed using the decision tool.

(6) GM has a new personal computer decision tool (TRANSPART II) that is currently in use at over 40 GM facilities. The savings at different facilities vary widely with documented examples ranging from $35 000 to $500 000 per year per application.

(7) GM Warehousing and Distribution Division can now effectively evaluate product-routeing strategies over its vast network. It is using the decision-tool extension for large networks to consider substantially more routeing options than it could consider previously. This technique is the only one the division could find that uses minimal data and properly captures freight scale economies.

These examples demonstrate the widespread use of the management science tools we developed for logistics decisions in GM. Many decision makers are applying these tools in their everyday work because they are easy to use and understand. Furthermore, our tools and their implementation have greatly enhanced the image of management science within GM.

16.15 MANAGEMENT SCIENCE LESSONS

As a result of our experience, we learned several management science lessons, which should increase the likelihood that decision tools will be used and decrease the time for their implementation.

First, regarding management science research, we learned that it is worthwhile to pursue results that allow simple decision models and principles to be developed. Formulating models that are simple functions of a few key parameters with clear physical interpretations help make decision tools transparent and meaningful to potential users. Transparency is important because decision makers justifiably want to understand the logic underlying decision tools.

Second, regarding decision tool development, we learned that tools evolving from the rigour of management science methods are more likely to be used if they do not require users to have sophisticated skills. Such tools should focus on quantifying trade-offs between key variables, using a minimal amount of data, facilitating sensitivity analyses, and presenting ranges of solutions graphically. They should aid in evaluating several options and highlighting the implications of decisions that are practical alternatives to optimal solutions. In this way, if for practical reasons an optimal solution cannot be implemented, the user can identify numerous options that are feasible in practice and nearly optimal.

Third, regarding decision-tool implementation, we learned that it is imperative that users share a sense of ownership in a tool A decentralized approach to decision-tool implementation facilitates this because it frees individual decision makers from having to accept the findings of a central group. Instead, it encourages them to generate their own findings, take pride in their individual accomplishments, and monitor the implications of their own decision.

Fourth, regarding both decision-tool development and implementation, we learned that personal computers are a powerful medium. They can reduce system development time, 'front-load' system benefits, reduce costs, and enhance the chances of a system being used.

Finally, regarding management science in general, we learned never to forget that people make decisions, not models or computers. Management scientists must therefore be exceptional listeners and view potential users as their most important resource. This certainly was the case for us, as evidenced by the contributions of Jim Schneider and Jerry Spencer. Jim's willingness and ability to clearly communicate Delco's challenge was instrumental in specifying research objectives. Jerry's initiative and foresight in proposing that TRANSPART be programmed on a personal computer was the key to gaining corporate-wide implementation.

In summary, our experience in reducing logistics costs at General Motors taught us several lessons for successful management science. These lessons are not unique to our experience. They reinforce lessons others have learned in the past, and reflecting on them can enhance the chances that future management science endeavours will have significant impact in practice.

16.16 ACKNOWLEDGMENTS

The accomplishments described here would not have been possible without the contributions of a large team of people. Clearly, Jim Schneider and Jerry Spencer played critical roles. In addition, listed by their affiliation at the time of their contributions, are

(1) Delco Electronics Division: Don Collins, Bob Costello, Tom Endres, and Brian Plante;
(2) Decision Technologies Division of Electronic Data Systems: Frank Babel, Greg Herrin, Bob Lawson, and John Lucas;
(3) GM Logistics Operations: Jerry Bodrie, Don Griffin, and Tom Matwiejczyk;
(4) GM Assembly Division: John Martin and Ray Taylor;
(5) GM Warehousing and Distribution Division: Dave Hansen;
(6) GM Research Laboratories: David Diltz, Tom Morrisey, Dick Rothery, and Bill Spreitzer.

Finally, most important are the users of the tools described here. Their contributions throughout this effort assured the acceptability of our tools.

16.17 APPENDIX: PROOF THAT THE NETWORK DECOMPOSITION METHOD IDENTIFIES THE OPTIMAL SHIPPING STRATEGY

Consider a network of two origins and many destinations and a corresponding subnetwork for one destination (Fig. 16.8).
Let

D = destination on subnetwork,
C_D^{DIR} = cost per unit time on a direct link to D,
C^{IN} = cost per unit time on an inbound link to the warehouse,
C_D^{OUT} = cost per unit time on an outbound link from the warehouse to D,
C_D^{SUB} = cost per unit time on subnetwork, and
C^{TOT} = cost per unit time on entire network.

 The subnetwork in Fig. 16.8 consists of two inbound links, two direct links, and one outbound link. Therefore, the cost per unit time on all links to D is

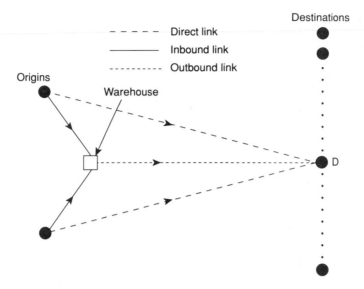

Figure 16.8 Subnetwork links for direct and warehouse shipping strategies.

$$\sum_{1}^{2} C^{IN} + \sum_{1}^{2} C_D^{DIR} + C_D^{OUT}, \tag{1}$$

where $\sum_{1}^{2}$ denotes summation of costs over two links. (Equation (1) assumes[1] C_D^{OUT} includes the inventory cost due to material-handling time at the warehouse.)

The direct and outbound links are different for each destination, but the two inbound links are common to subnetworks for all destinations. Therefore C^{TOT} is given by

$$C^{TOT} = \sum_{1}^{2} C^{IN} + \sum_{D} \left[\sum_{1}^{2} C_D^{DIR} + C_D^{OUT} \right], \tag{2}$$

where $\sum_{D}$ denotes summation over all destinations.

Consider one inbound link. The cost per part, C, on this link is (Blumenfeld et al. 1985).

$$C = PR \left(\frac{V}{Q} + T \right) + \frac{F}{V}, \tag{3}$$

where P, V, Q, T, and F are the part value, shipment size, flow, transit time, and freight rate, respectively, on this link, and R is the inventory-carrying charge. Therefore, the cost per unit time on this link is

$$C^{IN} = QC \tag{4}$$

$$= PRV + PRTQ + \frac{F}{V} Q. \tag{5}$$

For fixed V, this cost is linear in flow Q.

The flow Q on this link is made up of part demands at all destinations receiving these parts via the warehouse. Therefore, denoting the demand via the warehouse to destination D by q_D,

$$Q = \sum_D q_D, \tag{6}$$

and

$$C^{IN} = PRV + PRT \sum_D q_D + \frac{F}{V} \sum_D q_D. \tag{7}$$

Hence, for fixed V,

$$C^{IN} = PRV + \sum_D (PRTq_D + \frac{F}{V} Q_D) \tag{8}$$

$$= \text{Constant} + \sum_D C_D^{IN}, \tag{9}$$

where C_D^{IN} is the cost on the inbound link attributable to D.

Therefore,

$$C^{TOT} = \sum_1^2 [\text{Constant} + \sum_D C_D^{IN}]$$

$$+ \sum_D [\sum_1^2 C_D^{DIR} + C_D^{OUT}] \tag{10}$$

$$= \text{Constant}$$

$$+ \sum_D [\sum_1^2 C_D^{IN} \sum_1^2 C_D^{DIR} + C_D^{OUT}] \tag{11}$$

$$= \text{Constant} + \sum_D C_D^{SUB} \tag{12}$$

Thus, for fixed shipment sizes on the two inbound links, C^{TOT} is the sum of a constant and subnetwork costs. It can therefore be minimized by minimizing the costs on the subnetwork for each destination separately.

16.17 REFERENCES

Arrow, K.J., Karlin, S. and Scarf, H. (1958) *Studies in the Mathematical Theory of Inventory and Production*, Stanford University Press, Stanford, California.

Blumenfeld, D.E., Burns, L.D., Diltz, J.D. and Daganzo, C.F. (1985) Analyzing trade-offs between transportation, inventory and production costs on freight networks, *Transportation Research*, **19B**(5), 361–80.

Burns, L.D., Hall, R.W., Blumenfeld, D.E. and Daganzo, C.F. (1985) Distribution strategies that minimize transportation and inventory costs, *Operations Research*, **33**(3), 469–90.

Daganzo, C.F. (1984a) The length of tours in zones of different shapes, *Transportation Research*, **18B**(2), 135–45.

Daganzo, C.F. (1984b) The distance traveled to visit N points with a maximum of C stops per vehicle: An analytic model and an application, *Transportation Science*, **18**(4), 331–50.

Daganzo, C.F. (1985) Supplying a single location from heterogeneous sources, *Transportation Research*, **19B**(5), 409–19.

Hall, R.W. (1984) *Principles for routing freight through transportation terminals*, General Motors Research Laboratories, Research Publication GMR-4772.

Hall, R.W. (1985) Determining vehicle dispatch frequency when shipping frequency differs among suppliers, *Transportation Research*, **19B**(5), 421–31. 4517, forthcoming in Transportation Research.

Magee, J.F. and Boodman, D.M. (1967) *Production Planning and Inventory Control*, McGraw-Hill, New York.

Newell, G.F. (1980) *Traffic Flow on Transportation Networks*, MIT Press Series in Transportation Studies, No. 5, Cambridge, Massachusetts.

Zangwill, W.I. (1968) Minimum concave cost flows in certain networks, *Management Science*, **14**(7), 429–50.

CHAPTER SEVENTEEN

Logistics for service support in the computer industry

D. Little, J. Mosquera and A.M.A. Wild

INTRODUCTION

The ability of high-technology industries to swiftly repair electronic equipment which has failed can have an impact upon the business out of all proportion to the cost of repair. Providing such a service across a range of equipment which is geographically widely described has proved a considerable logistical problem.

The speed by which such companies provide service (field support) for their products, and the quality of the service, has a demonstrable impact on equipment sales. As product complexity and product mix increase, the consequences of down-time become more apparent and field-service maintenance (FSM) becomes a strategic issue. One extreme solution in providing adequate support is with a large engineer workforce and a high spare-parts inventory. This is not viewed as effective logistics management and creates a high service cost to the customer.

The majority of solutions to the management of this logistical problem centre on computerized control of the spares inventory, the allocation of key resources (spares and engineers), and the regular shipment of replenishment stock. Most solutions in the industry are characterized by reactive methods of dealing with demand changes.

Source: Little, D., Mosquera, J. and Wild, A.M.A. (1987) *Proc. 7th International Logistics Conference*, London, 30–35

A predictive approach to parts failure is comparatively uncommon, although several mathematical models exist (Clarke 1972). There are two categories of importance: the logistic support models and the multi-echelon inventory models. The former works typically ignore the multi-echelon structure or lack the capacity to measure system performance (Department of the Air Force 1971). The latter works are either analytical or simulation models. The analytical models (Sherbrooke 1968; Muckstadt 1960) cannot efficiently cope with the data and computing requirements of the FSM operation. Their major shortcoming is the inability to provide adequate performance analysis. The simulation work often, for simplicity, ignores the multi-echelon problem or places the emphasis of analysis in a different area (Clarke 1960; Hitzelberger 1985). Our research is concerned with analysis of the operating characteristics of the complete FSM system. The use of simulation is now seen as a flexible means of modelling many of the complexities to be found within FSM operations. It is also considered a robust means of exploring the many possibilities in which inventory may be distributed to support the operation.

This paper discusses the research work undertaken by Liverpool University. It draws upon a major survey conducted by the authors under the auspices of Midas Consultants (Mosquera and Wild 1987) and work within the UK Spares and Logistics function, ICL (UK) Limited.

17.1 THE MULTI-ECHELON STRUCTURE

The field-service logistics operation commonly uses a 'tree structure' method of spares distribution. Figure 17.1 shows a central stores at the apex supplying regional and local stores. The local stores directly supports the engineer activity which interfaces with the customer.

The very nature of demand for spares typically creates three classes of inventory; slow-, medium- and fast-moving items which are generally held at central, regional and local stores respectively. There will, however, exist some degree of duplication of spares at each echelon. The level of spares holding directly reflects the frequency of demand and the ability of the system to respond to the demand. The latter is a function of the products supported, distribution of customer sites and number of engineers.

The survey has shown that although four echelons of spares holding are identified, always one, and sometimes two echelons are omitted. Each echelon has a clearly defined purpose as follows.

Central stores usually procures and distributes spares. It controls the

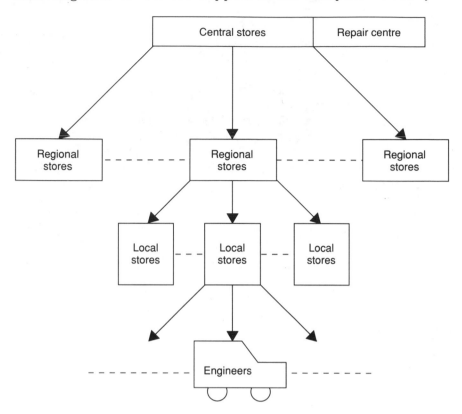

Figure 17.1 The multi-echelon structure.

flow of spares through the network and oversees the repair activity. It holds the slow-moving parts.

Regional stores hold medium-moving spares for a faster response to emergency demands within the region. It monitors and controls the field activity.

Local stores hold fast-moving spares to replenish the van and swap kits, and usually acts as the first-line support to the engineer.

In all cases, the travelling engineer is the interface between the customer and the FSM operation. He is ultimately responsible for both diagnosis and repair.

17.1.1 The repair activity

The repair activity handles the large volume of spares which are capable of being returned to an operational status. All other items are

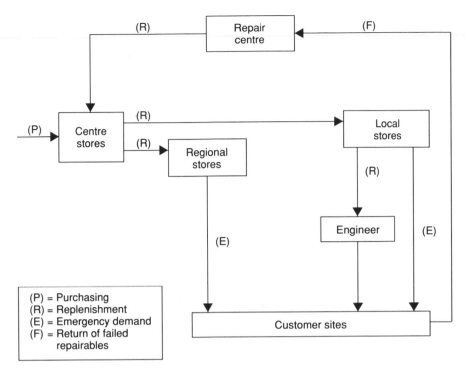

Figure 17.2 A typical inventory distribution path.

deemed consumable. The repair centre is usually attached to the central stores, although increasingly a limited repair capability is to be found within the local stores. Most repairables are cycled through the logistics system. The differing frequencies of demand necessitate that certain spares be repaired before others, effectively creating a priority repair system. In practice, these priorities are assessed informally.

Figure 17.2 shows a typical inventory distribution path which is, however, subject to much variation. Though simplified, the figure highlights those elements which a logistics control system account for: the multi-echelon structure, the distribution network and the feedback loop within it. The consequential balancing of internal supply to meet external demand becomes most critical at the local store/engineer interface.

Spare-parts logistics is concerned with having the correct parts and skills available at the right place and time to fix a failed system. In its effort to achieve this, industry has adopted many structures and logistic techniques. No one solution is correct, but all possibilities need assessment.

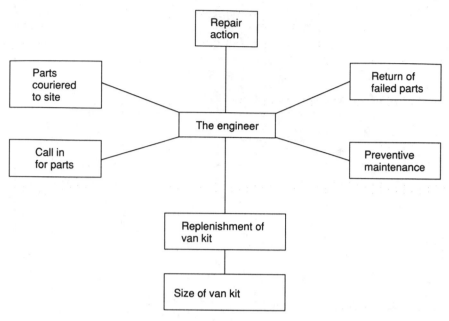

Figure 17.3 The engineer's environment.

17.2 MANAGEMENT OF FSM

The main objective of FSM may be broadly stated so as to maximize the availability of spare parts and engineer utilization, whilst minimizing the total operating cost. The primary measure of the function is the customer-service level achieved within a given time. Management of FSM covers four areas:

(1) The organizational structure
(2) The scheduling of repair activities
(3) The movement of spares around the system
(4) The performance monitoring of the system

There are several multi-echelon structures used by companies in the FSM operation to achieve this goal, based on the generic model depicted in Fig. 17.1. To effectively manage the system, its many varied activities must be reviewed in order to explore alternative strategies. This may indicate a need for a radical reappraisal of current working practices. Such a process requires some form of representational model, and also a high degree of managerial vision.

The person most directly involved in fault analysis and repair is the field engineer. His key activities are represented in Fig. 17.3. In an ideal world he would have all spares immediately at his disposal. Cost considerations alone make this impossible. One common solution is to give him a limited range of spares that he is most likely to require, such that he has a reasonable expectancy of repairing a fault each time he attends a call. This range of spares, referred to as a 'van kit', proves difficult to define. A van kit is a concept providing general cover over several products throughout a local area. The recent survey conducted by the authors has indicated that engineers utilizing van kits are averaging two calls per day.

Another solution is to withdraw all spares, except low-cost consumables (e.g. fuses, switches, etc.) to the local stores, making swap kits available to the engineer. A swap kit is a complete range of spares needed to repair a particular product. When an engineer is requested he either picks up a swap kit from local stores or, if he is already in the field, uses the kit he has to hand.

In this case the initial decision on which spares should be held is eliminated, but even here the logistics of spares supply and engineer allocation can become complex. In particular, the requirement that an engineer always returns a swap kit to stores is very limiting on engineer utilization. An apparent contradiction shown by the survey indicates that engineers utilizing swap kits are averaging three calls per day, slightly better than those using van kits. However, since scheduling of work can often be made twice daily, it is not unexpected to find swap kits proving more effective. In rural areas this would be good, however, since most engineers operate out of major conurbations, the figure is still considered somewhat poor.

Another problem concerning FSM and more especially the characteristic multi-echelon structure, is the level of sparing required at each echelon, and the consequential transport costs and lead times associated with such a decision. Routine replenishment of the lower echelons has been found to occur predominantly on an overnight basis, whereas supply from manufacture still requires scheduling. Concentrating solely upon the need to supply an emergency demand swiftly, the transport costs and time penalties of holding most spares at a central location are obvious. Basing one's assumption on the wish to provide a comprehensive service to the customer, it is critical to the manager that spares are located at an echelon that reflects demand and, thereby, maintains his ability to rapidly supply a spare to a customer site (typically four hours). Whereas lead-time consideration is not as important with routine replenishment, it is evidently a major factor when considering supply from manufacture and of emergency demands.

An added problem which makes the logistics system more complex is the existence of **repairable** inventory. These are high-cost spares which can be restored to their designed operating state without incurring enormous costs to do so. Since such a high proportion of inventory (80% or more) is repairable, one is not so much sparing purely for field demand, but to a demand which can be satisfied by the logistics operation as a whole. In this case, the inventory levels of the repairables are sensitive to the turn-round time (lead time) of the repair cycle.

There are three key activities demanded of the logistics manager:

(1) *Logistics control* is the fundamental activity in which a manager and his team are engaged – the management of the logistics system. Frequently the system is set up and allowed to run indefinitely within the operating parameters seen as appropriate at set-up. In such a system management tends to be reactive, where only identified problem areas are specifically dealt with as they occur. Implicit in this approach is an accumulation of information not readily being tapped. This information could provide the logic for opting to change a particular service structure or inventory distribution.
(2) *Performance monitoring* entails setting levels which are realistic and achievable. Against these, the performance of stores, engineers and inventory can be judged.
(3) *Demand prediction* and system performance analysis is an activity which has experienced little attention. It relates to the analysis of how the system is likely to perform given a different structure or a changing product base, and why it behaves the way it does. It requires that all knowledge be brought to bear in a form which allows strategic decisions to be made.

Activities (1) and (2) are very typical of the FSM operation, but they offer little insight into the problem of FSM management and no means of indicating how managerial objectives may be achieved. It is only through activity (3) and focusing on the information available from (1) and (2) that these higher aims may be achieved. We believe that simulation offers a very powerful route to achieving this goal.

17.3 PROBLEMS IN MANAGING THE FSM OPERATION

It is evident that the FSM logistics system, like many others, is a balance between a variety of competing factors. When optimized, one expects a significant amount of capital to be freed. The field-service manager is faced with a dichotomy when trying to balance the system logistic requirements with those of his contractural obligations. On the one hand he is expected to provide a high level of service to the customer and engineer. On the other hand he is expected to minimize investment in inventory (whilst affording a high availability of spares with the engineer), to maximize effective engineer utilization, to maintain short field engineer response times, to provide a fast logistics back-up for spares not readily available, and all this within a set of financial targets! Is it any wonder that managers accept high levels of inventory and spend much time chasing specific problems?

With such a variety of factors to consider, it is not surprising that one gets caught up in detailed appraisals of a single parameter, rather than assessing the performance of the operational system as a whole. It is for this reason that managers are searching for a relatively simple method of viewing the overall performance of the system without losing sight of the performance and effect of individual parameters. It is the contention of this research that the simulation approach provides a way to identify and manage FSM problems by combining relative simplicity with strong analytical capability.

17.4 DEVELOPING THE SIMULATION MODEL

The simulation model describes the operational system as perceived through discussion and observation. It is a representation of a multi-echelon structure comprising the main elements, activities and governing factors in the system:

The **elements** are

(1) The stores structure
(2) The engineers
(3) The inventory.

The **activities** are
(1) Response to customer calls
(2) The replenishment activity
(3) Handling emergency demands
(4) Managing the return of failed repairables.

The **governing factors** are

(1) The failure rates of spares
(2) The lead times
(3) The agreed response time
(4) The level of inventory held at each echelon
(5) Availability of spares (ex stock service)
(6) Repair centre capacity.

The purpose of the simulation is to provide a means of testing assumptions on system behaviour, and to assess the impact of changes on the operational system. Simulation provides an added benefit to the research in its ability to dynamically model the relationships between variables. It should be remembered that the simulation model concentrates on key activities.

Optimization of the model will be based upon the disposition of stores and the trial of new rules determining inventory flow. The objective of the model is to inform the user of benefits attainable through an organizational restructure or a redistribution of resources.

Modelling shall be performed in two stages as emphasized by Shannon (1975). These are

(1) Validation
(2) Verification.

The validation phase ensures that the operating logic of the simulation program is both accurate and consistent with the system processes (i.e. it is internally consistent).

Although the model may be allowed to run under ideal conditions, simulation allows any variable to have predefined degrees of randomness associated with it. The variables will be rigorously defined to represent the stochastic system behaviour present in multi-echelon systems. However, simplifications or generalizations are inevitable in areas where information is too complex or insufficient to draw clear conclusions.

The verification phase places its emphasis on determining the accuracy of both input and output information with that found in industry. Comparison of the model and system behaviours will then take place. Performance is to be measured against criteria accepted by the industry to be valid and of value. These are:

(1) *Service level* the ability to supply parts and labour in an agreed time.
(2) *Availability* the number of requests on stores filled immediately.
(3) *Investment* measured as the total investment in inventory.
(4) *Operating costs* the cost of supporting the logistics function.

17.5 CONCLUSIONS

We believe that the multi-echelon distribution system for field support is dynamic and does not lend itself to the traditional approach to organizational design. However, its complexities can be modelled successfully using simulation. Furthermore, the ability of some forms of simulation to sample stochastic variables from within a distribution provides greater realism to the model. The model then serves as a potential management tool, allowing one to examine more precisely the effects of organizational changes on system behaviour. Of particular interest is the influence of inventory levels on service level, engineer utilization, cost incentives or penalties in reducing inventory, elimination of an echelon or changes to the number of field engineers.

This ability to pose 'what if' questions relating to structure and inventory is invaluable, and allows managers to consider the implications of strategic decisions made in the logistics area.

17.6 ACKNOWLEDGEMENTS

The authors wish to thank Mr R. Cromwell, ICL (UK) Ltd for his valuable contribution to our work, and to the many companies who contributed to the survey.

This paper was presented at the 7th International Logistics Conference held in London in October 1987. We are grateful to IFS (Conferences) Limited for their permission to reprint the paper.

REFERENCES

Clark, A.J. (1960) The use of simulation to evaluate a multi-echelon, dynamic inventory model, *Naval Research Logistics Quarterly*, **7**(4).

Clarke, A.J. (1972) An informal survey of multi-echelon inventory theory. *Naval Research Logistics Quarterly*, **19**(4).

Department of the Air Force (1971) Optimum Repair Level Analysis, *Air Force Logistics Command*, Manual 800–4, June.

Hitzelberger, W.R. (1985) *An analysis of the inventory/repair decision in a multi-echelon environment*. The Ohio State University, Ph.D.

Mosquera, J. and Wild, A.M.A. (1987) *Comparative inventory survey in high-technology companies*. Midas Consultants, 15 Bolton Street, Ramsbottom, Lancashire, UK.

Muckstadt, J.A. (1960) A model for a multi-item, multi-echelon, multi-indenture inventory system. *Management Science*, **20**(4).

Shannon, R.E. (1975) *Systems Simulation: The Art and Science*. Prentice Hall, Englewood Cliffs, New Jersey.

Sherbrooke, C.C. (1968) METRIC: A multi-echelon technique for recoverable item control, *Operations Research*, **16**.

CHAPTER EIGHTEEN

BMW logistics: a step into the future

Hanns-Ulrich Pretzsch

INTRODUCTION

An integral logistic system was introduced at BMW AG Munich in 1976. This paper illustrates the organization structure of this function. Practical examples of forward looking logistic solutions are described. These include the newly created material planning system, Just-In-Time concepts, the central external automated warehouse of the Munich plant, and the logistic system of the new plant in Regensburg. Finally, the paper deals with computer integrated manufacturing, and the methods employed by BMW for the step-by-step realization of the CIM model. The paper shows that efficiency can be improved if the organizational prerequisites for an overall logistic concept are created with a company.

The automobile has celebrated its 100th anniversary, and is still enjoying great popularity. The same applies to the automobile manufacturers. That is why I would like to start by giving you some brief facts about BMW:

(1) In 1986, the company manufactured 450 000 passenger cars and 32 000 motorcycles.
(2) Turnover was approximately DM 15 billion.
(3) In the last ten years production and turnover increased continually by about 60% and 200% respectively.

Figure 18.1 shows BMW's production development compared to the entire German automobile industry.

Source: Pretzsch, H.-U. (1987) *Proc. 7th International Logistics Conference,* London, 3–9

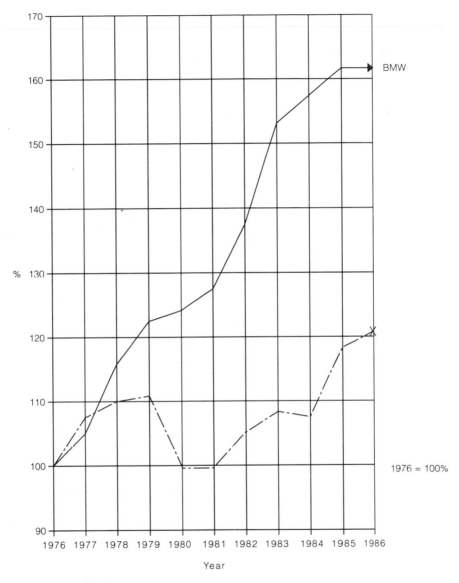

Figure 18.1 Automotive production: BMW cf. all German manufacturers 1976–86.

Passenger cars are produced in three assembly plants, all of which are located in the southern part of the Federal Republic of Germany, in Bavaria. Motorcycles are manufactured in the Berlin plant. The different assembly plants are closely linked.

18.1 BMW LOGISTICS

In the mid-1970s, we at BMW set ourselves the goal of reorganizing all those functions which were either directly or indirectly involved with material management. A team of experts was formed to conduct a detailed analysis of all existing structures, tasks, procedures, responsibilities, personnel expenditure and material costs of the company. The result was an organization form unprecedented in the industry at that time. We introduced this organization at BMW in 1976 and called it logistics. Years later industrial logistics found its way into other companies as well and now, universities, colleges, management consultants and international congresses are intensely preoccupied with the logistic concept and its development.

It is no exaggeration to say that BMW was, and still is today, one of the precursors in the field of logistics.

At BMW, logistics is seen as a cybernetic function with cross-sectional character, structured along the lines of control-loop principles.

Job assignment was based on the following principles:

(1) Decentralized as far as possible
(2) Central as far as necessary.

This principal is illustrated in Fig. 18.2.

The central jobs comprise mainly the planning and controlling functions, although operational processes may be included if this proves to be more economical for the company. Examples of such jobs are as follows:

(1) Drawing up the production programme;
(2) Controlling customer orders received from the sales department;
(3) Completing material planning;
(4) Planning and implementation of facilities for material flow;
(5) Planning and purchasing of all transport services;
(6) Planning and realization of all data-processing systems;
(7) Elaborating, implementing and checking of goals.

Decentralized logistical tasks are carried out by the plants on location. Organizationally, these tasks are grouped together to form the

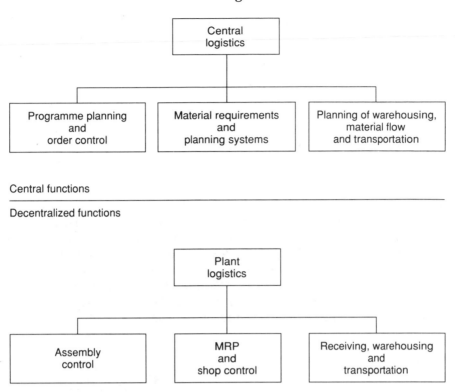

Figure 18.2 Organization of logistics.

plant logistics departments which report directly to the relevant plant manager. The main tasks are as follows:

(1) In-plant parts production control;
(2) In-plant assembly control;
(3) Material call-offs from other plants;
(4) Material call-offs from suppliers;
(5) Handling of physical logistics from receiving to returning of empty bins.

Table 18.1 shows a current quantity structure of passenger-car production. It serves to illustrate the complexity of logistical tasks at BMW.

Looking at the number of parts and combinations which are possible with the options; engine and model derivatives, the number of variants is almost unlimited. In practice, not all variants occur and the frequency with which certain variants do occur differs greatly. Neverthe-

Table 18.1 Quantity structure of BMW logistics

Basic types	4
Models	200
Engine variants	1400
Options	3000
Parts	100 000
Call-off's from suppliers	200 000
Shop orders	18 000

less, all processes and systems must be designed flexibly enough to cover all possible combinations.

For example, when we introduced the new 7-series a year ago, the number of outside mirror variants increased to over 300 compared to the previous model's 12 variants. You can imagine what effect this has on the bills of material, material call-offs, bins, staging on the assembly line and the spare parts business. The trend towards more individually styled cars is growing steadily, at least in BMW's market segment. The same applies to the demands made on logistics.

18.2 EXAMPLES OF FORWARD-LOOKING LOGISTIC SOLUTIONS

From the range of forward-looking logistic solutions, I would like to describe a few select examples in greater detail to provide you with a general picture of our activities.

18.2.1 The material planning system

In 1978 we started to develop a completely new data-processing (DP) material-planning system. It had to meet the following requirements:

(1) Recording of all planned primary requirements from the production programmes;
(2) Automatic generation of bills of material;
(3) Minimum explosion time (less than 1 hour);
(4) Consideration of existing stock and orders which have already been issued;
(5) Online requirements planning for select parts via the display unit in exceptional cases;
(6) Requirements proposal via display unit;
(7) Consideration of incoming vehicle orders;
(8) Daily recalculation on the basis of current parameters;
(9) Implementation of simulation calculations.

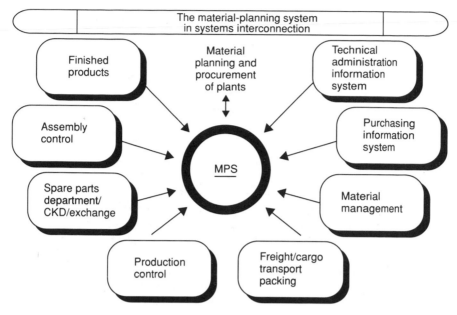

Figure 18.3 Inter-connections in the material–planning system.

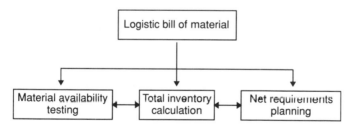

Figure 18.4 Elements of the material-planning system.

In 1978, there was nothing to model our system on, so we had to develop everything ourselves. It took about five years before we were able to introduce the new material-planning system step by step in 1983. It had to be integrated into a fairly advanced systems landscape.

Figure 18.3 illustrates this system landscape (clockwise).

The material-planning system consists of four main sections, shown in Fig. 18.4.

These four sections are closely connected and mutually dependent. With the introduction of the material-planning system, we were able to achieve marked reductions in material stocks and expenditure for manual material planning, as well as greater flexibility.

Over and above that we created the data processing basis for later just-in-time processes.

18.3 JUST-IN-TIME CONCEPTS

Even today, the European automobile manufacturers differ from their American and Japanese counterparts by their greater manufacturing penetration. In the USA, there was a trend towards specialization, i.e. different plants concentrated on different components, e.g. engines, chassis and even body components. These plants supplied several assembly plants which did not manufacture any, or only very few, components. This usually resulted in a build-up of large stocks of material and parts and expensive transportation services. The structure in Japan was similar, although there, one of the main goals was stock minimization. This led to the development of the well-known Japanese methods synonymous with the word 'kanban'.

The structure of the automobile and supplier industry in Europe and the USA is such that Japanese kanban operations cannot simply be adopted indiscriminately. The same goes for BMW. That is why very similar processes were developed in the USA and in Europe which can be summed up by the term just-in-time. For the sake of clarity, I will briefly explain the traditional material-planning process (Fig. 18.5).

The production plan usually covers several months. This volume is split up on parts level via explosion of the bill of material. Production and the supplier are informed about the requirements for several months in advance on a monthly basis. Usually, weekly quantities are indicated. Current fluctuations in demand are either absorbed via the stock in hand or *ad hoc* arrangements are made by telephone.

In the just-in-time concept (Fig. 18.6), the requirements information also covers several months, although it serves as a forecast only. Actual requirements are determined on the basis of assembly orders received in the plant. This is done on a daily basis, usually covering a time span of 1–3 weeks. (This necessitates short explosion times for the bills of material, because there is very little time between two productions days.)

The requirements information which is worked out on a daily basis is passed on to the job shop or the supplier. That is where teleprocessing is needed, otherwise this process would be far too time consuming. In other words, the automobile manufacturer's computer communicates directly with the supplier's computer.

The first few days of the requirements schedule should only be

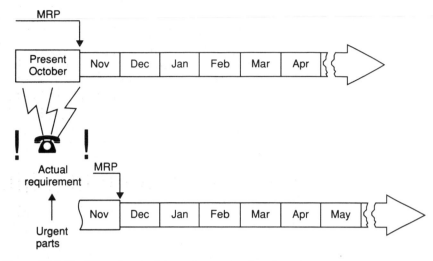

Figure 18.5 Traditional material-requirements planning.

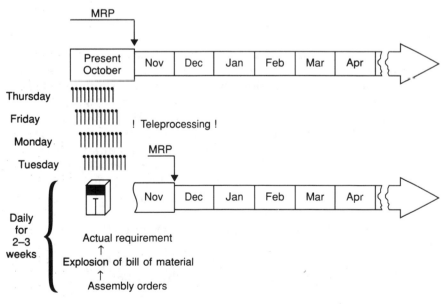

Figure 18.6 Just-in-time concept.

changed slightly, or not at all, so that the supplier has enough time to react if necessary.

At BMW, we have been using such just-in-time processes within our own plants for many years, for example, in seat production and engine assembly. The just-in-time process is new for purchased parts. We believe that just-in-time is meaningful and feasible for approximately 10% of all parts representing 60% of the total material value.

BMW has introduced just-in-time for purchased parts successfully for transmissions, carpets, wiring harnesses, etc. The introduction of teleprocessing between automobile manufacturers and suppliers is meaningful also for parts which cannot be produced and supplied according to the just-in-time concept. We have already put this into practice on a large scale.

The co-operation between automobile manufacturers and suppliers under the auspices of the 'Verband der Deutschen Automobil-industrie' VDA (German Society of Automobile Manufacturers and Suppliers) is extremely helpful in this regard. Teams are formed to standardize DP-interfaces, to mention but one example.

18.4 LOGISTIC STRUCTURE CONCEPTS

In this part of my paper I would like to outline two examples, namely the central external warehouse of our Munich plant, and the logistic concept in our Regensburg plant which was opened in the spring of this year.

Firstly, let me explain the situation at our plant in Munich. Our main factory in Munich is also our oldest assembly plant. This is where the 3-series models and the majority of our engines are produced. The plant was built at the beginning of the century in the open countryside outside Munich. Today, it is completely enclosed by the city. Rising production volumes and the growing demand for more production space slowly pushed the necessary storage areas into different external warehouses. As a result, the complete flow of material became more and more involved and uneconomical. The obvious solution of establishing a central storage area within the plant itself, or in the direct vicinity of the plant, had to be ruled out. That is why we decided in favour of a central external warehouse, about 20 km away from the plant.

The unusual feature of this solution is that the warehouse is not run by BMW, but by a forwarding agent. The firm 'Schenker':

(1) Rented the premises;
(2) Set up the warehouse according to BMW requirements;

(3) Manages the warehouse;
(4) Supplies the Munich plant with the necessary components.

The warehouse is equipped with the latest facilities and all computers are directly linked to BMW's computers.

Transportation between warehouse and plant is carried out with specially developed trucks. Emphasis was placed on environmental acceptability, with the result that irritation of residents could be reduced considerably. As far as we know, the inclusion of a forwarding agent in this form is unprecedented in the automative industry and has attracted the interest of many experts. Colleagues from the other German automobile manufacturers and from many different branches of industry have had a look at this solution.

Secondly, I would like to describe the logistic structure of our latest assembly plant in Regensburg. Here, we have been able to realize the latest knowledge in automobile production. All logistics areas are assigned to the assembly areas. About 70% of the material flow from receiving via the warehouse to the assembly station is automated. Material transportation is handled by means of an automatically control-led high bay warehouse and automatic guided vehicles (AGV). Naturally, all this is controlled by hierarchically arranged interconnected computers.

The building of the Regensburg plant has also prompted about 20 suppliers with more than 2500 employees to set up new production sites in the vicinity of the plant, up to now a rather sparsely industrialized area. These are good prerequisites for the realization of just-in-time concepts.

The seat manufacturer Schmitz and Company, who produce all the seats for our Regensburg plant is a good example. The seats are received in plant just prior to fitment. Schmitz and Company gets our production order only two hours prior to fitment via teleprocessing. Figure 18.7 illustrates the process schematically. The entire process is handled without seat stocks and trucks are loaded and unloaded automatically.

This brings me to the last part of my paper.

18.5 CIM AT BMW

The examples mentioned have already shown how important the use of data processing has become for the resolution of logistic problems. When BMW logistics was founded in 1976, it was one of the prime

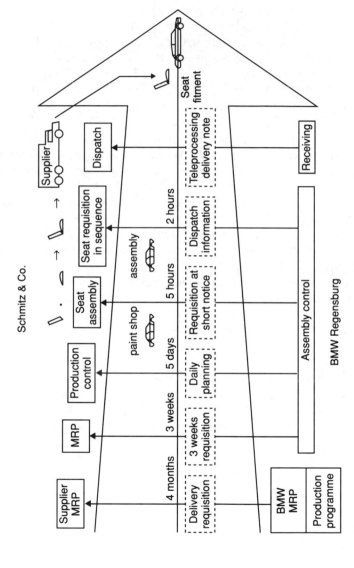

Figure 18.7 Synchronous delivery at BMW.

objectives to establish a general, integral DP structure. This was basically achieved within logistics with the introduction of the material-
planning system.

Logistic data-processing systems form an important and integral part
of all CIM models. Regarded in this way, logistics at BMW may be seen
as the starting point of the CIM concept. Although J. Harrington had
published his book *Computer Integrated Manufacturing* in 1973, the CIM
idea only became popular in 1985. However, even in 1973 Harrington
pointed out that two of the five CIM components are:

(1) Computer-aided material management; and
(2) Computer-aided production programme compilation.

By definition, both form an integral part of BMW logistics. At BMW,
we have defined our CIM concept as a system with two main axes
(Fig. 18.8):

(1) The product-related axis (vertical);
(2) The production-related axis (horizontal).

The product-related axis comprises mainly those activities which are
carried out only once for the product in question, e.g. design and
development. The appropriate equipment is usually summed up in the
term CAD.

The production-related axis comprises those activities which are
repeated frequently, and thus make other demands on the data-
processing systems. It includes operations which are continually
repeated during the manufacture of a product. The production planning and control system is an important constituent.

At BMW, annual expenditure for CAD activities alone is about DM
60–80 million. If the other CIM relevant volumes are added, the
amount is trebled. To gain practical experience, we have selected certain projects which we are deliberately developing according to CIM
principles. CIM activities are embedded in the data-processing system
as a whole. A decision committee at top management level takes the
necessary forward looking decisions. This underlines the importance
attached to the CIM philosophy.

18.6 CONCLUSION

With the introduction of logistics in 1976, BMW took a great step into
the future. Now after 11 years it is evident that a decisive competitive
advantage can be gained by a closed, logically structured logistic con-

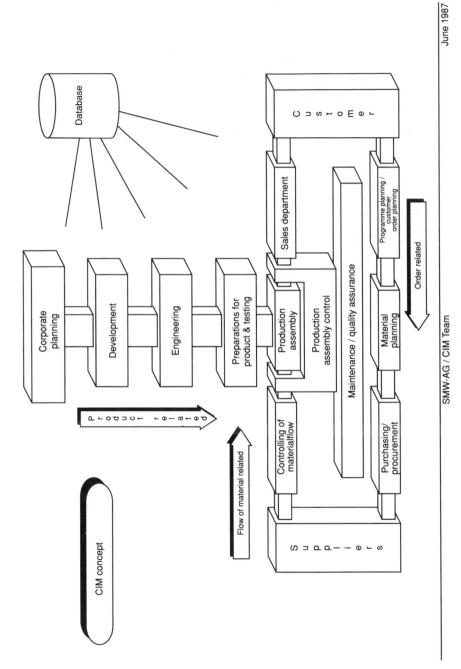

Figure 18.8 CIM at BMW.

June 1987

SMW-AG / CIM Team

Database

CIM concept

Corporate planning

Development

Engineering

Preparations for product & testing

Production assembly

Production assembly control

Maintenance / quality assurance

Sales department

Controlling of materialflow

Material planning

Purchasing/ procurement

Programme planning / customer order planning

Product related

Flow of material related

Order related

Customer

Suppliers

cept. Within the bounds of this paper I have only been able to touch on a few important examples. Nevertheless, I hope that I have been able to convince you that the services of BMW logistics are certainly comparable with our cars' image.

CHAPTER NINETEEN

The single European market: optimizing logistics operations in post-1992 Europe

J.H. Van der Hoop

The European Communities have set out an ambitious programme to create a single market and abolish the still existing fragmentation along national lines that can be found in every aspect of business. Only by achieving a real single market can Europe survive as a viable player in the international market place.

The EC White Paper that in 1985 mapped out the course to the single market identified close to 300 areas which would need EC legislation.

Assessing the present situation a two-speed development can be observed.

In the political arena steady, if slow, progress is being made because of each country's attempts to shape the EC regulations to its own best advantage. At the same time, a concern is arising of how far national autonomy should be traded for EC autonomy. This is particularly valid for such sensitive areas as financial and fiscal policies and welfare policies. An extra matter for concern is that the presently existing European legislative machinery still has a long way to go to be able to replace the national legislative bodies.

If the political field can therefore be expected to move slowly, in the business area the situation is completely different. The major players are not awaiting the outcome of the political and regulatory mills, but have started the groundwork for a single market in practice. Key words are economy of scale and market share. The number of take-overs

Source: Hoop, J.H. Van der (1989) *Proc. Council of Logistics Management*,
First presented at the 1989 Annual Conference of the Council of Logistics Management, St Louis, USA

across European borders has risen dramatically, and new forms of strategic alliances are being probed. For the medium-sized and smaller companies the focus will have to be on niche marketing and networking. At the same time a number of victims, corporations unable to cope with the new competitive structure, can be expected.

The single European market will offer a host of challenges and opportunities for the creation of an optimal distribution structure. More than ever a strategy is needed which integrates the manufacturing, marketing, finance and logistics objectives of the firm, which in the European context have to be firmly interlinked.

19.1 THE FRAMEWORK

Although a great number of uncertainties will continue to exist for some time the parameters for a logistics structure in the European arena are becoming visible.

Although the optimal structure will obviously be different for individual firms or industry groups, the framework for the organization of the supply chain, which will be valid for most players in this market, can be derived from the present developments and expectations.

(1) Production is being rationalized in the sense of allocating a limited product range to a specific plant for production on a Europe-wide basis rather than a wide product range on a regional basis. This means a rescheduling of product lines and inter-plant networking with the aim of achieving the best economies of scale. It also means the reduction of the total number of plants. Obviously this will change the product flows.

(2) Sourcing of materials and components is being rearranged. On the one hand new and more distant sources are coming within reach, on the other hand the number of sources will be rationalized in order to create reliable and economic supply lines. With rescheduled manufacturing and therefore more concentrated supply flows sourcing from outside Europe locations will also be easier to accomplish.

(3) It can be expected that the national European submarkets will for a long time to come retain a number of their individual characteristics, particularly as to demand for products and services, which can best be catered for by nationally organized marketing and sales services.

(4) In order to achieve the needed economies of scale and control of the more complex product and information flows it would seem

that within the firm not only will corporate finance be a centralized function, but also overall materials planning and logistics.

Translating the issues of economy of scale and the service levels required into logistics operations, the focus of attention will have to be on control and information, location and level of inventory, distribution centre functions and available third-party service options to achieve the selected customer service targets.

19.2 LOGISTICS CONTROL

To achieve an effective logistics system, both from a cost and a service perspective, centralized control is necessary to manage and mesh the converging and diverging materials flows. Moreover, flexible and fast response to the diverse requirements from the various submarkets can be realized only when manufacturing, sales and logistics planning is integrated into real supply-chain management.

Centralized logistics control should also enable total logistics costing, with allocation of generated cost to relevant market segments. Not only is this conditional for judging profitability of filling diversified market and service demands, it will most likely also be the major base for price differentiation on a single-market basis versus national basis.

Another essential issue to be tackled here is standardization of materials-flow information which in practice tends to be based on different parameters.

These compelling arguments will have to override counter-arguments from separate entities in the chain against relinquishing some of their autonomy.

Centralizing logistics control, however, does not mean that the total European distribution operations should be centralized: the country-related differences will often lead to leaving some operations (such as order handling, local delivery operations, customer-service monitoring, VAT and administration) under local responsibility. Interestingly, this will impact the definition and measurement of profit centres.

19.3 INVENTORY CONTROL

One of the major issues in structuring logistics for the single European market is how to control inventory in the total supply chain. Breaking through the national boundary segmentation should result in a leaner and more flexible use of inventory. There are two main routes to achieve this:

(1) By centralizing stock, as discussed below, both the aggregate stock can be reduced and availability can be better controlled.
(2) By applying the principle of postponement the aggregate stock can be further reduced, while inventory value and therefore inventory-carrying cost will be lower when holding inventory earlier in the chain.

Postponement in this sense means postponing final commitment in form, time or place to the moment actual demand or order is known. This is particularly relevant in Europe where, if not the product itself, assembly, conditioning, packaging and labelling will continue to be customized to submarkets. Here also evolves another function of the European distribution centre: processing of products flowing through the centre. In this sense integration with the manufacturing function is required.

19.4 CENTRALIZING STOCK

An important feature of the single European market is the improved possibility for centralizing stock in one or only a few locations. This will enable rationalization of the location of stock in the supply chain on the basis of logistics considerations rather than on the now common basis of national territory.

However, as usual there is no single easy solution to the question of how to organize stock centralization and a number of practical aspects have to be considered, such as where, how, why and why not, and finally at what service levels should such central stock be held.

Where? Should the central stock be held at the plant or in or between markets? This question is particularly relevant in the relatively small European area.

How? There are a number of options, such as: concentrate all stock, leave critical items in national stock (trading off local market requirements against optimal effectiveness), convert national stockpoints into transfer points.

Why? Centralizing stock will significantly reduce the sum of nationally held inventories, and enable improved stock and cost control. It will further lead to optimizing (consolidating) transport configuration, another key issue in the European market, and will allow application of the principle of postponement.

Why not? There may be specific reasons which counteract the advantages of centralization of stock. Distances to some (sub)markets and the impact on lead time to some key market areas may influence the decision on how far the total number of stock locations can be reduced. Regulatory formalities that will still exist may cause delays. Feasibility will be influenced by the physical product and order characteristics. Divestment and redundancy of storage activities may be unacceptable, as may be the fact that centralizing stock takes away responsibilities (for instance for inventory levels) considered essential by the local (national) entity.

At what service levels? One of the essential issues in the European arena will be to decide on the level and diversity of service that one can afford to offer the various European markets. On the one hand this requires thorough customer service audits into the sensitivity of the service elements in each of the submarkets, on the other hand it needs imaginative measures to create more commonality in distribution operations to the various submarkets (e.g. in packaging and handling units, shipment size, consolidation and scheduling).

19.5 EUROPEAN DISTRIBUTION CENTRE FUNCTIONS

In a European context the distribution centre serving the total or a large part of the market will need to combine a number of functions:

(1) It will serve as the central stock holding.
(2) It will have a consolidation and de-consolidation function, serving as a hub in the supply chain for the incoming flows from diverse sources, and for the rearranged distribution flows to the various markets. This will serve the need for optimum transport consolidation, but will also ensure that time-different supplies can be combined into complete deliveries of orders.
(3) It will serve as an important information hub, combining order and supply information, as well as generating vital management information on actual usage and availability. Obviously this can only be achieved when full use can be made of electronic data interchange (EDI) links.
(4) It should be equipped to process, assemble, repack and label the goods moving through the distribution centre in order to achieve the advantages of postponement.

A crucial question is whether a European distribution centre can ensure the same customer service level as the local distribution centre. This depends to a large extent on the reliability of transport arrangements that can be made. Practical experience shows than even in the pre-1992 period with the available mix of transport services all major European markets can be served within acceptable lead times with only some exceptions for the perimeter areas.

Two service options can be considered when centralizing operations: scheduled delivery and direct distribution from the distribution centre to the final customer in the country of destination. These options can be used in a trade-off between transit time, transport cost and reliability of service. It is interesting to note that the possibilities of consolidating transport with consequent lower transport rates, as well as the fact that border crossing rates are relatively lower than domestic rates, to a large extent outweigh the cost of the increased transport volume.

19.6 DISTRIBUTION CENTRE LOCATION

Closely connected with the consideration of a European distribution centre is the question of where this should be located from a service and cost perspective.

In a European context the selection criteria have a somewhat different weight or are of a different nature.

The major criteria are:

(1) Transit time and cost to market hubs – these do not always correspond to the actual distances, but are influenced by traffic-lane circumstances. Consequently the centre-of-gravity model does not always apply.
(2) Operational cost and productivity which can be achieved – there are significant differences between countries.
(3) Available skills – particularly in the area of language capabilities and international experience.
(4) Availability of competitive services: transport, warehousing, documentation and administration, communication and EDI.
(5) Investment/divestment and incentives.

19.7 THIRD-PARTY DISTRIBUTION SERVICES

Finally, when looking at an optimal distribution strategy for Europe, the question of whether the use of third-party service providers can contribute to an effective operation needs to be discussed.

In this respect it should be realized that particularly in the transport area the use of transport providers, transport organizers and freight forwarders in international and intra-European distribution has historically been a viable and proven way of distribution. As far as warehousing and distribution centre operation is concerned, third-party providers were until recent years far less common.

What are the main reasons for the trend to contract out part of the distribution operation?

(1) The need is felt to concentrate on core business and adding value in the developing European environment, where multiple, highly competitive submarkets exist.
(2) The use of third party providers improves adaptability in an uncertain and changing market place.
(3) From a perspective of resource management it is preferable to convert fixed assets allocated to non-core activities variable costs.
(4) With third-party arrangements it is possible to clearly place risks (notably risks of utilization and risks caused by lack of specific skills, know-how and experience) where they can most economically be borne: service providers can usually better handle these risks by having a broader customer base.
(5) Although not often the primary reason for contracting out, an added benefit is the transparency of costs. A rational rate structure facilitates cost allotment to distribution consignments (and hence to market segments), and offers a good basis for profitability accounting and pricing decisions.

Are third-party distribution services available on a European scale?
It should be understood that even in the pre-1992 era, distribution on a real European scale was being organized. The single European market will further facilitate the way this has to be done. Third-party providers are adapting to the opportunities by creating Europe-wide controlled networks, offering one-party agreements for specific distribution services. These can replace the systems built on a series of separate, sequential service contracts with individual contractors in various countries. Two developments can be seen:

(1) Transport, forwarding and storage companies are strengthening their networks by either acquiring or setting up their own operations in key countries, or by forging closer operational and commercial relationships with independent counterparts.
(2) Service companies in a particular field are extending their activities to related fields, so broadening their service package.

In addition, service contracts, tailored to specific requirements of the customer, become more common. These longer-term contracts are not any more primarily based on rates, but also on qualitative conditions and on a structured exchange of information between both parties. The rapidly developing transport and distribution EDI message standards will considerably facilitate the use of third-party service providers.

19.8 SUMMARY

The development of the Single European Market offers challenges for distribution management, but also new opportunities. It will require a closer integration with manufacturing, marketing and finance. The major goals of economy of scale and effective customer service can be met by the selective use of centralizing materials control and creating one or more European distribution centres with stocking, consolidation, information and materials-processing functions. The use of third-party service providers will facilitate optimization of a European distribution system.

Undoubtedly the strength of the logistics structure will be decisive for competitive positions in the Single European Market in the areas of achieving economies of scale, determining supply-chain leadership, pricing and market service.

CHAPTER TWENTY

Formulating and implementing a global logistics strategy

John H. Roberts

In the last few years, ICL has developed from being a mainframe computer business to a full range supplier of information systems for the corporate, departmental-office and single-user markets.

This expansion in product and service range has been extremely rapid and has increased the complexity of the logistics environment from one which was dominated by internal manufacture to today's situation which requires the integration of products from ICL plants and vendors located in all continents, to meet customers' requirements all over the world.

ICL's goal is to be a leading supplier of high-quality information solutions to customers seeking to maintain and improve their competitive edge through their information technology infrastructure. To achieve our goal the following six strategies have been developed:

(1) *Integrated solutions* ICL is committed to providing 'solutions', as opposed to just hardware 'boxes' or software packages, by providing and developing the best new technologies and products available. The timely production and supply of those solutions is provided by our manufacturing and logistics capability.

Source: Roberts, J.H. (1990) *International Journal of Logistics Management*, 1(2), 53–8

(2) *Market strategy*   ICL will focus investment and resources to develop open standard IT infrastructures to meet the needs of vertical industry markets. There will be continued international expansion, with the whole of Europe being developed as our home market.

(3) *Open framework*   ICL will use open standards in designing our products so that they can be integrated easily into solutions.

(4) *Collaborations*   ICL will capitalize on our own investments by collaborating with other companies in technology, product development and marketing. One specific element of this strategy is our commitment to increase the proportion of components sourced from European companies.

(5) *Expertise*   ICL will increase investment in our expertise as systems integrators in the design, development and implementation of integrated solutions,

(6) *Organization*   ICL is committed to the continual evolvement of our commercial policies, processes and information systems to respond rapidly to changing market needs and thus maintain our excellent business performance.

20.1 LINKING CORPORATE AND LOGISTICS STRATEGY

By presenting this view of ICL's corporate strategy, I have attempted to provide the background scenario for which we are developing and implementing our logistics strategy. By their very nature, high-level strategies contain perceived 'motherhood' statements and it is therefore important that this corporate strategy is fully understood so that lower-level supporting strategies underpin it. Revisiting the six corporate strategies, I would highlight the following seven phrases as being the key drivers of our logistics strategy:

(1) *Provider of 'solutions'*   Increases complexity of logistics operations,

(2) *Vertical industry markets*   Each needs 'tailored' logistics solution,

(3) *International expansion*   Requires global logistics infrastructure,

(4) *Europe as home market*   Need new mindsets, culture awareness, etc.

(5) *Collaborations*   Each one causes us to revisit current logistics strategy,

(6) *European sourcing*   Requires focused purchasing proactivity

(7) *Business performance*   Requires optimization of logistics service and costs.

With these points in mind the following global logistics strategy has been developed at ICL.

20.2 ICL LOGISTICS STRATEGY

20.2.1 Forecasting/planning

For finished products (i.e. hardware, software and literature) ICL has a well-established centralized planning process that runs on a monthly cycle. We have no current plans to amend this process significantly, although it is being constantly tuned and improved.

With typical lead-time demands from our customers of between two and four weeks, and typical total procurement leadtimes of up to nine months, the criticality of optimizing forecasting accuracy cannot be over-stressed. Additionally, with product life cycles reducing, product introductions and product demises occur with increasing regularity, and, of course, these two phases offer the biggest forecasting challenges.

The complexity of forecasting, and therefore the opportunity to get it wrong, is directly related to the difference between procurement and delivery leadtimes. The delivery leadtimes for most of our products are several degrees of magnitude better than those of our competitors. This situation is regularly reviewed with the sales operations to determine real customer requirements but, to date, we have been offered no relief in this area!

A good barometer of forecasting accuracy is inventory performance. Over the last few years ICL has climbed to the top position in the industry while maintaining product availability, and hence service levels. This gives us confidence that our forecasting process is right, albeit with many opportunities for operational improvements. For example, our pull-feed policy for shipping products to countries outside the UK, in nearly all cases based on firm customer requirements, is fundamental in maintaining a lean and mean international inventory pipeline. Because we do not formally relate these actual requirements to the appropriate country forecast of several months earlier, the country operations have little or no practical incentive to improve for forecasting accuracy – financial sales forecasts are as good as can be expected, but the related product mix forecasts leave much room for improvement. To address this we are actively encouraging the enhancement of the status of country logistics personnel from the traditional 'Cinderella' role to one of true business partner who understands the importance of accurate forecasting and can contribute positively in this area among others.

I mentioned earlier that one of the key drivers of our logistics strategy was our corporate strategy of seeking collaborations. Our recent international expansion has required us to readdress our planning process to ensure the appropriateness of centralization. Each new situation is analysed separately. For example, for our activities in North America through the acquisition of Datachecker, we have developed a parallel planning system that allows the flexibility to make the detailed decisions where they belong, i.e. in the USA, but with a 'check-and balance' link into the centralized UK planning process. For our joint venture in Denmark, RCI, we are strengthening their internal control process, but currently keeping totally separate from the UK process.

Our top-level spares forecasting has traditionally been based on the rolled-up replenishment demand on our centralized spares operation by all the country operations. The centralized operations could be up to three stocking echelons higher than the one that sees the real customer demand, hence the perceived demand at that level can easily be driven more by the stocking policy of the intermediate echelons than by true customer requirements. To combat this we have recently transferred ownership of spares inventory from the many country operations to the worldwide spares division within manufacturing and logistics. Our new materials and repairs system (MARS) was implemented through-out the UK during 1989, and is planned for progressive introduction outside the UK, commencing 1990. By accessing these new MARS systems, material planners in the UK will have visibility of true customer usage and will therefore be able to use this information in their forecasts, thus ensuring worldwide optimization of spares inventory.

Recognizing the increasing importance of forecasting and planning during the product introduction and demise phases, and the corresponding decreasing size of the stable mid-life phase, our next opportunity is to review our currently separate planning operations in M and L with a view to integration to ensure full exploitation of our enhanced information systems capability.

20.2.2 Purchasing

We have a well-communicated European sourcing policy, within our purchasing division, which reads:

'We will give preference to European vendors who satisfy our requirements for Quality, Cost-of-Ownership and Service'.

To quantify our objectives, we have a target of 70% European Product Content by the end of 1992, with an interim target of 50% by the end of 1990. These compare with 26% at the beginning of 1988, 32% at the end of 1988 and 40% at the end of 1989.

There are three reasons why we just had to break away from dependence on non-European sources.

(1) to reduce risks
(2) to achieve lower costs and better customer satisfaction
(3) to build viable local sources of supply

(a) Reducing risks

The risks we are trying to reduce are of two kinds: firstly financial losses resulting from currency fluctuations and secondly disruption of supplies.

With our home market in Europe we should ideally be purchasing in European currencies with comparatively little movement between them. Instead we found ourselves dealing in dollars and yen, which over the lifetime of a contract or an order, might vary significantly against the currencies in which we sell in Europe.

Disruption of supplies was even more worrying because it might happen as a result of events entirely beyond our control: changes in US controls on high-tech exports, quotas or punitive duties imposed as a result of international trade conflicts, or restrictions resulting from new commercial alliances by our suppliers over which we had no influence.

(b) Lower costs and greater customer satisfaction

The lower costs of European sourcing are not to do with prices! They are rather a combination of the absence of import duties, the absence of official controls on high-tech trade, lower transport costs and shorter lead times.

As well as saving money, the European sourcing gives us logistics benefits which we can pass on to our customers in the form of shorter lead times and more flexibility in accepting orders.

(c) Growth of viable European sources of supply

By focusing on European sources we aim to build up viable European sources of supply so that we can start to get the benefits I have described in new lines of components and over a long period.

This is especially so where the suppliers need volume in order to compete effectively. For example, the majority of makers of large disk drives are US-owned (with manufacturing in the Far East): the only major European supplier is Siemens. It is no surprise therefore that Siemens and ICL are trying to build a long-term relationship for the supply of these drives. An even more striking example is in semiconductors. Although ICL is not a manufacturer of semiconductors, we are giving every encouragement to the European Community's JESSI R&D project to build adequate, competitive European sources of very powerful submicron semiconductors.

20.2.3 Production logistics

Traditionally, manufacturing organizations focused on what they believed were the key factors determining their performance, e.g. standard hours, direct labour efficiency, annual factory cost rates, factory output value, overhead recovery on direct labour, etc.

The problem in the IT industry was that the importance of these factors virtually disappeared as outsourcing increased and silicon technology rapidly penetrated the hardware. Direct labour content fell to an insignificant level and manufacturing effectively developed into a material-handling operation with 80% of costs being in material.

The measurement focus and systems did not change, however, and this led to poor decision-taking which in turn reduced competitiveness. For instance, factory managers looked to fill up their plants 'willy nilly' just to reduce factory rates without considering how they could best support their company in the market place. Investment in automation was made to reduce direct labour costs – already insignificant.

The primary focus was output value, with no regard to the impact that would have on inventory and customer service. As this approach drove manufacturing down a path on which labour cost and performance were the key factors, the competition from the Far East made it seem as though the best decision was to close manufacturing altogether and outsource completely. However, to have done this would have missed the point entirely of the potential benefit to the company of an inhouse manufacturing capability. Hence, a major reappraisal was needed.

The environment in which ICL sits is one where we are focused on particular markets (for example Retail and Local Government) with stringent requirements. To be a player in these markets we have to be able to satisfy demanding customers whose needs will change rapidly, and the technology will change rapidly. To support successfully a market driven company puts a whole different set of disciplines on a manufacturing organization.

ICL's conclusions as to what was needed from its manufacturing operation in the market place in the 1980s and 1990s, can be summarised as:

(a) Customer service

The prime requisite must be the capability to deliver to the customer what he ordered, on the promised date, every time. This ethic must be applied throughout the organisation. Every 'supplier' within the manufacturing chain has a customer for whom he must meet that commitment – in items shipped, not value. This is a major change in mindset for a manufacturing manager.

(b) Quality

Nothing less than the highest level of quality in all aspects of service will be acceptable. Total quality management is essential. This means visible commitment from the Chairman downwards.

(a) Product cost

Costs should be measured regularly by product, not organization, to allow a focus on where the competitive issues are and goals to be set by product. Target price and target costs are the issues.

(d) Market responsiveness

To support a market-led company in a rapidly changing market requires a need for a highly responsive manufacturing organization. This will need special focus on key manufacturing technologies such as CIM, FMS, rapid product introduction, and aggressive cycle times. The problem was that none of the established measures focused on these key factors and therefore no attention was being given to their development.

Running through all of these objectives is the common theme of flexibility. This is a source of competitive edge that European Manufacturers will do well to build on. Offshore competition is still weak in this area, but is developing fast. To be flexible means that every member of the Manufacturing team has to understand that (and be prepared for) each day being different. Nothing is fixed. That is what makes manufacturing so exciting.

As the major task is the management of material, the emphasis must be on an efficient international logistics chain with inventory pushed back to raw material, minimum handling, awareness of everyone of the level of inventory under his influence, and value added only at the last possible moment. The lower the inventory level within the system the higher the service level to the customer.

The key driver of inventory and service is cycle time, whether it is product introduction cycle time, manufacturing cycle time, administration cycle time or supplier lead times. By focusing attention on these times and introducing systems and processes to dramatically reduce them, bottlenecks and inventory can be driven out.

The JIT philosophy has been a very successful tool for us in this process, both as a mechanism and a philosophy. It has educated us to focus only on what is required. Our supervisors have got used to having idle operators in preference to idle material. Excess capacity is planned in, not regarded as a cost penalty.

With inventory reducing, problems are exposed. Managers begin to realize the relationship between Inventory (or lack of it) and customer service.

Automation must be focused on what is important to the organization. If material management and service is important then automation should be geared to improve these factors. We have focused on the concept of flexible manufacturing cells connected by automated material handling.

Our recent collaborations and acquisitions have also challenged us to establish all these same philosophies within their manufacturing operations, and we are very much on the learning curve in our skills at recognizing the different needs and cultures worldwide.

We are also rapidly establishing 'screwdriver assembly' operations, primarily in third world and Eastern bloc countries, thus allowing products to acquire the appropriate local added-value content. Again these need to embrace the philosophies of service, quality, cost and flexibility while, at the same time, satisfying the multitude of local requirements.

20.2.4 Configuration, customization and hangaring

This area offers, perhaps, the biggest logistics challenge. As noted earlier, ICL's traditional direct labour content has fallen significantly as outsourcing has increased. In its place there has been an increased demand for final assembly and test activities and to help us make the right logistics decisions we have subdivided these under the three headings of configuration, customization and hangaring. Confusingly, people tend to use these terms interchangeably but, although the physical activities involved are very similar, their purposes are different and the logistics solution equally so.

Configuration is the act of final assembly to produce a limited range of standard catalogue products. The two most obvious examples in our product range are our personal computers and retail point-of-sale tills. In the case of the personal computer, the standard processor, which is procured from the Far East, is configured with a variety of store sizes, disk drives and communications interfaces to provide a range of 'deliverables'.

Customization is the act of taking one of these 'deliverables' and carrying out a value-added activity, usually chargeable to the customer. This could be anything from re-spraying to match the customer's decor, to loading and running up some customer-specific software.

The differentiation between these two activities is somewhat subjective as they merge in the middle, but as the ideal logistics solutions are 180° different, it is imperative that a policy decision is made as to where the line is drawn and then this decision is adhered to by all parties. In order to optimize the balance between, on the one hand, service levels and flexibility, and, on the other hand, logistics costs and inventory levels, configuration should be carried out as close to the supplier as possible, while customization is done as close to the customer as possible. Failure to do this will result in dissatisfaction throughout the supply chain with elements of both activities occurring at various stages in between the two ideal extremes.

Hangaring is the third element I mentioned and again different people will define it differently, even within the same company. To me this is the act, carried out immediately prior to customer installation, of networking all the elements of a system, each themselves previously fully tested, to ensure total system compatibility and conformance to requirements. To categorize this whole activity as 'price of non-conformance' (PONC), and therefore something to be eliminated is, perhaps, the symptom of taking too simplistic a view. In this age of modular design, plug-and-play functionality and increasing reliability of electronic technology, the real need to 'hangar' should be severely limited to highly complex situations. Far too often the need for expensive hangaring activities is based on historical experience of product quality and unquantifiable perceptions. In many cases this usually well-meaning activity not only incurs unnecessary costs but actually introduces quality problems. In summary, all hangaring activities should be reviewed with the intention of elimination. If there are genuine quality issues with individual elements of a system, these should be addressed at source, with a root cause solution put in place.

20.2.5 Order fulfilment

A key prerequisite to any order-fulfilment process is a common understanding between 'supplier' and 'customer' of agreed lead times and levels of service. When does a lead time start and finish? In supply logistics we offer a worldwide online availability schedule for all finished products, quoting current lead times which reflect any specific supply issues. The clock starts when a firm order is entered on the systems and stops when the consignment is despatched from our UK warehouse. To avoid dissatisfied salesmen, those of us within the supply chain, either corporately or within the relevant sales operation, need to ensure entry and distribution time from the UK warehouse.

To ensure this common understanding within the spares world, our UK-based worldwide spares division have established formal service and trading agreements with the customer-service operations within the UK and mainland Europe.

As I stated when we were looking at forecasting and planning, our corporate strategy for international growth, both organically and through collaborations, presents many logistics challenges. As with forecasting and planning, our order fulfilment process remains centrally managed within the UK. We aim to manage the added complexity caused by global trading through the use of information systems rather than a multiplicity of processes and people. Our Japanese and USA warehouses appear to our UK-based order-fulfilment staff as just another location on their database, from which they can allocate stock and arrange shipment worldwide without the goods coming anywhere near the UK.

Advances in technology within the literature and software replication areas are now offering us exciting opportunities to reduce our *P/D* ratio (procurement leadtime: demand leadtime) to less than 1, thus eliminating the need for much error-prone forecasting. With the right organization, systems and processes in place, we can make available, cost effectively, most of these products within a few days, not just in special panic mode but as the norm. This enables us to establish a make-to-order policy, thus dramatically reducing inventory holdings and obsolescence costs, which traditionally have been unacceptably high.

For the more established product offerings (e.g. mainframes, mini-computers, retail systems) ICL's lead times offered to customers have always been extremely competitive and this fact has been further supported by a recently commissioned independent market research survey. By definition, our order-fulfilment systems and processes have supported this capability. Over the last few years the emergence of commodity products like the personal computer have forced us to satisfy even shorter customer lead times (is 24 hours lead time a genuine customer requirement?), Until recently we have been satisfying these demands using our established order-fulfilment systems and processes, buffering with inventory as required. During this year ICL logistics, in response to the changing market place, is establishing a fast-track order-fulfilment process, bypassing some of the more time-consuming existing processes, and enabling us to better support the global requirement for short lead-time commodity-type products.

20.2.6 Warehousing

Moving, handling and storing goods costs money so we are constantly exploring efficiency improvements. A purpose-built Corporate Spares Warehouse was opened in 1987 at Stevenage in Hertfordshire and in 1989 a state-of-the-art warehouse for finished hardware and software products was established on the same site. These two centralized operations gave a springboard from which we could review the optimum strategy for global de-centralized warehousing.

The business requirements for spares inventory and finished goods inventory are very different and our warehousing solutions need to reflect this difference. Spares inventory is only any use if it is within, say, two hours of the customer site. All other spares inventory within the pipeline is there to support and replenish this multiplicity of locally based stock-holdings. With the exception of commodity-type products, finished goods inventory need to be with the customer in a matter of weeks as opposed to minutes/hours as for spares. These two requirements set the stage for our global warehousing strategy which needs to drive as much of the total spares inventory holdings as possible to the decentralized local stores, to optimize customer service, and as much of the finished goods inventory in the opposite direction to centalized stores, to optimize flexibility.

On mainland Europe, ICL established a central European distribution centre for spares in Holland in 1988, to support the five countries of Holland, Belgium, Germany, Switzerland and Austria. This acts as a base for a centralized team of inventory managers and analysts who are creating systems to provide pan-European visibility of inventory enabling the optimization of spares holdings under their direction. The creation of this distribution centre was a planned short-term pilot to establish credibility and confidence in the principle of centralized spares management among the country management teams. This objective has been achieved with service levels to the country stores being improved while country stock-holdings have been reduced by pulling back slow-moving and excess items. Additionally this DC has been piloting the direct replenishment of local stores, bypassing the country-level warehouse.

We are now at the next stage of the European spares warehousing strategy, planning the steps and timescales towards an end-game of two stockholding echelons only – a corporate spares warehouse in the UK directly replenishing locally based stores. This will necessitate the phasing out of the central European distribution centre and 12 country spares stores, fully exploiting better information flows, improved European distribution infra-structure and the elimination of delays at national boundaries as we approach 1992.

For finished goods we see the existing country warehouse structure as being the most appropriate. These warehouses provide the service directly to the customer, without the intermediate 'branch' stores, and are progressively providing more local added-value customization. This should become their prime purpose, with stock-holding being restricted to strategically held commodity-type products.

I mentioned earlier our USA and Japanese warehouses. These should be considered as an extension of our Stevenage warehouse. They are used to stock products sourced locally, both made-in and bought-out, that we wish to 'direct ship' to somewhere other than the UK, thus saving transport costs and time.

20.2.7 Transport

In transport and distribution we expect the competitive pressures released by 1992 will cause a levelling of tariffs. To exploit this effectively we are reviewing our whole distribution network, in Europe and world-wide. The 'UK vs. overseas' mentality is being broken down by merging the former UK transport unit with the export/import service unit to form distribution networks. As well as running day-to-day operations the combined unit is required to think strategically so as to get the most out of 1992. What we're trying to cultivate is a totally objective view of distances, times and tariffs in Europe irrespective of inter-state borders. The political view of separate countries has to be replaced by a view of where our suppliers and markets really are.

Because of the high value of IT equipment the prime drivers for defining the most appropriate distribution network are speed and flexibility. Opportunities to 'direct-ship' non-UK-sourced products to non-UK-based customers are continually being sought but, apart from some Far East to Australasian activity and intra-USA activity, we have openly struggled to establish significant volumes. With the added complexity, decreased flexibility and drive to provide totally integrated solutions to customers what initially so often looks such an attractive proposition, in practice turns out not to be so. But we can certainly be smarter in this area and are confident our newly formed distribution networks department will realize opportunities for improvement as they formally establish a global distribution infrastructure.

20.2.8 Repair

Again the question often tabled is 'centralize or decentralize?'. But centralize/decentralize what? The physical location, the policy making, the management control? ICL has been reviewing its repair activities in recognition that there are improved efficiency opportunities. With fierce competition in the market place, margins are being squeezed world-wide and country operations are, quite rightly, challenging internal corporate charges for services such as repair. To stop local decisions being made that adversely effect ICL's overall cost efficiency, it is recognized that policy decisions on 'what is repaired where' should be co-ordinated centrally and form part of a non-contradictory global plan. Many decisions on 'what to repair where' are straightforward: if very expensive test equipment is required, then single-source repair is logical; for straightforward repairs requiring no special equipment, one wouldn't recommend flying product half-way around the world. Other decisions are not so easy and we are currently reviewing our repair policy in Europe and questioning the need for significant capacity in Holland and France as well as the UK.

The final decision will be based on the individual cost analysis, not forgetting the additional inventory holding cost associated with having extended pipelines of both good and defective material. Whatever the outcome of this analysis though, policy making and management control and planning will remain centralized.

20.2.9 Information systems

I have deliberately included 'information systems' as a separate paragraph, to emphasize the message that the key to logistics success in the 1990s is to substitute information for inventory as the main trade-off for achieving customer service, and this must become a mind-set in managers along the supply chain.

The strategic investment in information technology is the largest lever available to logistics management in the competitive battle on service and inventory and cost performance.

Possibly the most important feature of the ICL supply chain is the flow of information. Information management is a mandatory activity in the business of logistics, whereas inventory is a result of imbalance processes. ICL believes that the cost of inventory is greater than the cost of managing information effectively. As a consequence, the logistics strategy contains a predominant emphasis on developing information technology applications to enhance logistics performance. The best example of this might be where conventional wisdom uses inventory to provide flexibility and buffer against variable demand and supply.

ICL believes it is more profitable to improve the content and speed of communication, thereby reducing lead times, and increasing the flexibility and responsiveness of the organization to the variable demand and supply, but with less inventory.

20.2.10 People

None of what I have been saying is possible without the right people with the right skills. This is even more acute today in view of the Company's successful International growth and the developments anticipated to impact global trading during the 1990s.

In a company the size of ICL which has an organization structure characterized by matrix relationships, the achievement of logistics objectives cannot be left to the specialists in materials or distribution management. It is imperative that senior management, from the managing director down, recognize the role logistics has to play in assisting any major multinational player achieve competitive advantage. In ICL this is the case and management education throughout the Company now treats materials and logistics management as one of the key ingredients in the successful management mix. A comprehensive awareness education programme on the role of the supply chain has begun to raise the effectiveness of managers in their contribution to logistics.

Currently ICL has separate logistics organizations in each of our twelve mainland Europe operations, reporting into the country management teams. At a corporate level in the UK we have three 'logistics' divisions. We have come a long way in our logistics operations in the last few years through co-operative use of matrix management and influence management techniques. In 1988 I, as international logistics manager, was given the functional responsibility of working proactively with country management teams to develop the appropriate global logistics management infrastructure; a European spares manager was appointed to ensure the optimization of spares management and establish the central European distribution centre; a European purchasing manager was appointed to establish enhanced professional expertise within the local country operations, enabling a co-ordinated cost-effective European purchasing policy to be implemented; and a European logistic management team of representative managers from the

country operations and the UK was created. Whereas all these initiatives are helping us integrate operations, exploit economies of scale
and improve communications throughout the supply chain, we now
need to look at our organizational structure if we are to practise what
we preach concerning integrated logistics, before organizational
boundaries become a major restraint to future progress.

Index